HOW TO DRAW MANGA

Drawing Yaoi

HOW TO DRAW MANGA
Drawing Yaoi
By Ai Kozaki

This book was first published in Japanese in 2006 by Graphic-sha Publishing Co., Ltd.
1-14-17 Kudan-kita, Chiyoda-ku, Tokyo 102-0073 Japan.

Artwork: Ai Kozaki
Original layout and cover design: Kazuki Kamiyama
Planning and editing: Sahoko Hyakutake (Graphic-sha Publishing Co., Ltd.)
Editor: Yuko Sasaki
English edition layout: Shinichi Ishioka
English translation management: Língua fránca, Inc. (an3y-skmt@asahi-net.or.jp)
Overseas edition project coordinator: Kumiko Sakamoto (Graphic-sha Publishing Co., Ltd.)

First printing: June 2007
Second printing: June 2008

ISBN: 978-4-7661-1781-3
UPC: 8-24869-00103
Printed and bound in China

Drawing Yaoi

Drawing Yaoi

Table of Contents

Cast of Characters

This volume features seven main characters whose profiles may be found again at the end of the book.

Dr. *Bishonen*

Dr. *Bishonen* is the headmaster of *Bishonen* Academy. While Dr. *Bishonen* is small in stature, he is a highly capable individual and is able to teach a wide range of *bishonen* subjects, ranging from how to draw *bishonen* to the history of *bishonen*. Rumor has it that Dr. *Bishonen* was quite an attractive young man, himself, when he was a lad. Now, he sets his personal needs aside in order to dedicate his energies to educating his successors. He is drawn at a 1:2 head-to-body ratio.

Bontaro Hei

Bontaro Hei is a new student who transferred mid-school year. He has a cocky attitude and has just earned the title of "*bishonen*." He is studying what it means to be a *bishonen* under Dr. *Bishonen*'s tutelage. He is still a freshman and is drawn at a 1:7 head-to-body ratio.

Kosaku Inochigake

Kosaku Inochigake is a senior (third year student) at *Bishonen* Academy. He belongs to a mysterious organization and is always found engaged in some kind of mission. He reflects a style ca. 1960s and is drawn at a 1:4 head-to-body ratio.

Otsuteru Yumebakari

Otsuteru Yumebakari is a senior at *Bishonen* Academy. Giving to wildly fanciful declarations, he is effeminate and is drawn in a style ca. the 1970s. Otsuteru is drawn at a 1:5 head-to-body ratio.

Nentaro Sho

Nentaro Sho is a junior at *Bishonen* Academy and is Jotaro's twin brother (Nentaro is the older twin). Nentaro is a passionate young man and can become a little too fiery at times, but he is a kind soul and looks after the other boys. He is drawn at a 1:6 head-to-body ratio and reflects the style of a *shonen manga* character from the 1980s.

Jotaro Sho

Jotaro Sho is a junior at *Bishonen* Academy and is Nentaro's twin brother (Jotaro is the younger twin). He can be a little of a reprobate, but he is an affable guy. He is drawn at an implausible 1:9 head-to-body ratio in the style of a *shojo manga* (*manga* targeted at girls) character from the 1980s. Jotaro is popular amongst the ladies.

Sugita Hinekure

Sugita Hinekure is a freshman at *Bishonen* Academy. Like Bontaro Hei, who is also a freshman, Sugita is drawn using a 1990s-to-present-day style. He is a shady character and does not have a single friend. Sugita is drawn at a 1:8 head-to-body ratio.

美少年先生之昔

美

Chapter 1
The Basics of Sketching

Introduction

Beginning artists often find themselves running into obstacles when drawing characters, even when attempting to draw the figure over and over again. Possibly you, the reader, have encountered the same problem and wondered if you were simply lacking talent. Well, don't give up. Mere luck, knowledge, and proper practice will enable anyone to draw characters just as the artist imagines. This book contains valuable lesson modules that will allow the reader to draw breathtaking, young male characters. These lessons cover everything from the basics in sketching to figure stylization. But before we do anything else, let's start by dispelling a few dilemmas that have been vexing our main characters.

Agony 1

How should I start? – From Bontaro Hei

When I try to draw a complicated position (like a belly-to-back suplex wrestling move or a figure-four leg lock wresting move, at first it develops nicely. But, somewhere during the drawing process, the key portion suggesting movement just appears stiff. In the end I give up and just opt for a standard, run-of-the-mill position instead. Do you have any advice?

Solution

Dr. *Bishonen*'s Solution

Your problem lies in where to start drawing to give your figure form, m'kay? When drawing a difficult pose or position, you should start by drawing the key points comprising that pose, m'kay? For example, when drawing a figure seated in a chair, start by drawing the backside and lap in a seated position on the chair. If you were to draw a character performing a figure-four leg lock, you would start with the figure's legs and arm grasping the opponent's leg. If you were to draw a character performing a belly-to-back suplex, and you intended to show the character arcing his or her back in a bridge, you would form the figure starting with the upper body and arced neck. In any case, if you have the habit of starting with the head when drawing, stop it now. Your artwork will improve much more quickly, m'kay? Incidentally, it seems that you're quite a pro-wrestling fan, Bondaro.

Agony 2

My under drawings progress into a mess. – From Kosaku Inochigake

I draw so many layout lines that my under drawing (sketch) becomes full of black lines, and I don't know which are the correct figure contours. The paper grows into a mess of black lines, just like my heart. What should I do to lighten things up?

Solution

Dr. *Bishonen*'s Solution

Sketching plenty of layout lines is a good thing, m'kay? It will help your artwork improve faster. When you are producing an under drawing, go ahead and sketch as many lines as necessary until you arrive at a contour you find satisfying. However, if you draw so many lines that you are no longer able to recognize which are the desired contours and which are trial-and-error lines to be erased, then you do have a problem that needs to be addressed. In such cases, use a light table or the like and, with a pencil, trace over the sloppy under drawing, m'kay? Traced lines tend to be highly refined. The fresh sheet of paper will allow you to draw smoother strokes. You will feel better about your under drawing, and you will feel invigorated to do your best. As you gain experience sketching, the time it takes until you arrive at the final lines in their desired positions will gradually shorten, and your under drawings will become cleaner. Incidentally, I included the under drawings pictured below, which were drawn by the lovely Ai Kozaki for your reference, m'kay? Just looking at how chaotic her sketches are should build your confidence, m'kay? To be honest, I'm more worried about your glum frame of mind.

Under Drawing for the Character Group Image on P. 143

Under Drawing for the Back Cover

Layout Sketch of the Front Cover

Agony 3

Nothing I draw looks three-dimensional. Am I cursed?

— From Otsuteru Yumebakari

I have plenty of confidence in my ability to give the figures form, but for some reason, I can't create the illusion of volume. I am rich and have a sensitive aesthetics, so I can't help but think that someone who is jealous must have cast a curse on me. Dr. *Bishonen*, do you have any idea of someone who might have done this to me?

Solution

Dr. *Bishonen*'s Solution

I don't think anyone has cursed you, m'kay? I think you, yourself are the problem, so you can rest assured and stop worrying about curses. Most likely, you are not modulating your stroke thicknesses when you sketch, m'kay? Even supposing you have accurately captured a figure's form, if all of the lines are identical in weight, the figure will appear flat, m'kay? Depending on the circumstances, you could change nib widths or modulate the pressure applied to your pen or pencil in order to achieve a sense of volume, m'kay? Use heavy strokes for objects or parts that are close to the picture plane and fine strokes for parts that are far from the picture plane. Main lines should be heavy. Clothing creases and hair strands should be delineated in fine strokes. Heavy strokes should be used for bulging parts and mounds, etc. There are many ways to modulate stroke thickness, m'kay? And, if this doesn't fix your problem, then perhaps you really are cursed, m'kay?

Agony 4

My artwork doesn't look stylish. — From Nentaro Sho

My characters always end up dressed in T-shirts and jeans. All I wear myself are T-shirts and jeans, so I am totally hitting a wall trying to think of other fashions. I want my characters to look stylish. What should I do?

Solution

Dr. *Bishonen*'s Solution

This is also a common problem, m'kay? Remember that T-shirts and jeans can come in countless variations. For example, they can have a tight or baggy fit. Jeans come with low-rise waists, boot-cut legs, and various other styles. Paying particular attention to such details is a step towards becoming fashionable, m'kay? The fastest shortcut would be to copy an ensemble directly out of a fashion magazine. For those strapped for cash, another option is to use a free mail-order catalog as reference, m'kay? In addition to clothing, any item of everyday use appearing in these magazines and catalogs will also make effective supplements your artwork. Magazines and catalogs are incredibly useful, m'kay? You should not rely solely on your ability to create something entirely new in your head but look at reference sources and use your imagination, m'kay? Get into the habit of creating stockpile not only of clothing but also of appealing articles and goods that you encounter in real life on a regular basis. This will help you visualize when you sit down to draw, m'kay?

Agony 5

I have trouble drawing front and back views of faces. — From Jotaro Sho

I am a genius southpaw. That is to say, I'm left handed. And yet, I have trouble drawing heads facing the left and facing forward. They come out all distorted. All the right-handed yo's tell me they can't draw a head facing the right. There must be something wrong with society. Was my generation born too early? Hey, Doctor B, what's that all about?

Solution

Dr. *Bishonen*'s Solution

Eh hem...I think it speaks poorly of today's youth to blame society constantly for everything under the Sun, m'kay? All right-handers struggle drawing heads facing the right, and all left-handers struggle drawing heads facing the left, m'kay? All you can do to improve is practice, m'kay? Here is a way to prevent the face from becoming distorted: draw a face→flip over the paper so that you can see the face through it→adjust those areas that appear distorted→flip the paper back over→with the paper again situated so that you can see the areas adjusted on the flip side→correct the same areas on the front side accordingly.
As you repeat this process over and over again, the distortions should disappear, m'kay? However, you should not get yourself so worked up over a few facial distortions here and there. If you find yourself pressed for time, flip the sheet of paper over, and draw the side of the face you do best. Then, flip the drawing over and trace over the face on the front side. This is a faster method, m'kay?

Agony 6

I can't draw smiling faces.

— From Sugita Hinekure

For some reason, when I draw smiles, they always come out as sly smirks.

Dr. *Bishonen*'s Solution

Hang in there.
For now, why don't you practice smiling in a candid, straightforwardly cheerful way while you draw, m'kay?

Solution

And now, let's start!

The Human Skeleton

The skeleton diagram depicted below should be used as reference in capturing the structure of the human form. Look at the skeleton along with the diagram illustrating the musculature of the human body appearing on p. 40 when drawing.

Human Skeleton Diagram

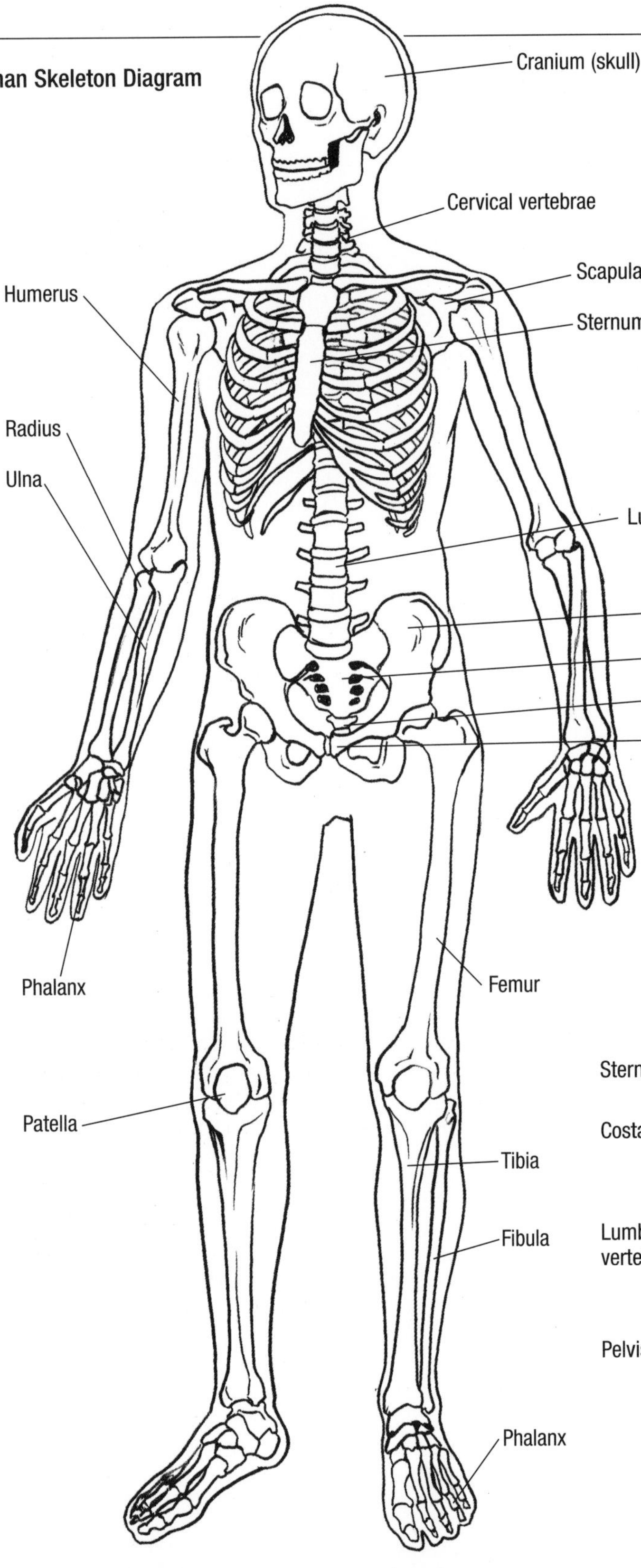

Cranium (skull)
Cervical vertebrae
Humerus
Scapula
Sternum
Radius
Ulna
Lumbar vertebrae
Ilium
Sacrum
Coccyx
Pubis
Pelvis
Phalanx
Femur
Patella
Tibia
Fibula
Phalanx

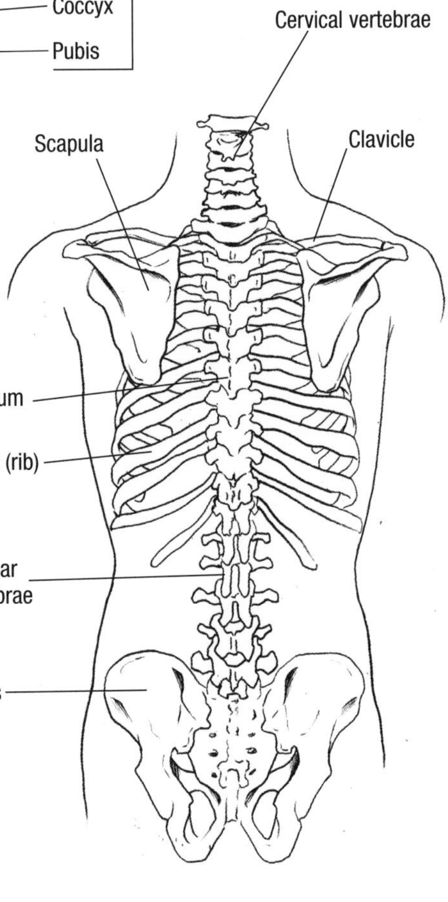

Cervical vertebrae
Scapula
Clavicle
Sternum
Costa (rib)
Lumbar vertebrae
Pelvis

Mastering the Human Skeleton

Correctly Positioning the Chest and the Clavicles

While individual differences do exist, the bones of the body have standard rules in their positioning. Height does not affect these positions. If you remain constantly mindful of basic figure proportioning, you should be able to draw any *bishonen* as you intend.

Joint Positions

This rule does not change, regardless of the individual's body type or age, so be sure to memorize it.

Position the chest's bottommost line one-quarter of the way down the figure (starting from the top of the head).

Position the navel along or just underneath the waistline. Never situate the navel above the waistline.

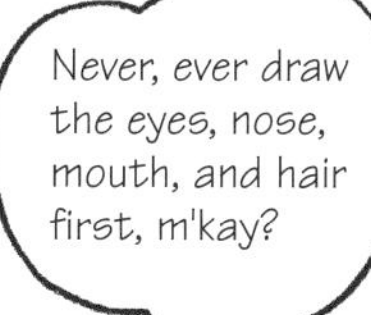

Never, ever draw the eyes, nose, mouth, and hair first, m'kay?

This is extremely critical.

Elbows are waist-level.

The groin should be located halfway along the figure's total height. Determining the groin's position first will help to position the other body parts.

Position the knees halfway along the legs total length. Legs generally appear more attractive if the lower half is longer than the upper half.

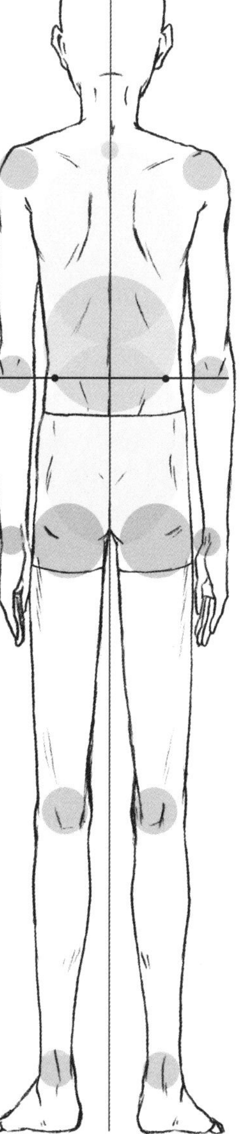

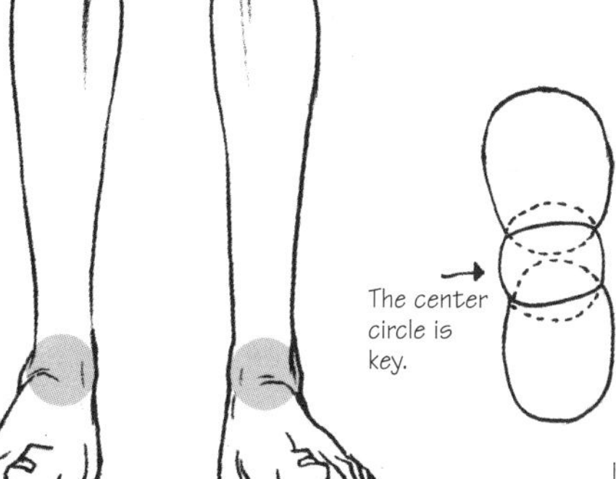

Three Circles of the Torso

Conceive of the torso as composed of three circles. The torso twists and bends with the center circle as the pivot.

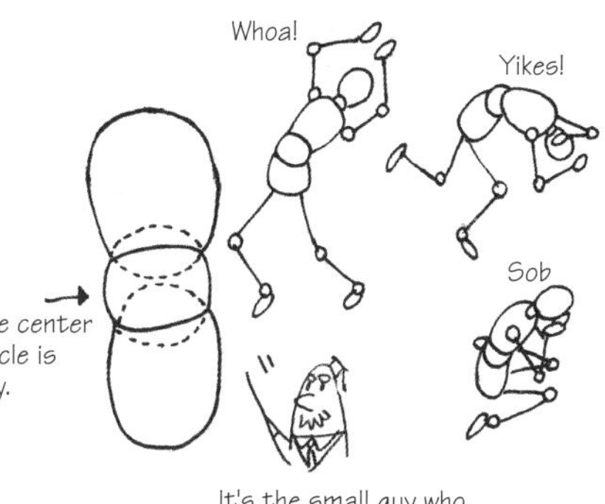

Whoa!
Yikes!
Sob
The center circle is key.
It's the small guy who usually takes control, m'kay?

Drawing a Standing Figure

Let's try drawing in a systematic fashion a well-proportioned figure using the "Golden Section of *Bishonen* Proportions" using the three circles that form the torso.
Try your hand at drawing a figure, following the numbers provided just as if it were a "follow the bouncing ball picture drawing" song.

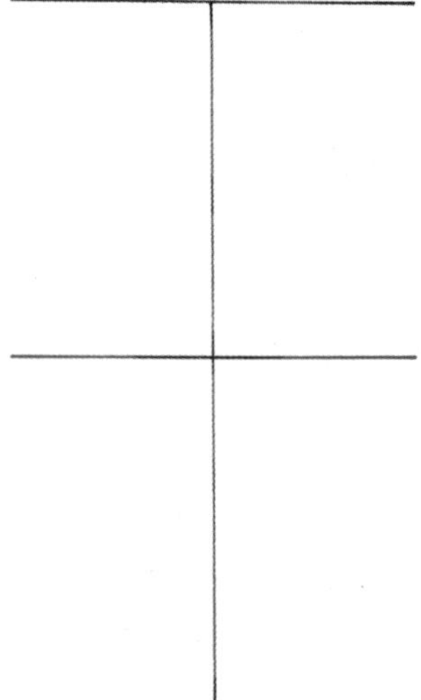

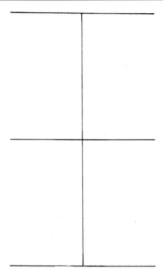

1 Draw a grid using three horizontal and one vertical line. The top line denotes the shoulder line. The bottom line denotes the groin's position. Draw one more horizontal line midway between the two.

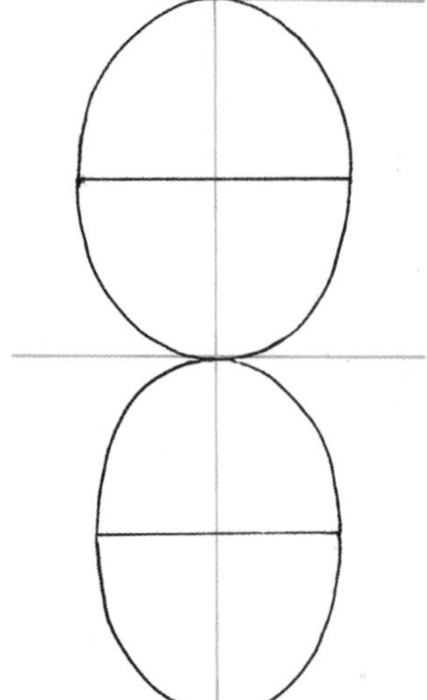

2 Draw two ellipses, making the upper ellipse slightly wider than the lower. Draw two horizontal centerlines, bisecting each ellipse. The narrower these two ellipses are, the thinner the resulting human figure will be. The wider these two ellipses are, the plumper the figure will appear.

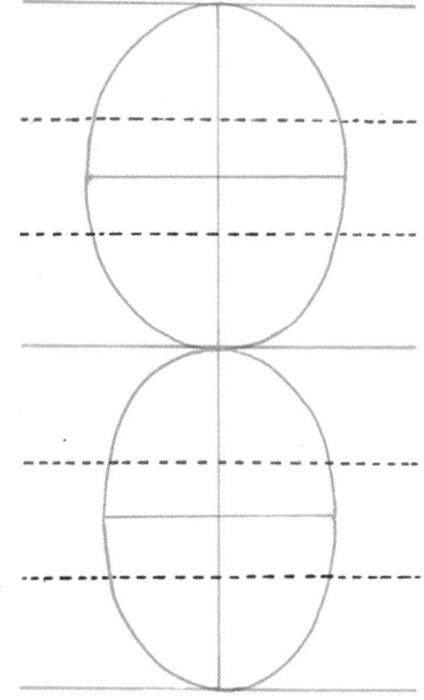

3 Divide each ellipse into three equal parts.

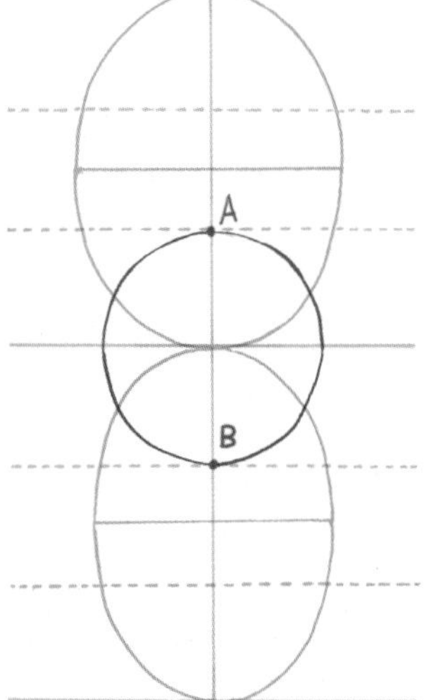

4 Draw a circle with one-third the length of each ellipse as the circle's radius.

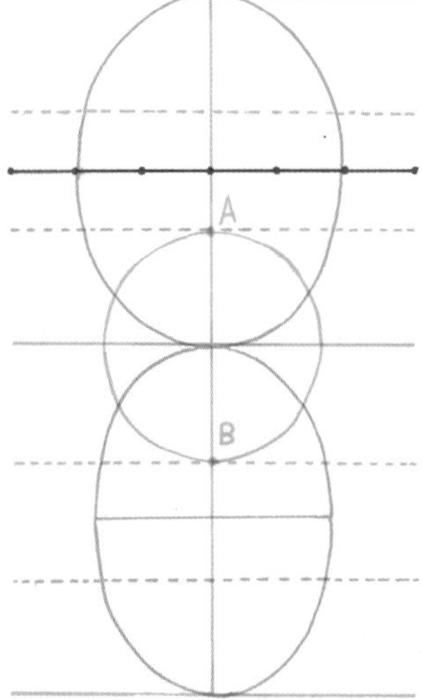

5 Divide the horizontal centerline of the upper ellipse into four equal parts. Add a line equal to one-fourth the length of the centerline to each of the right and left sides of the ellipse. These lines denote the shoulder width and arm thickness.

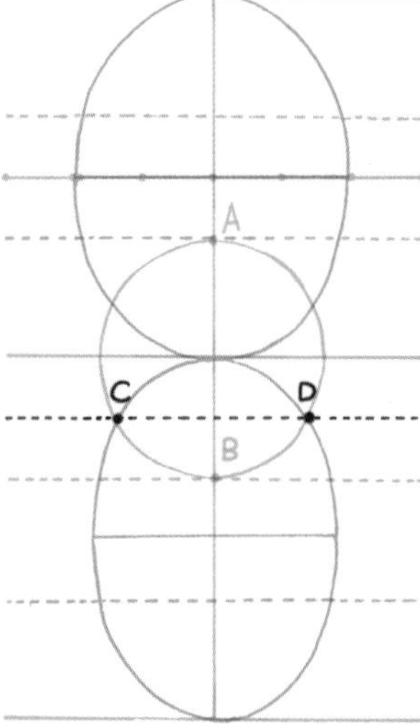

6 Draw a line connecting points C and D, where the lower ellipse and the center circle intersect. This line marks the narrowest region of the torso, the waist.

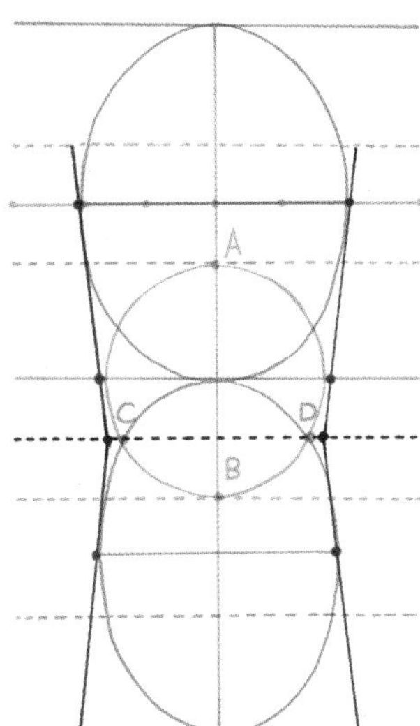

7 Draw two lines touching both the upper ellipse and the center circle. Have the lines intersect points C and D. Continue by drawing two lines touching the lower ellipse.

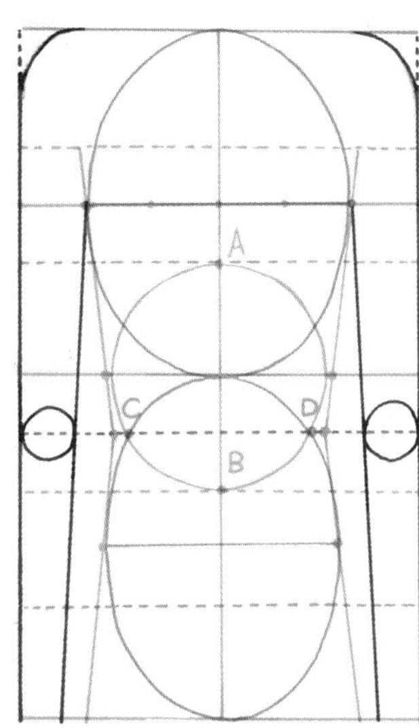

8 Draw arms according to the positions of the shoulders established in step 5. Draw the elbows level with the waist.

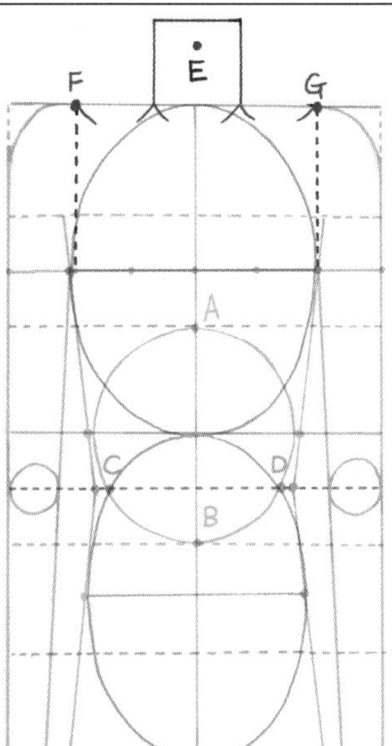

9 Draw a square so that one of its sides divides a line connecting points F and G into three equal parts. Draw the square resting on the ellipse. Mark point E. E will become the figure's chin.

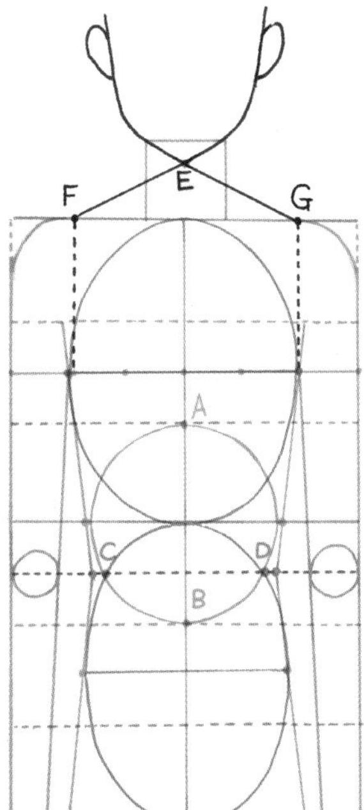

10 Connect points E, F, and G using lines. This will mark the Adam's apple. A prominent Adam's apple results in a more masculine character. Draw the head with E marking the axis.

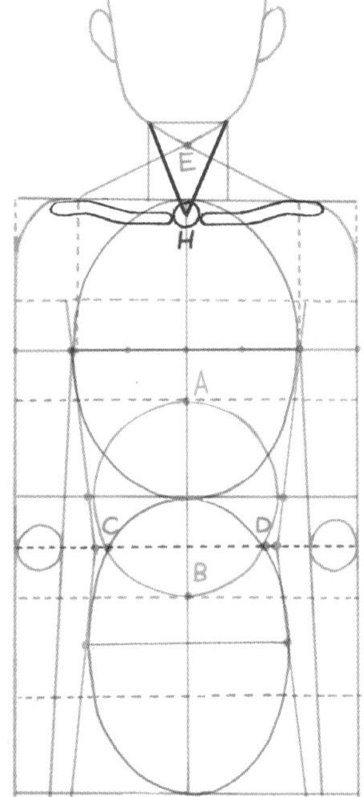

11 Draw the clavicles from point H. The clavicles should have a shape reminiscent of bicycle handlebars. Connect point H to the square's two upper corners. This forms the neck.

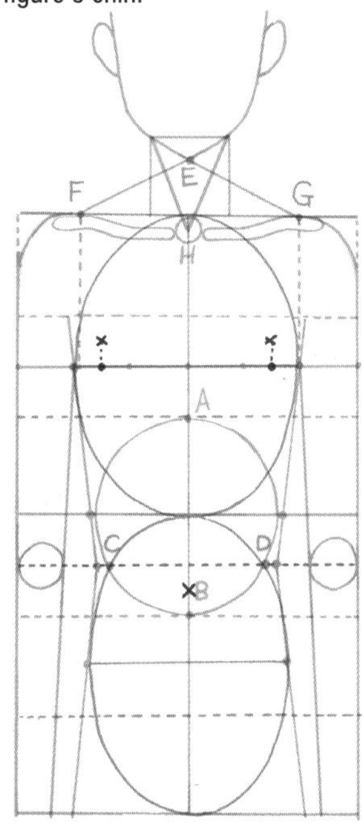

12 Draw two points along the upper ellipse's centerline, which was created in step 5. Position the points so that they divide the centerline into four equal parts. These two points denote the areoles. Draw the navel just below the waist. Congratulations. You have now finished.

Evoking a Sense of Texture

Give the figure a sense of texture using the diagram drawn in steps 1 through 12 as a point of departure. It is not necessary to go this far and use a ruler to achieve a precise sketch. However, the positions of the body parts deduced following steps 1 through 12 will form the basis of every figure, so be sure to memorize them.

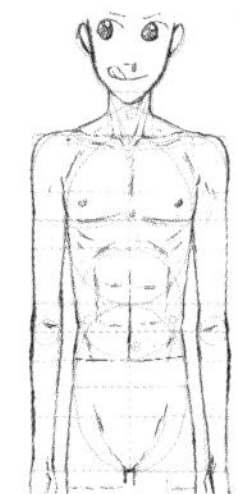

Drawing a Figure with Volume

Although you have now learnt how to proportion a frame for a human figure using a diagram; you still need to create more than just a forward facing figure standing erect. On this page, you learn how to draw a figure with a sense of three-dimensionality using the three-stage process illustrated below. Imagine that you are sculpting as you proceed.

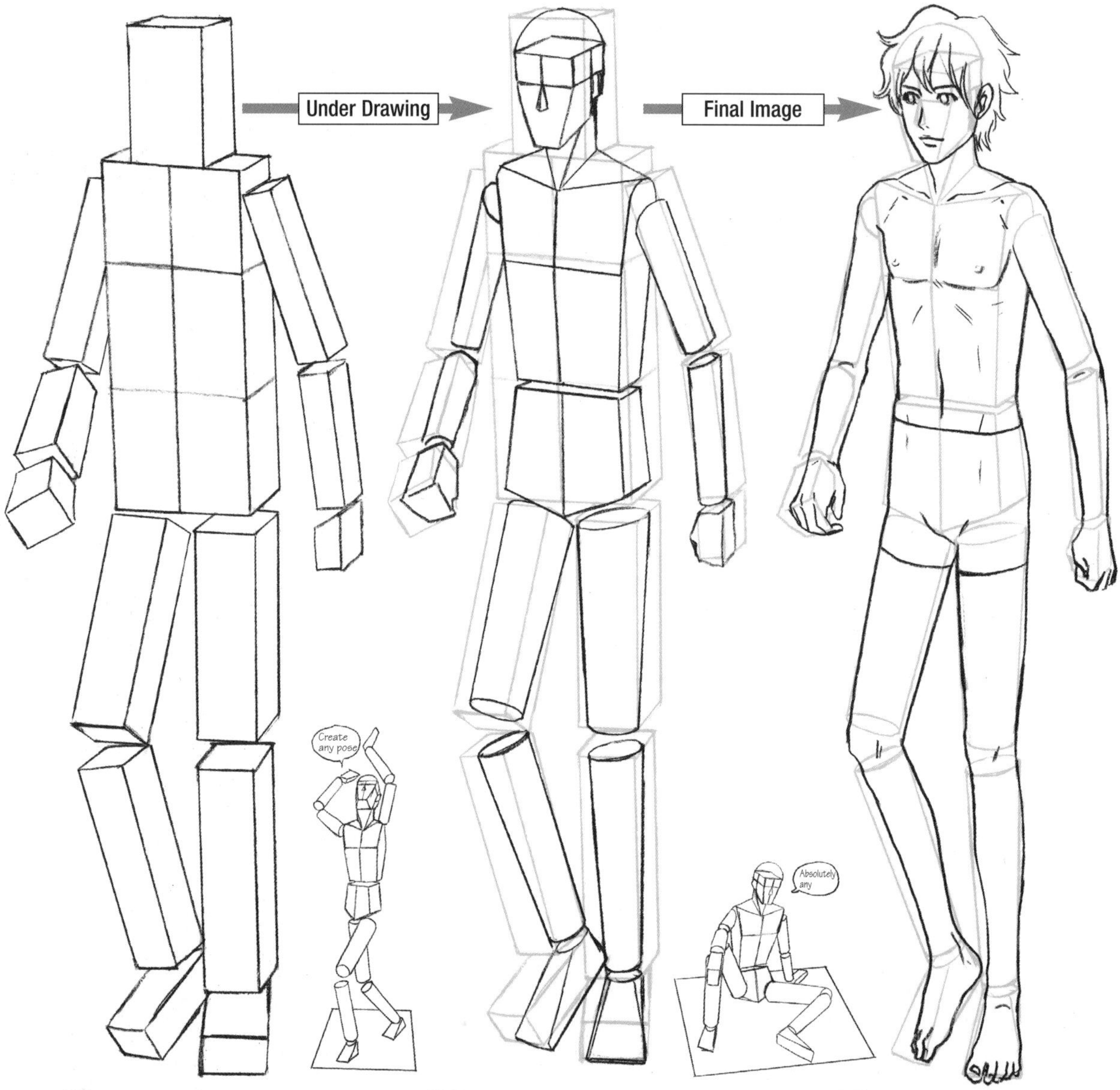

Under Drawing

Final Image

Create any pose

Absolutely any

1 Block Figure Stage

Start by drawing the upper body, lower body, head, arms, and legs using cubes and rectangular solids. Sketch the block figure in the target pose. Refrain from drawing the hair, eyes, or nose at this time. You might feel the urge to go ahead and add the facial features, but hold back.

2 Robot Stage

The above shows the block figure created in the previous stage sculpted and carved in a rough manner. As the above figure indicates, the surfaces at this stage have been given more detail. Take careful note of the positions of the joints and torso parts learned in the previous lesson module. Continue to suppress any urge to add the hair and facial features at this stage. If you successfully complete this stage, then you are as good as finished with your figure. You have nothing left to fear.

3 *Bishonen* Stage

In this stage, flesh out the robot figure drawn in the previous stage. Draw the figure with gracefully undulating sinews and exquisite hair and facial features.

Head-to-Body Ratios

Draw a wire figure, while adhering to the proportions (position relationships between the waist, joints, and chest, etc.) covered on pages 13 to 15. Start with as basic forms as possible and gradually fill in the details.

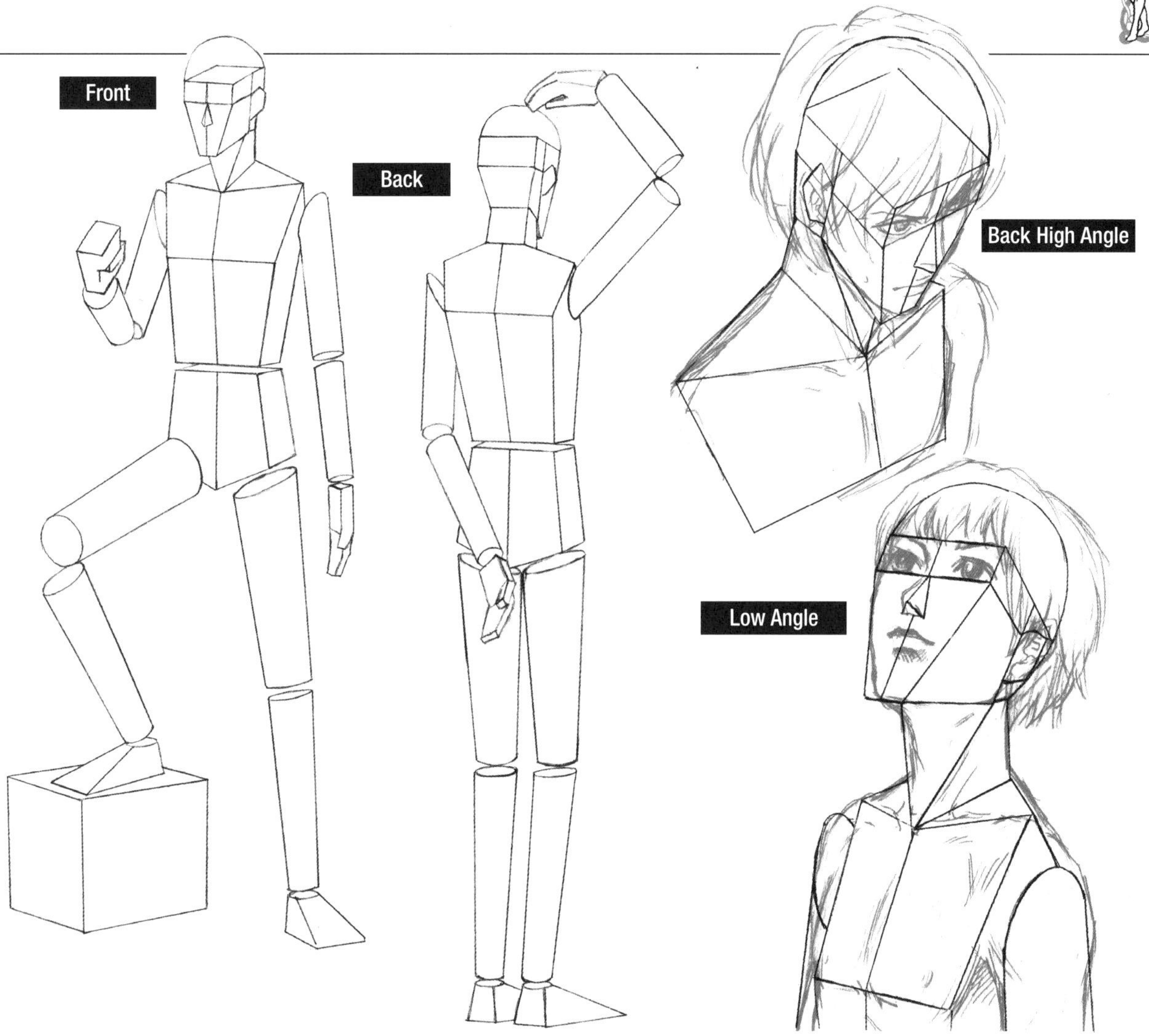

Front

Back

Back High Angle

Low Angle

Practical Wisdom from Dr. *Bishonen*
Are layouts really that important?

The following three are the most common agonies encountered by young artists:

Drawing takes planning!

"I always end up drawing the same pose time after time."
"I can't get the entire figure to fit on the paper."
"The figure looks awkward."

The above phenomena occur because inexperienced artists have the tendency to start from the head and jump right into drawing the details. When constructing a house, you would not immediately start building it. First you would draft a blueprint. In much the same way, when you create a drawing, you need to plan. Where is the character? What kind of person is the character? What does the character look like? How is the character posed? If you establish these factors first, and then construct the character starting with the figure's basic structure, you will be able to avoid drawing the same composition over and over again, and you will always be able to fit the entire figure on the paper. An artist would never disregard a character's body in favor of the head. Hair and facial expressions that match the figure's pose may always be added later after drawing the body. The lessons covered on pages 13 to 17 can be likened to a blueprint. Professional artists refer to this type of design plan as a "layout," and you might hear an artist refer to "creating a layout" or "sketching a layout." There is no need to get uptight about drawing a layout and drag out a ruler or straightedge. Just make it a habit to sketch a quick layout before diving into the details.

Dude, there's something weird about you.
Really?

Character A was drawing according to a plan.

Character B was drawn without a plan.

Changes in the Basic Structure Owing to the Head-to-Body Ratio Front View

The figures below resulted from adjusting the head-to-body ratio without changing the height. Note how the positions of the waist, groin, knees, and elbows shift as a result. The length and girth of the torso remains virtually the same. Only the size of the head and the length of the legs change. In other words, the torso from the groin to the neck maintains the same structure, regardless of the head-to-body ratio. Basically, if you are able to draw a torso as covered in the preceding lesson module, you should be able to create any head-to-body ratio you desire.

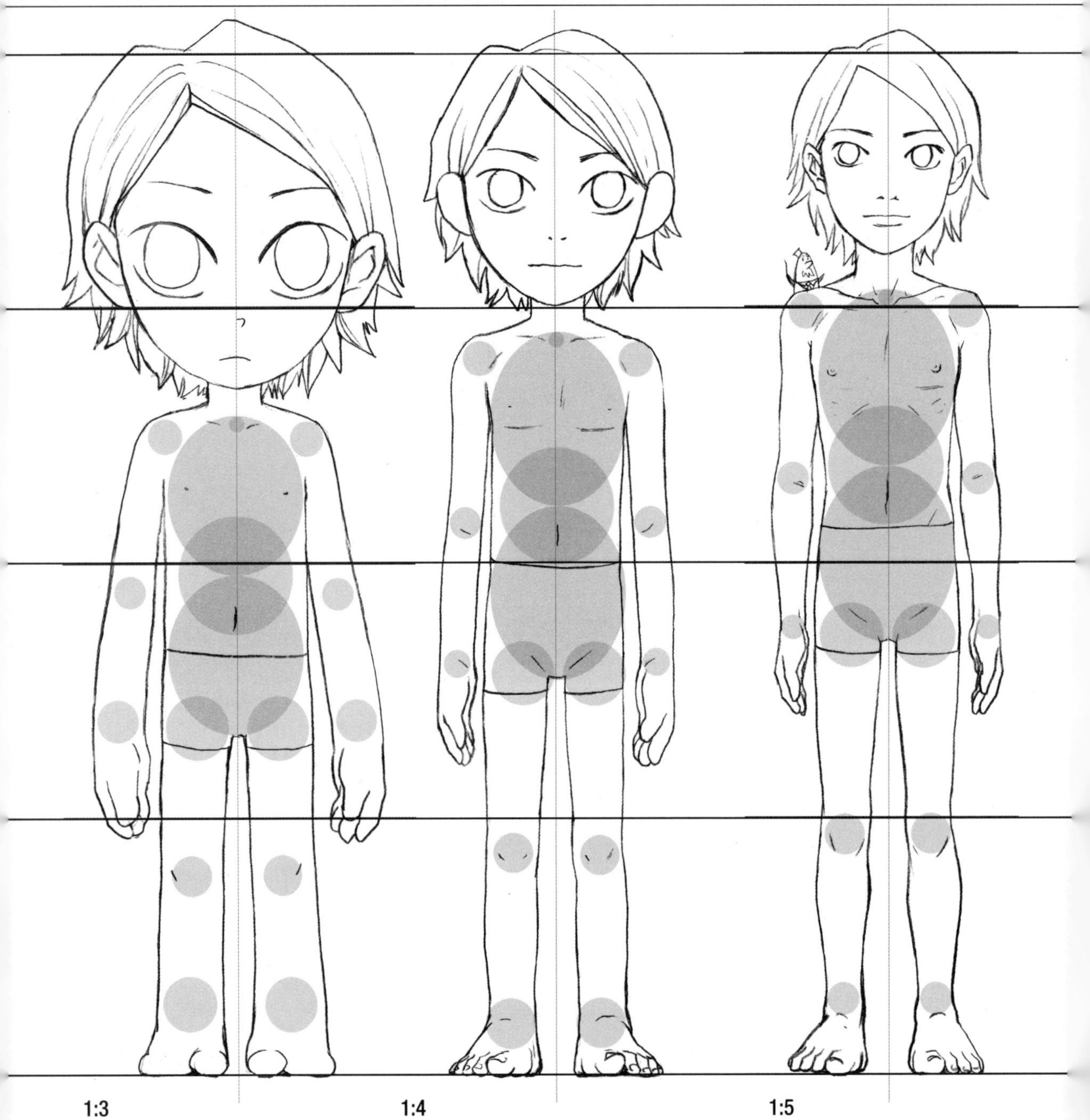

1:3

A real person with these proportions would appear grotesquely deformed. Characters with these proportions are geared toward slapstick *manga*. Of the six figures, this is the only one whose torso is somewhat shortened. The character's head, torso, and legs are the same length, so that the figure's total height may be divided into three equal segments.

1:4

People with 1:2, 1:3, and 1:4 head-to-body ratios do not exist in real life. They are targeted toward slapstick *manga*. If the arms and legs were drawn more realistically, the character would appear gawky and scrawny. However, eliminating curves in the torso, thickening the wrists and ankles, and giving the character great, big eyes results in a visually balanced character. Adding stomach muscles and other details would make the character appear creepily awkward. Try to stylize the character in a systematic manner.

1:5

In real life, we find children with this head-to-body ratio. It is suited to humorous *manga*.

POINT 1

Body Parts That Change along with the Head-to-Body Ratio
- The legs' length
- The head-to-body proportioning

POINT 2

Body Parts That Are Never Affected by the Head-to-Body Ratio
- The arms' length with respect to the torso
- The positions of the torso's features (e.g. the navel, the stomach muscles, the areoles)
- The positions of the joints with respect to the torso

Knees—Positioned slightly above the halfway point along the leg
Elbows—positioned at waist-level
Ankles—Positioned at groin-level
Etc.

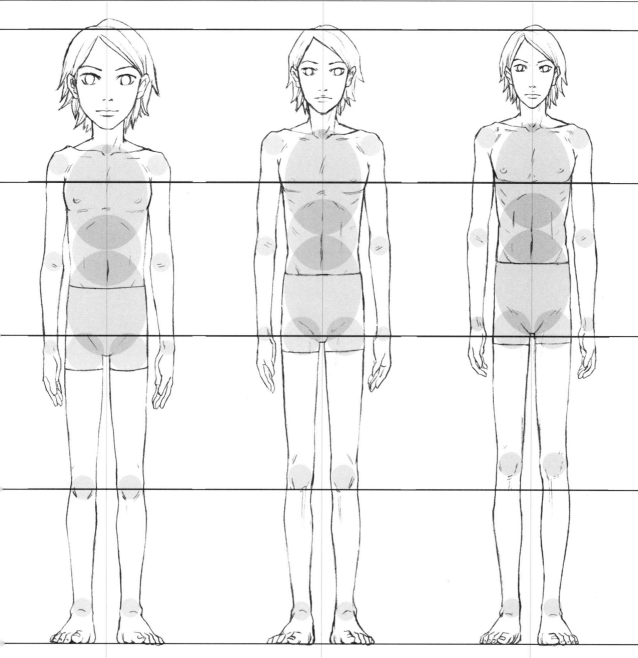

1:6
This head-to-body ratio is suited to humorous *manga*.

1:7
This head-to-body ratio appears frequently in *manga* and is suited toward dramatic *manga*. Unlike the 1:3 head-to-body ratio and similar proportioning ratios, straight, pole-like arms and legs will make characters with this proportioning to look like a scrawny wimp that is smooth all-over, so maintain awareness of adding hip bones, clavicles, and other skeletal details, a tapering curve to the waist, and muscular detail to create moderately undulating contours.

1:8
Again, this head-to-body ratio does not truly exist in real life; although, we do find celebrities and models with these proportions. It is a ratio common to *manga* and is geared toward dramatic *manga*.

Low Angles

Draw guidelines, dividing the figure into four sections. The guidelines should be drawn in consideration of the perspective and should give the illusion that the four sections are equal in height. Draw the various body parts in the same locations as you would when drawing a front view. Double-check the positions of the chin, waist, groin, elbows, knees, and elbows in relation to the guidelines.

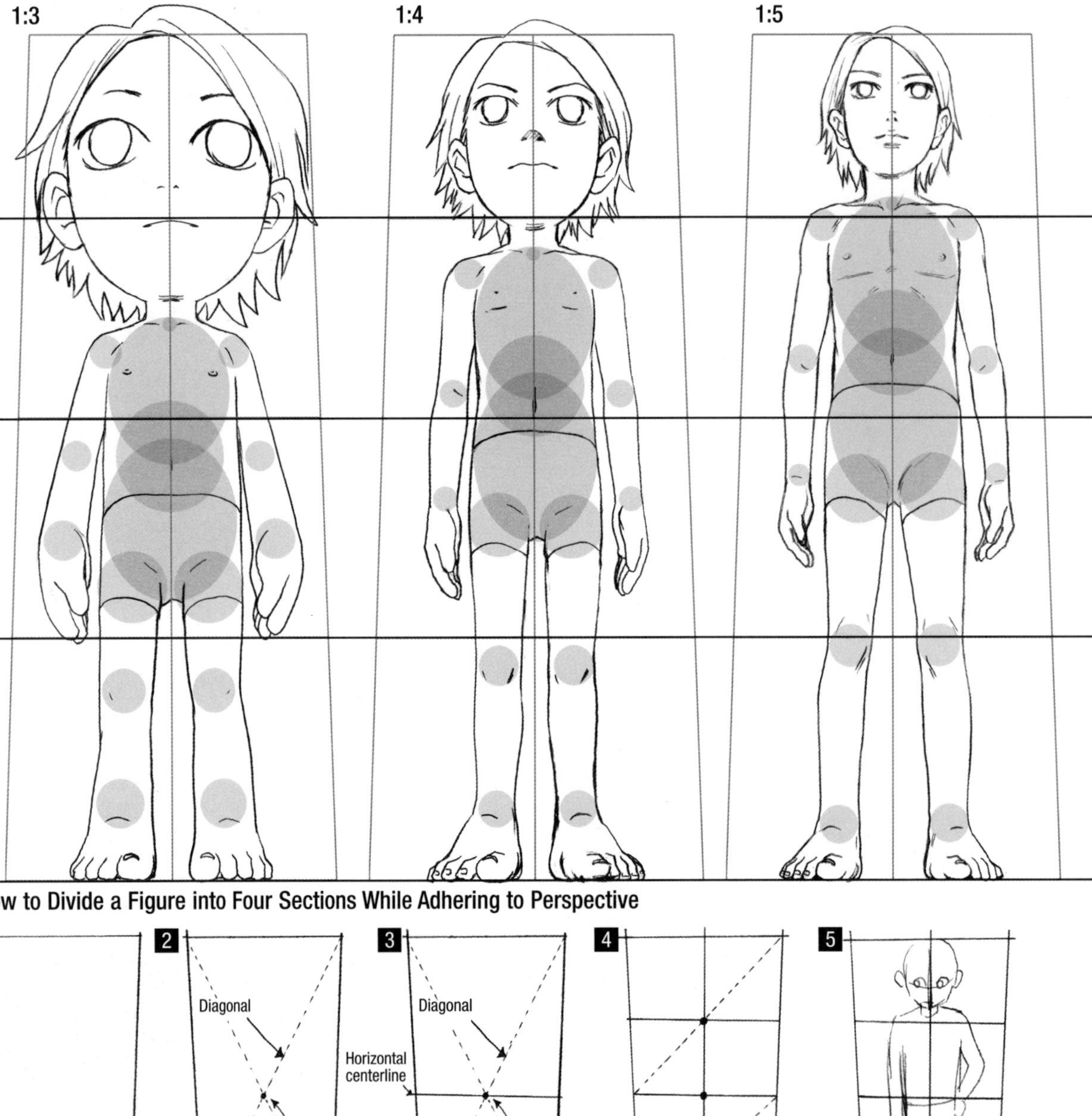

1:3

1:4

1:5

How to Divide a Figure into Four Sections While Adhering to Perspective

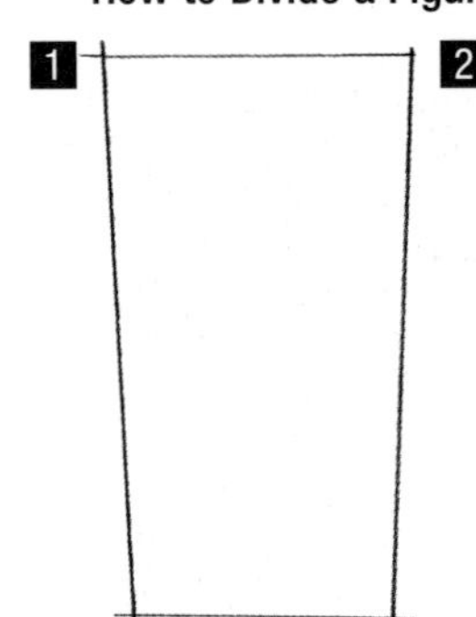

Draw a quadrilateral according to the angle of perspective desired.

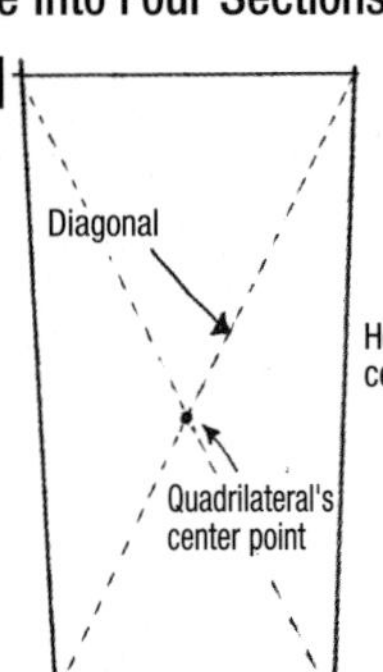

Draw diagonals from corner to corner. The quadrilateral's center is the point where the two diagonals intersect.

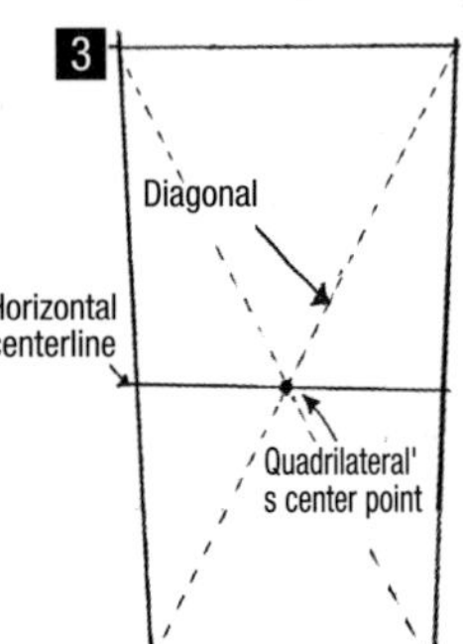

Draw a horizontal line parallel to the top and bottom lines through the center point. You have now divided the quadrilateral into two, visually "equal" sections.

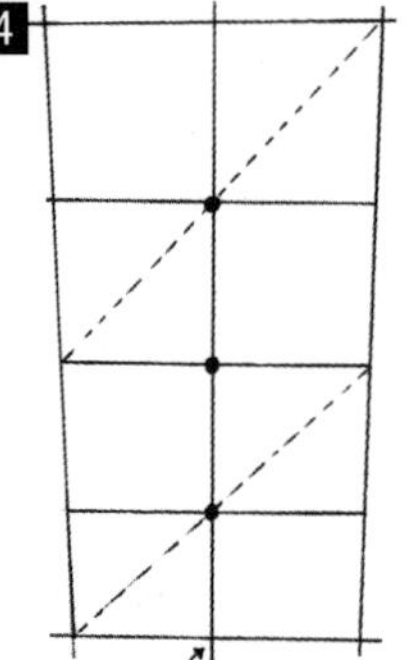

Repeat the steps using in numbers 2 and 3 to further divide the quadrilateral. Draw a vertical line connecting each of the center points to create a vertical axis for the figure.

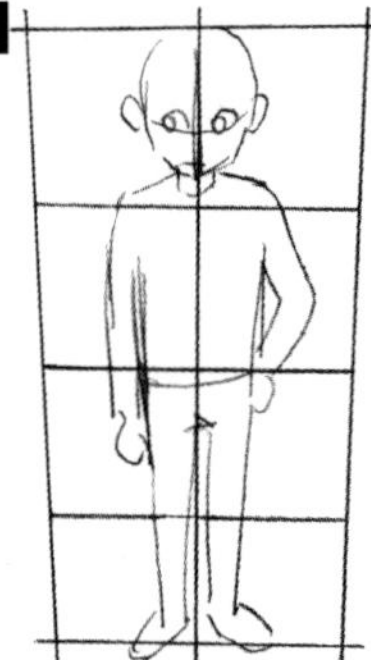

You have now successfully divided a figure into four sections according to the angle of perspective. This is an extremely handy technique, which may also be applied to drawing backgrounds and props.

POINT

In a low angle composition, the clavicle becomes a physically alluring point. Draw the clavicle so that it is straight or has a slight upward curve.

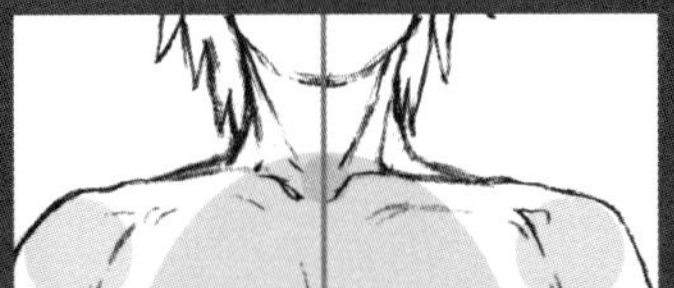

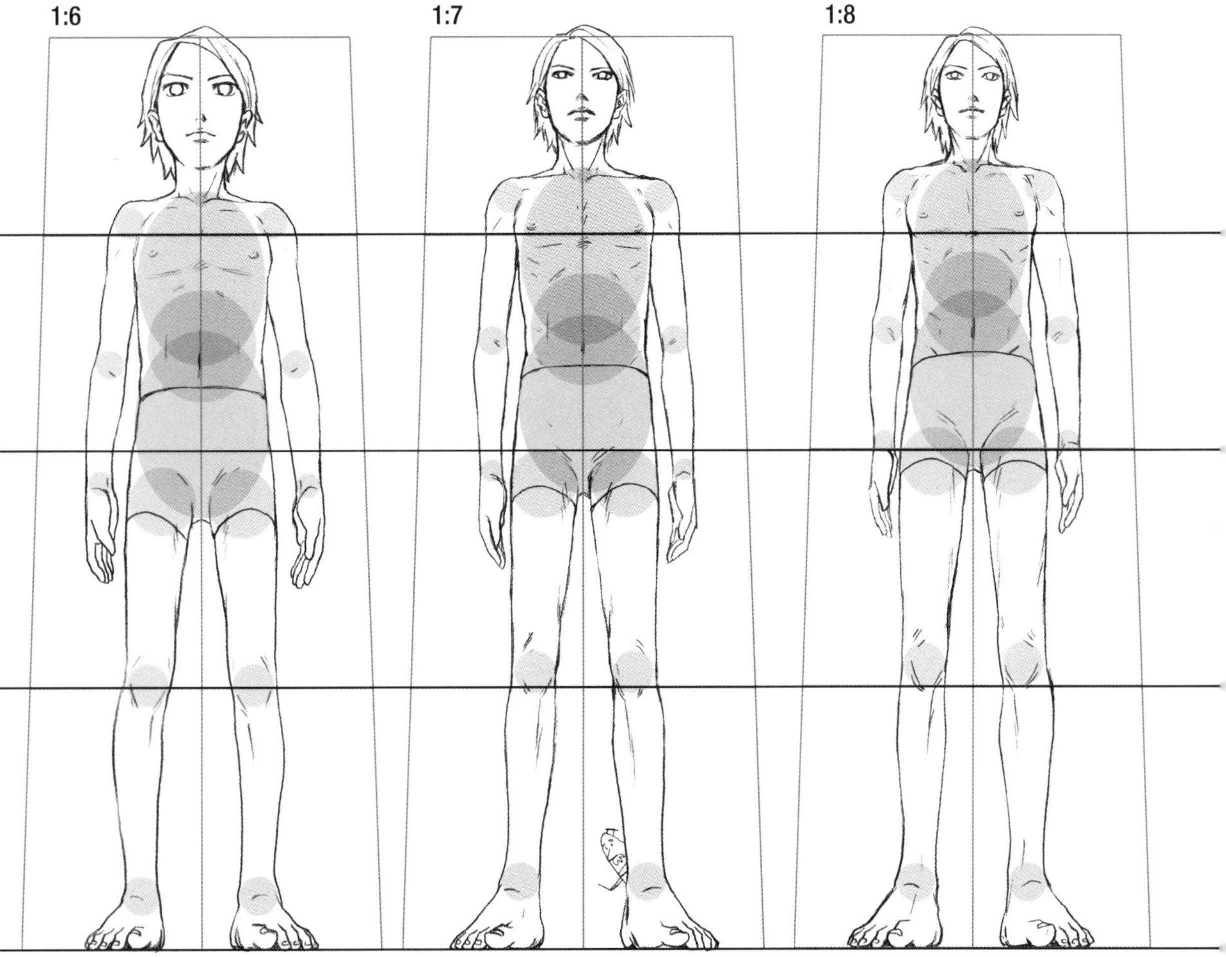

1:6

1:7

1:8

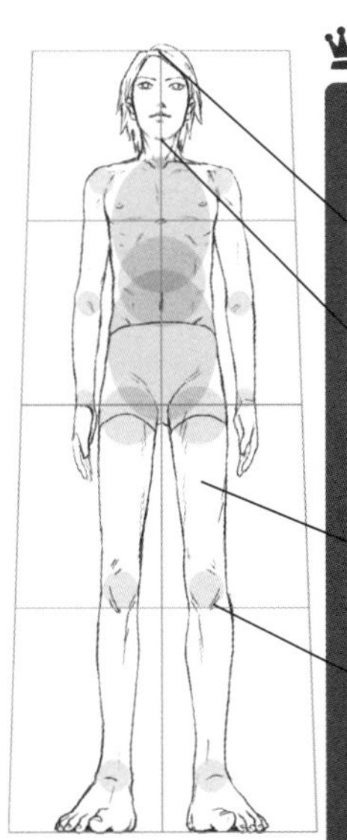

POINT

Comparing a Low Angle to a Standard, Straight-on Angle

- The head is smaller in the low angle composition.
- The ears' positions are the same.
- The mouth and chin are distanced farther from each other.
- The more exaggerated the low angle, the longer the legs become.
- The lower half of the leg becomes significantly longer.

The various body parts become larger in size as the eye travels from the top of the head to the feet.

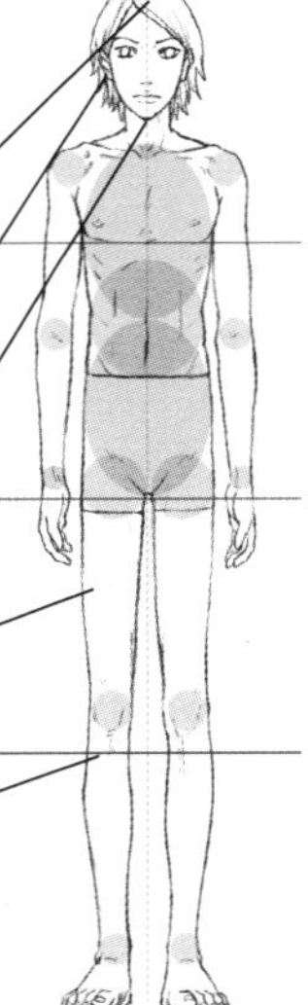

POINT

The Jaw and Chin Are Key in Low Angle Compositions

Triangular forms play a key role in low angle compositions. The more exaggerated the low angle, the more gradual the angle of the jaw line will appear, visually creating a triangle.

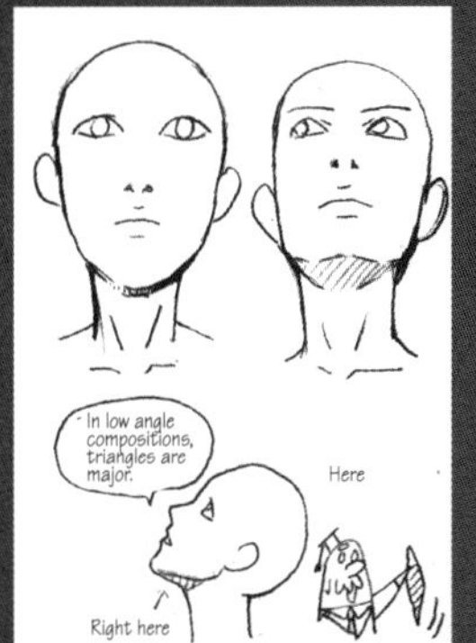

High Angles

As with low angle compositions, draw guidelines, dividing the figure into four sections. The guidelines should be drawn in consideration of the perspective. Draw the various body parts in the same locations as you would when drawing a front view. Double-check the positions of the chin, waist, groin, elbows, knees, and elbows in relation to the guidelines.

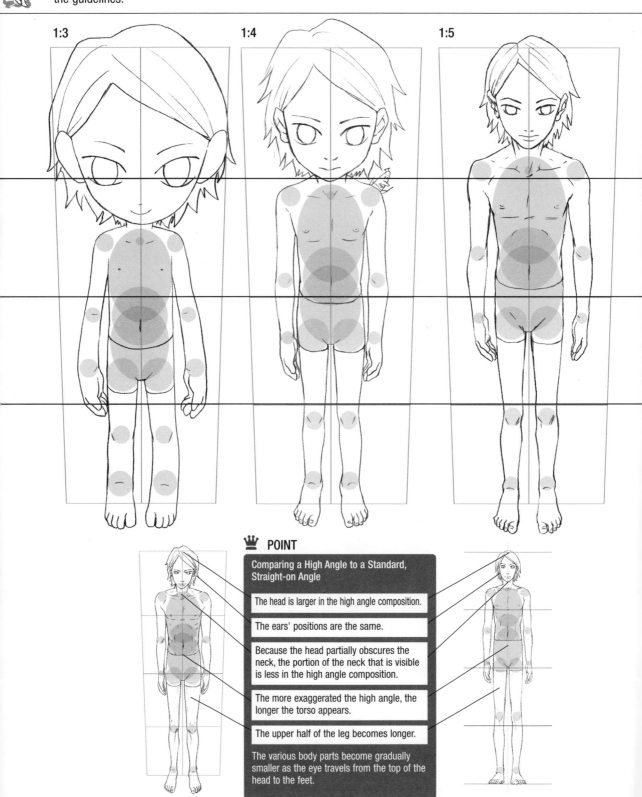

1:3

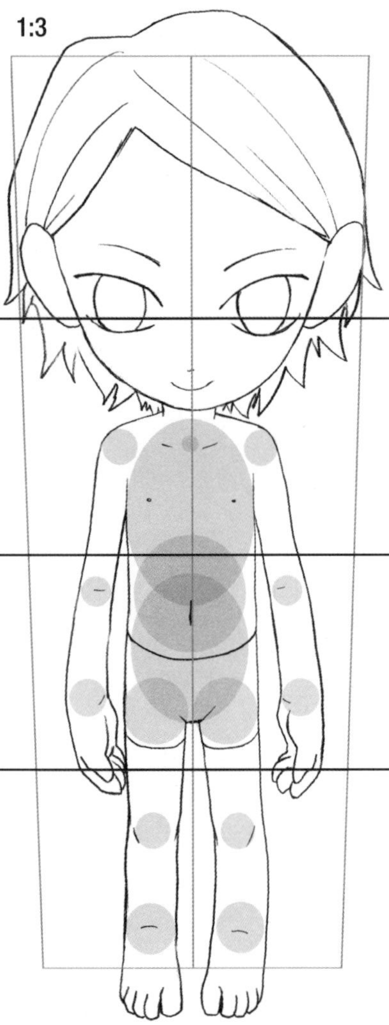

1:4

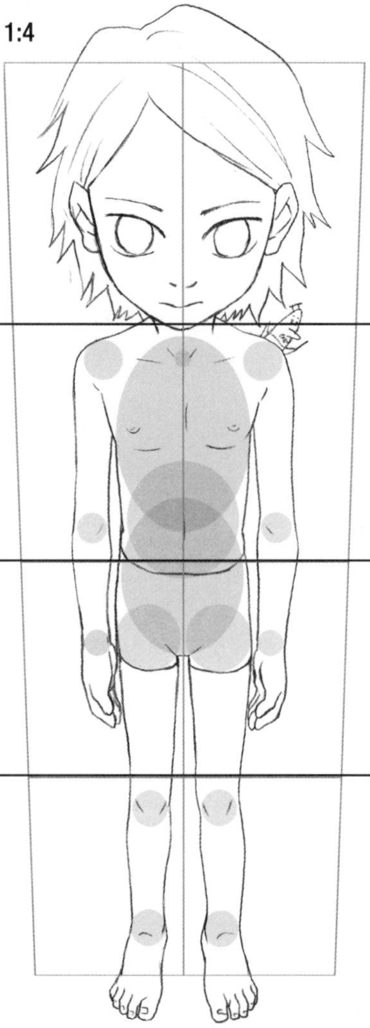

1:5

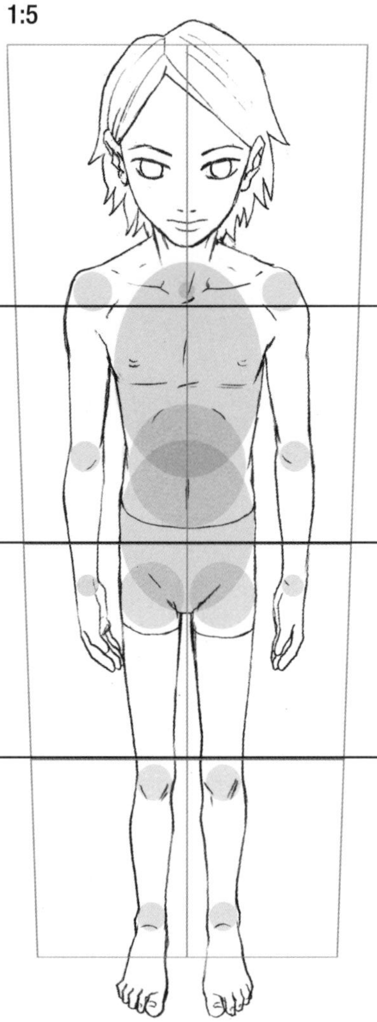

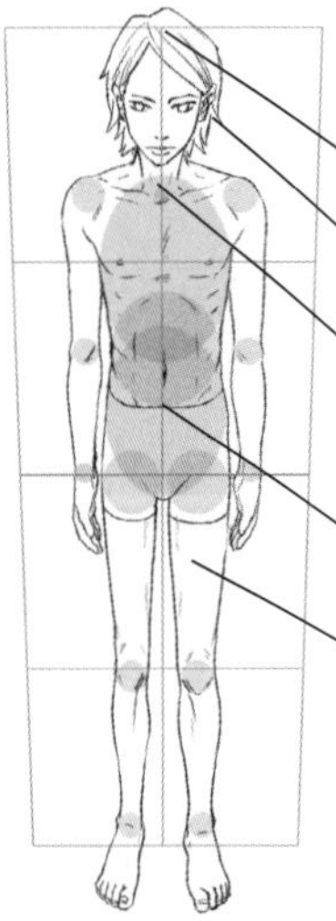

POINT

Comparing a High Angle to a Standard, Straight-on Angle

- The head is larger in the high angle composition.
- The ears' positions are the same.
- Because the head partially obscures the neck, the portion of the neck that is visible is less in the high angle composition.
- The more exaggerated the high angle, the longer the torso appears.
- The upper half of the leg becomes longer.

The various body parts become gradually smaller as the eye travels from the top of the head to the feet.

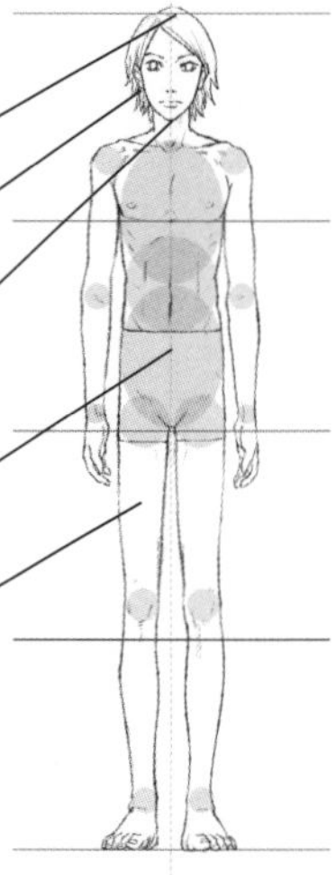

POINT

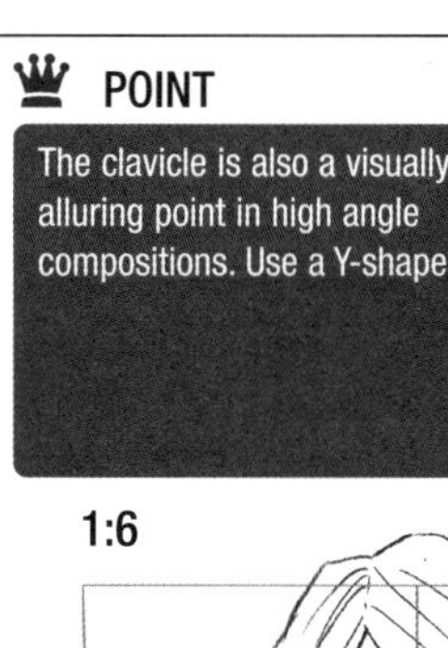

The clavicle is also a visually alluring point in high angle compositions. Use a Y-shape.

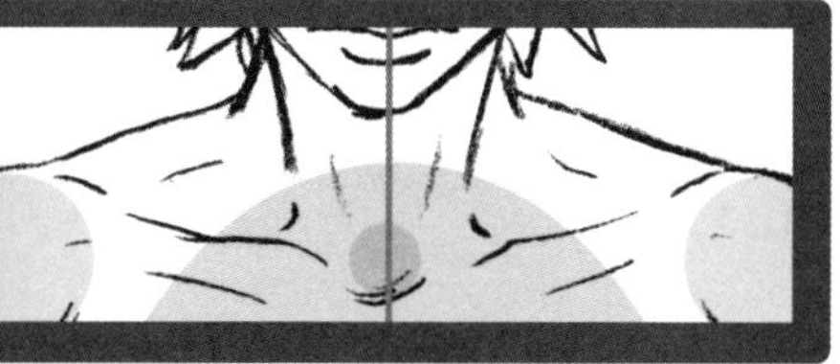

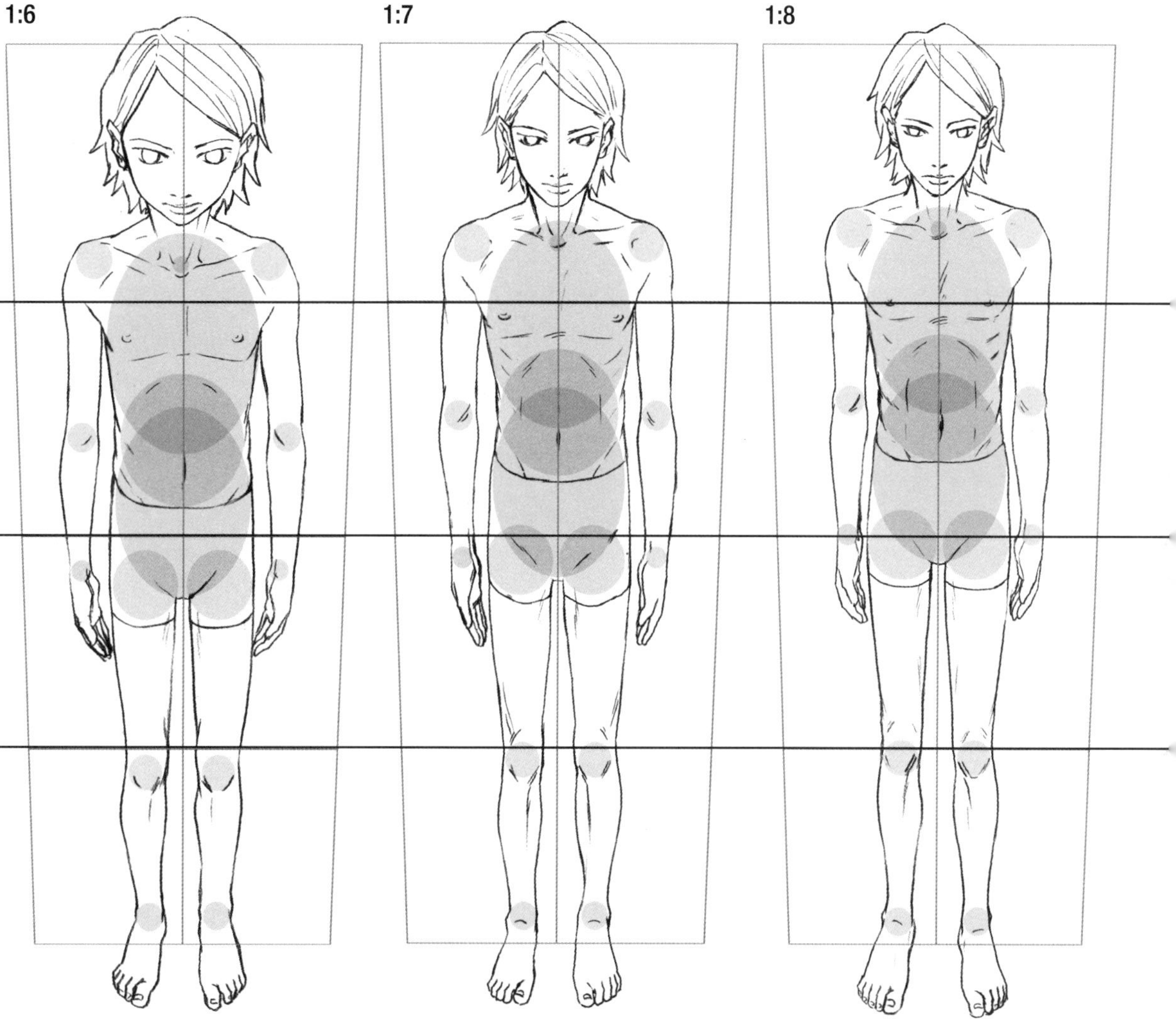

1:6

1:7

1:8

POINT

From a High Angle, Facial Features Become Concentrated toward the Bottom of the Head

Shortening the distances between the eyes, eyebrows, chin, mouth, and other facial features creates the look of a head composed at a high angle.

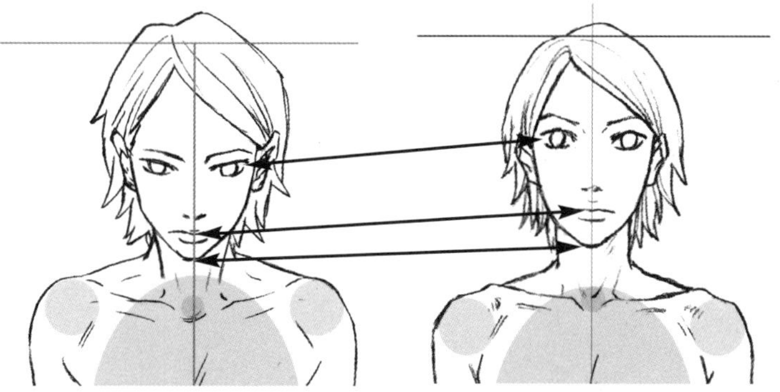

Changes in Form According to the Direction Faced

Memorizing the basic forms of the various body parts will enable you to compose them from any angle. As you were instructed earlier in the lesson module covering the block figure, simply replace the body parts with the simple forms illustrated below.

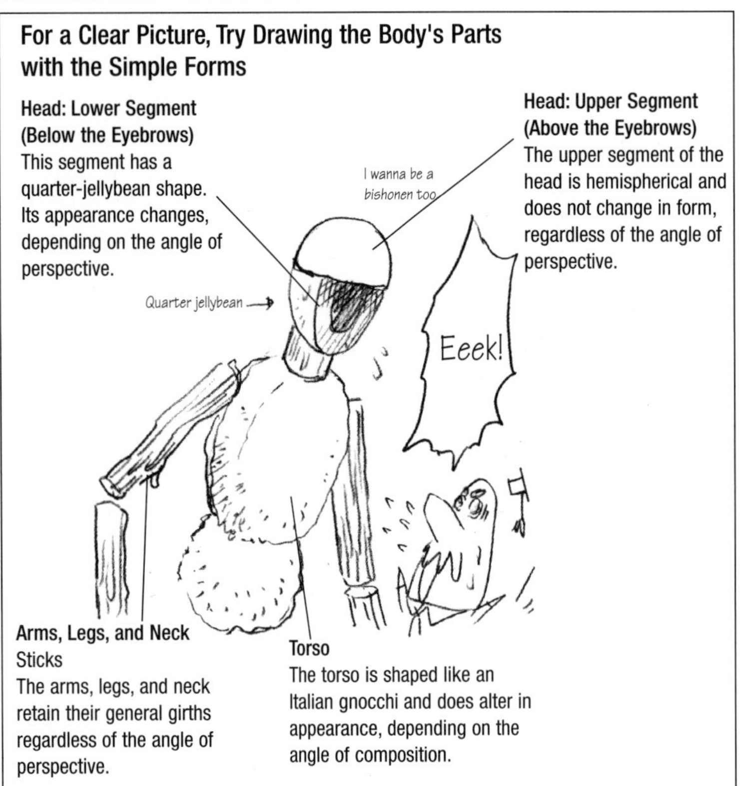

For a Clear Picture, Try Drawing the Body's Parts with the Simple Forms

Head: Lower Segment (Below the Eyebrows)
This segment has a quarter-jellybean shape. Its appearance changes, depending on the angle of perspective.

Head: Upper Segment (Above the Eyebrows)
The upper segment of the head is hemispherical and does not change in form, regardless of the angle of perspective.

Arms, Legs, and Neck
Sticks
The arms, legs, and neck retain their general girths regardless of the angle of perspective.

Torso
The torso is shaped like an Italian gnocchi and does alter in appearance, depending on the angle of composition.

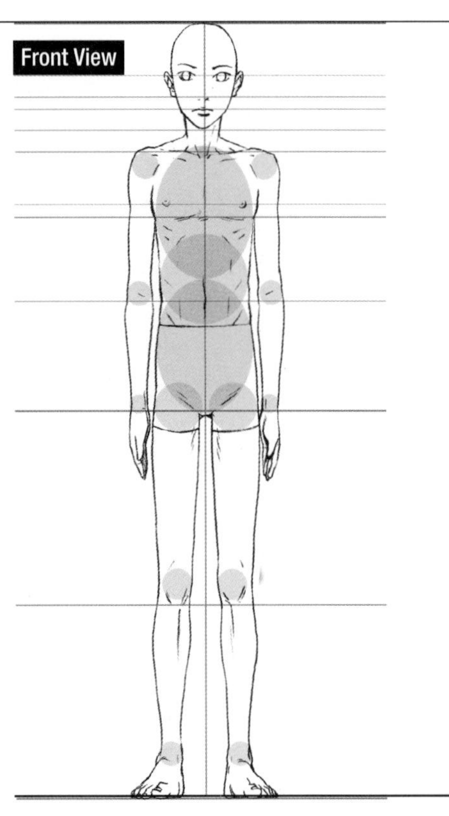

Profile View

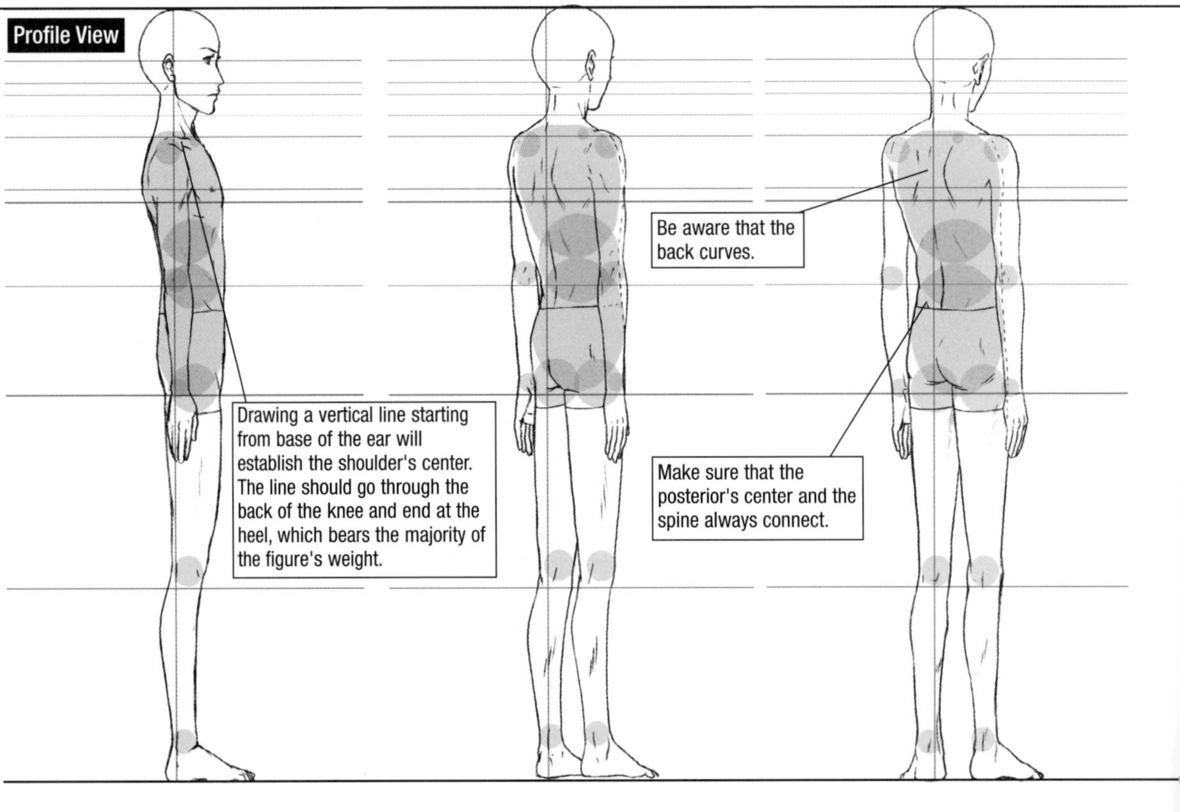

Drawing a vertical line starting from base of the ear will establish the shoulder's center. The line should go through the back of the knee and end at the heel, which bears the majority of the figure's weight.

Be aware that the back curves.

Make sure that the posterior's center and the spine always connect.

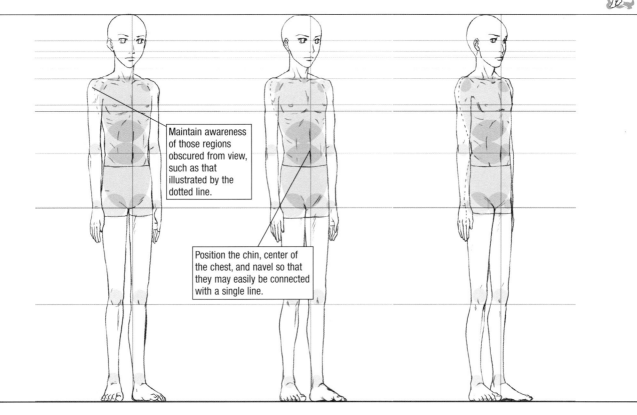

Maintain awareness of those regions obscured from view, such as that illustrated by the dotted line.

Position the chin, center of the chest, and navel so that they may easily be connected with a single line.

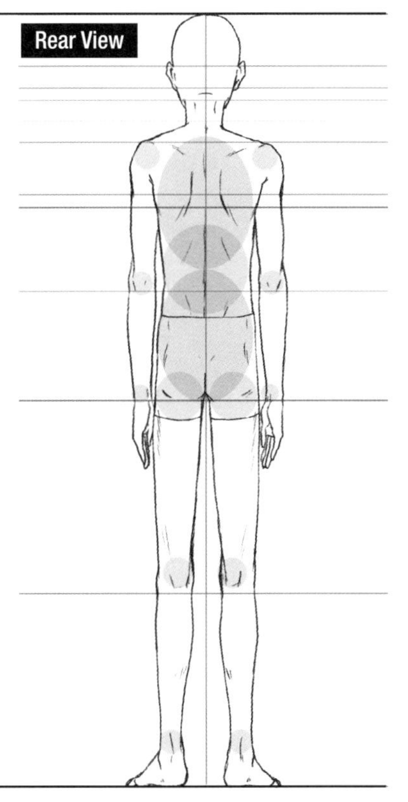

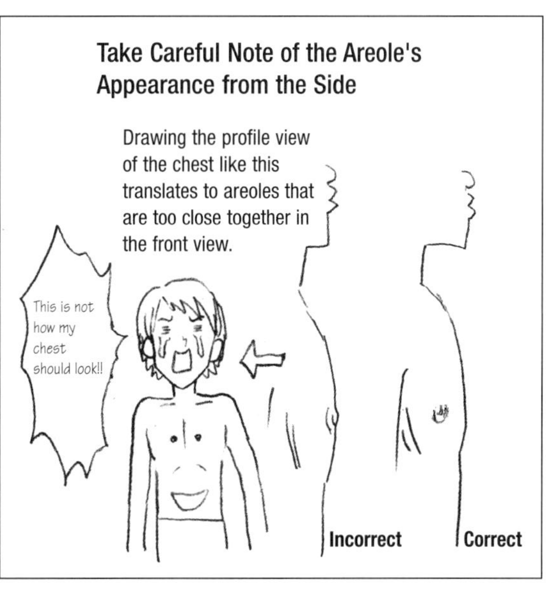

Take Careful Note of the Areole's Appearance from the Side
Drawing the profile view of the chest like this translates to areoles that are too close together in the front view.
This is not how my chest should look!!
Incorrect
Correct

Learn the Skeletal Structure's Distinguishing Features

Once you have mastered the human body's skeletal structure, the only thing left is adding the characteristics that distinguish the individual body parts. Memorizing the forms of the body's parts will make them much easier to draw.

01:Clavicles and Scapulae

Clavicles

Clavicles have a shape reminiscent of a bicycle's handlebars. Accentuating the bony projections appearing inside of the circles below results in a lean, angular look.

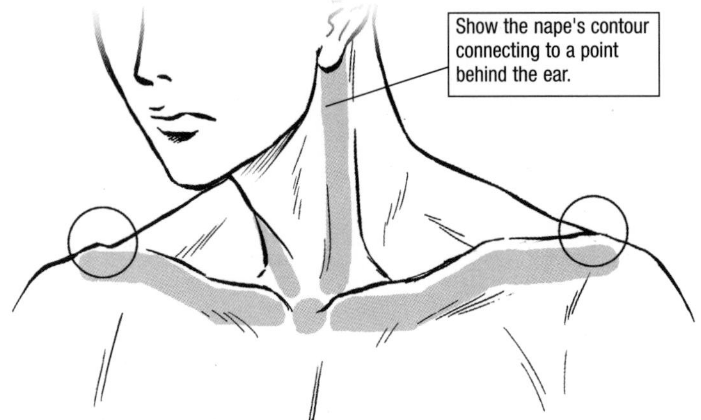

Show the nape's contour connecting to a point behind the ear.

POINT

Omitting the Adam's apple creates the look of either a preadolescent or androgynous character.

Don't you think the clavicle looks like a handlebar?

Scapulae

The scapulae are positioned on the back as shown. You might have not noticed this yourself, but the scapulae shift around in conjunction with the shoulders. However, the scapulae do not shift downward.

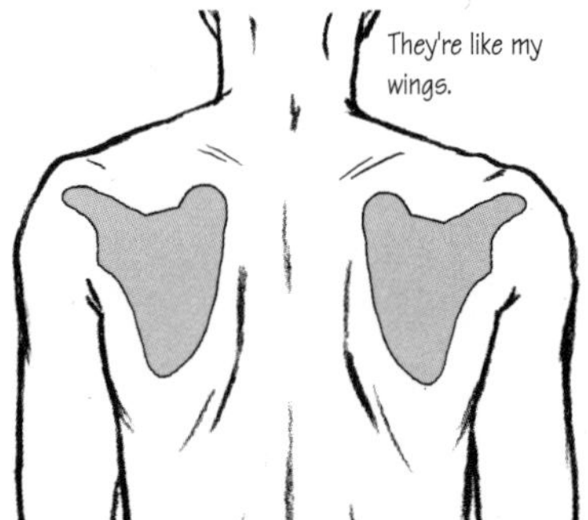

They're like my wings.

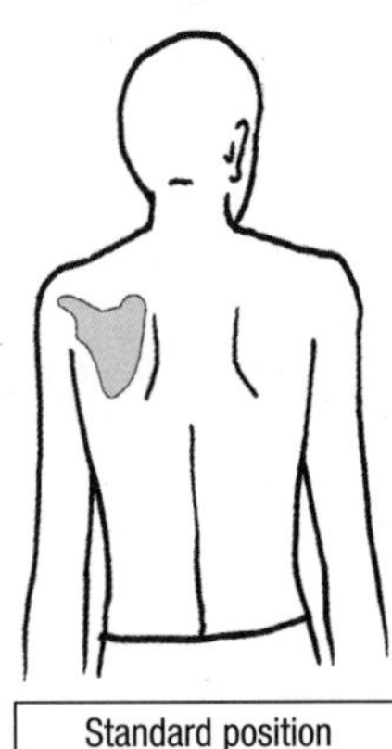

What about my clothes?

Standard position

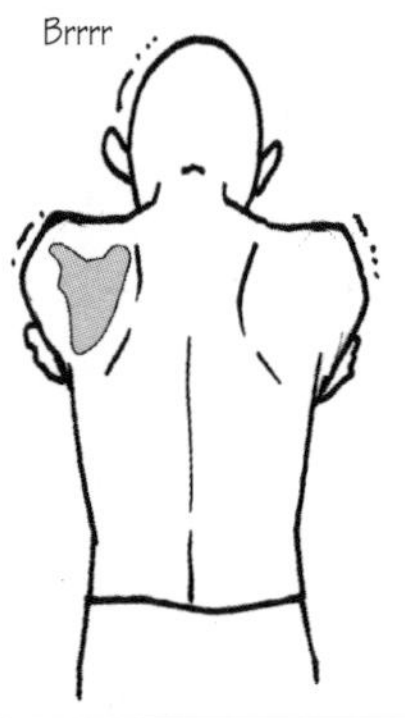

Brrrr

Rotating the shoulders forward causes the scapulae to shift apart.

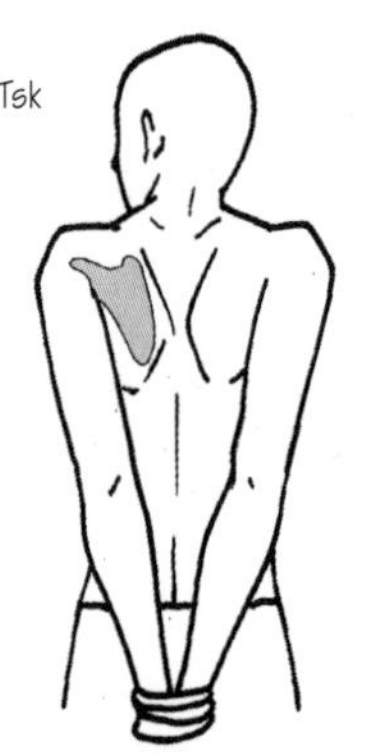

Arcing the shoulders back causes the scapulae to shift together.

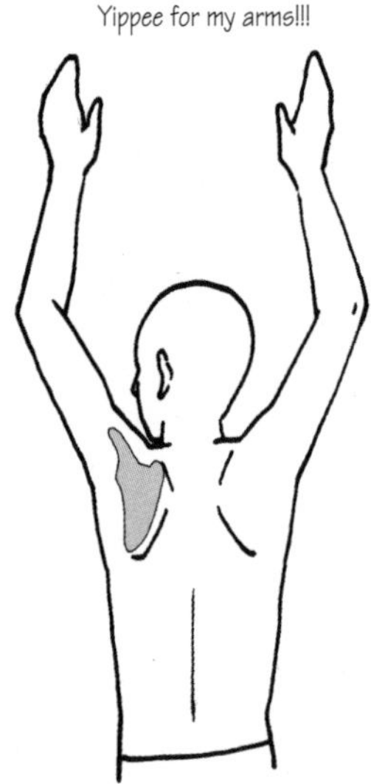

Yippee for my arms!!!

Raising the arms causes the scapulae to rise.

02:Skeletal Structure of the Arm

Crossing Bones: The Radius and Ulna

The radius and ulna cross according to the direction faced by the palm.

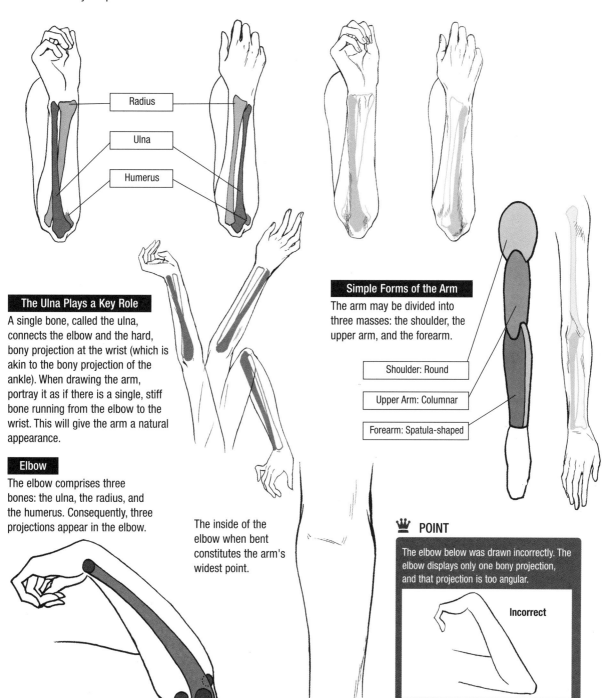

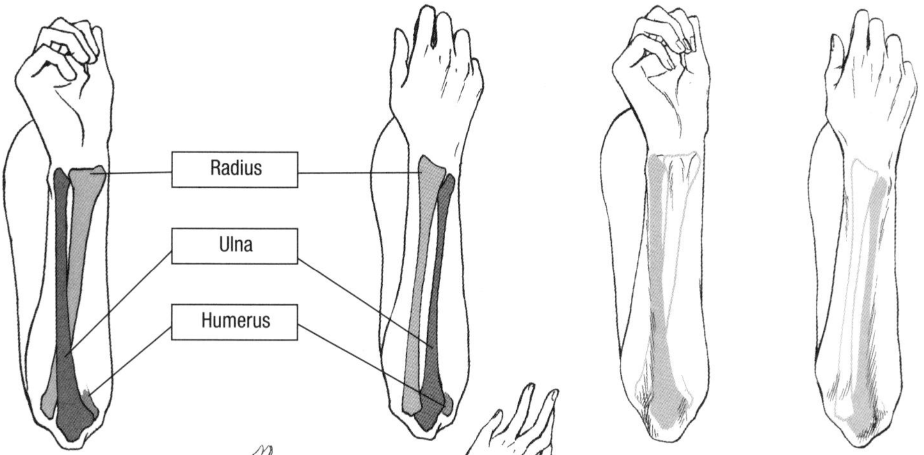

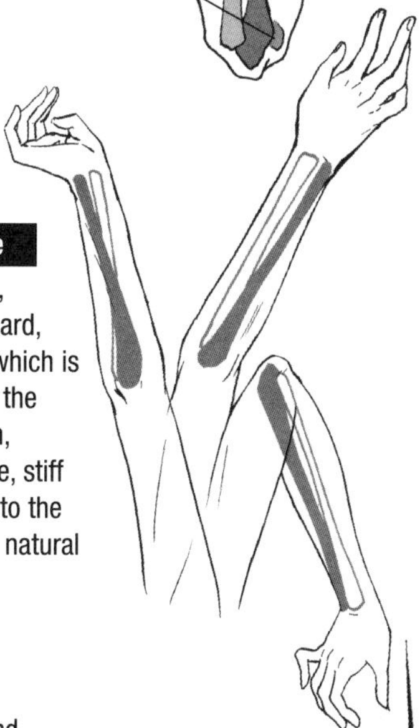

The Ulna Plays a Key Role

A single bone, called the ulna, connects the elbow and the hard, bony projection at the wrist (which is akin to the bony projection of the ankle). When drawing the arm, portray it as if there is a single, stiff bone running from the elbow to the wrist. This will give the arm a natural appearance.

Simple Forms of the Arm

The arm may be divided into three masses: the shoulder, the upper arm, and the forearm.

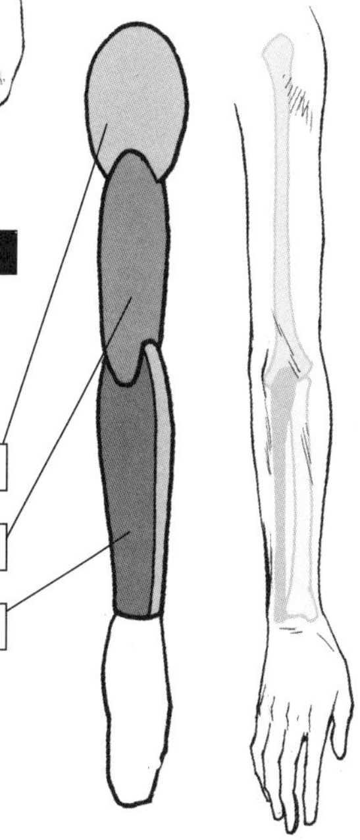

Elbow

The elbow comprises three bones: the ulna, the radius, and the humerus. Consequently, three projections appear in the elbow.

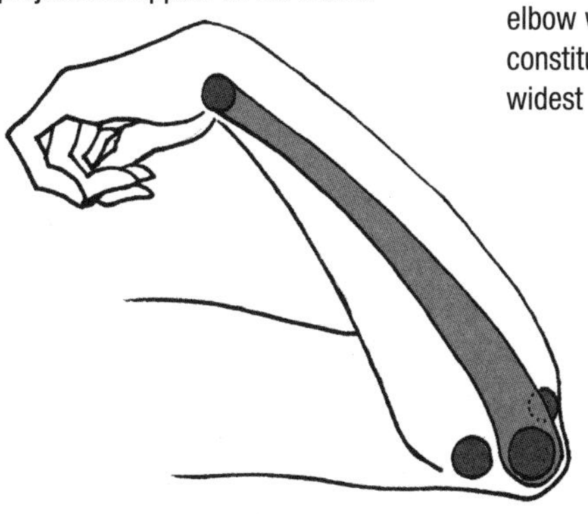

The inside of the elbow when bent constitutes the arm's widest point.

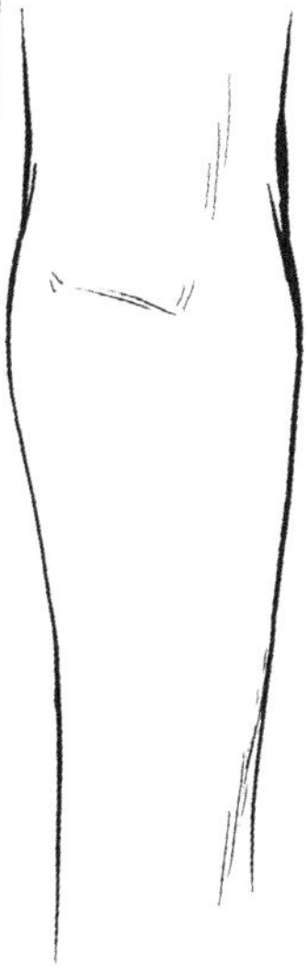

POINT

The elbow below was drawn incorrectly. The elbow displays only one bony projection, and that projection is too angular.

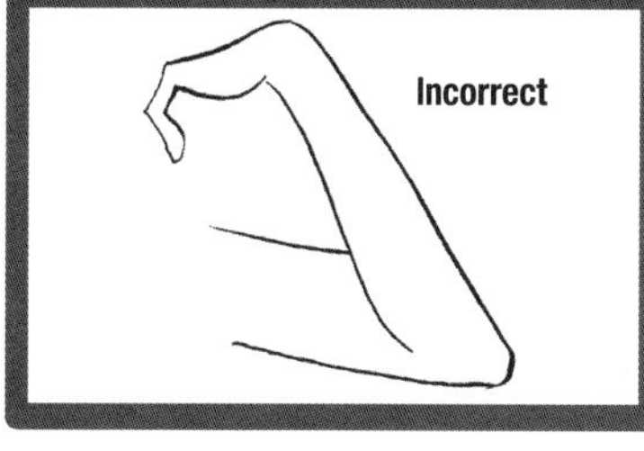

03:Skeletal Structure of the Leg

The Shin and Ankle

The arrows below illustrate that four curved contours describe the inside of the leg, while three describe the outside.

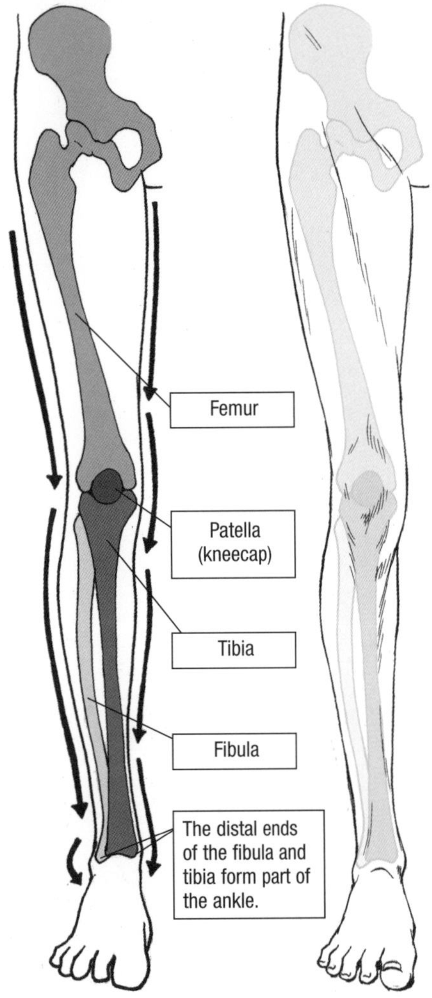

Femur

Patella (kneecap)

Tibia

Fibula

The distal ends of the fibula and tibia form part of the ankle.

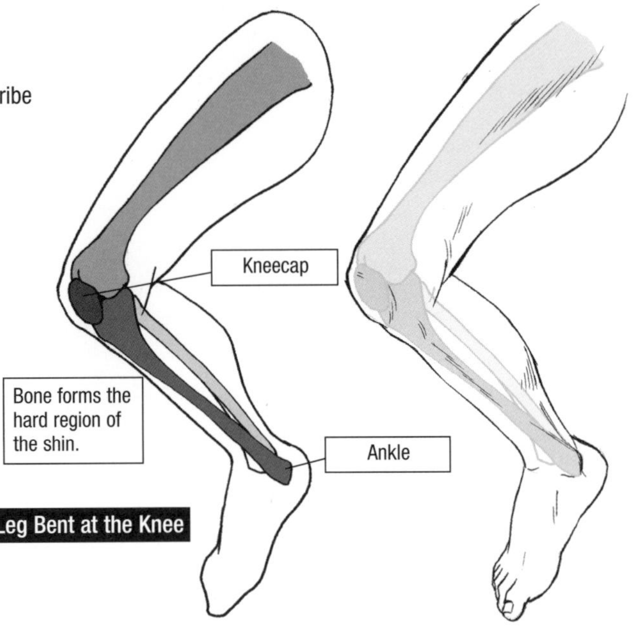

Leg Bent at the Knee

Kneecap

Bone forms the hard region of the shin.

Ankle

Three Hills of the Knee

The knee comprises three hills formed by the kneecap (the largest of the three) and the fibula (forming the remaining two smaller hills located underneath the kneecap). The two hills of the fibula may be omitted when drawing the knee.

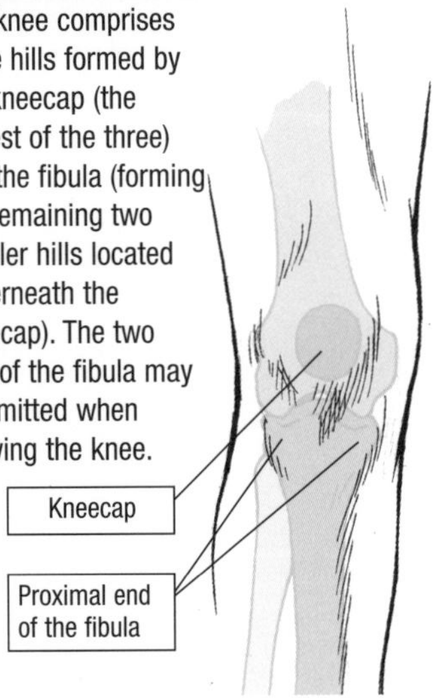

Kneecap

Proximal end of the fibula

Rear View of the Knee

An "H" is visible behind the knee.

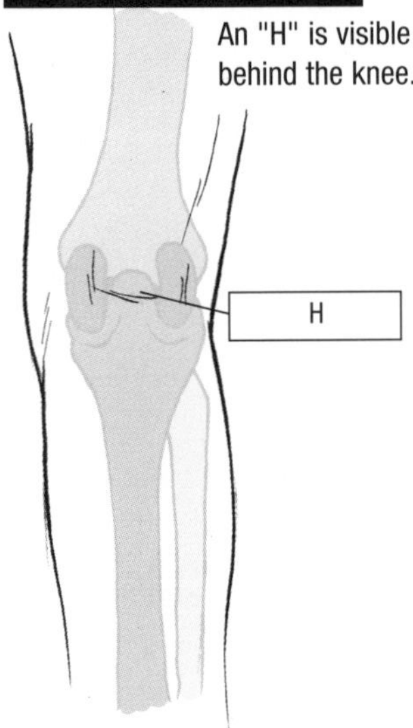

H

Dr. *Bishonen*'s Jolly Joint Workshop

The girths of the calf and thigh confuse some artists and cause them to make the knee and elbow too narrow when attempting to recreate the arms and legs' sinuous curves. However, given that the joints are articulations of bone to bone, logically speaking, the joints should not be narrower than any other body region where bones appear as a group. In fact, the joints should be more solid and chunkier than other body regions. They are vital to creating a sense of presence. Show attention to making the areas before and after the joint narrower to create undulating contours.

Joints should be chunky and stiff, m'kay?
Gross!
Weirdo!

Joint Motions

This lesson module shows poses illustrating the actual motions of the leg and arm joints, maintaining awareness of the skeletal structure's distinctive characteristics covered in the preceding lesson modules.

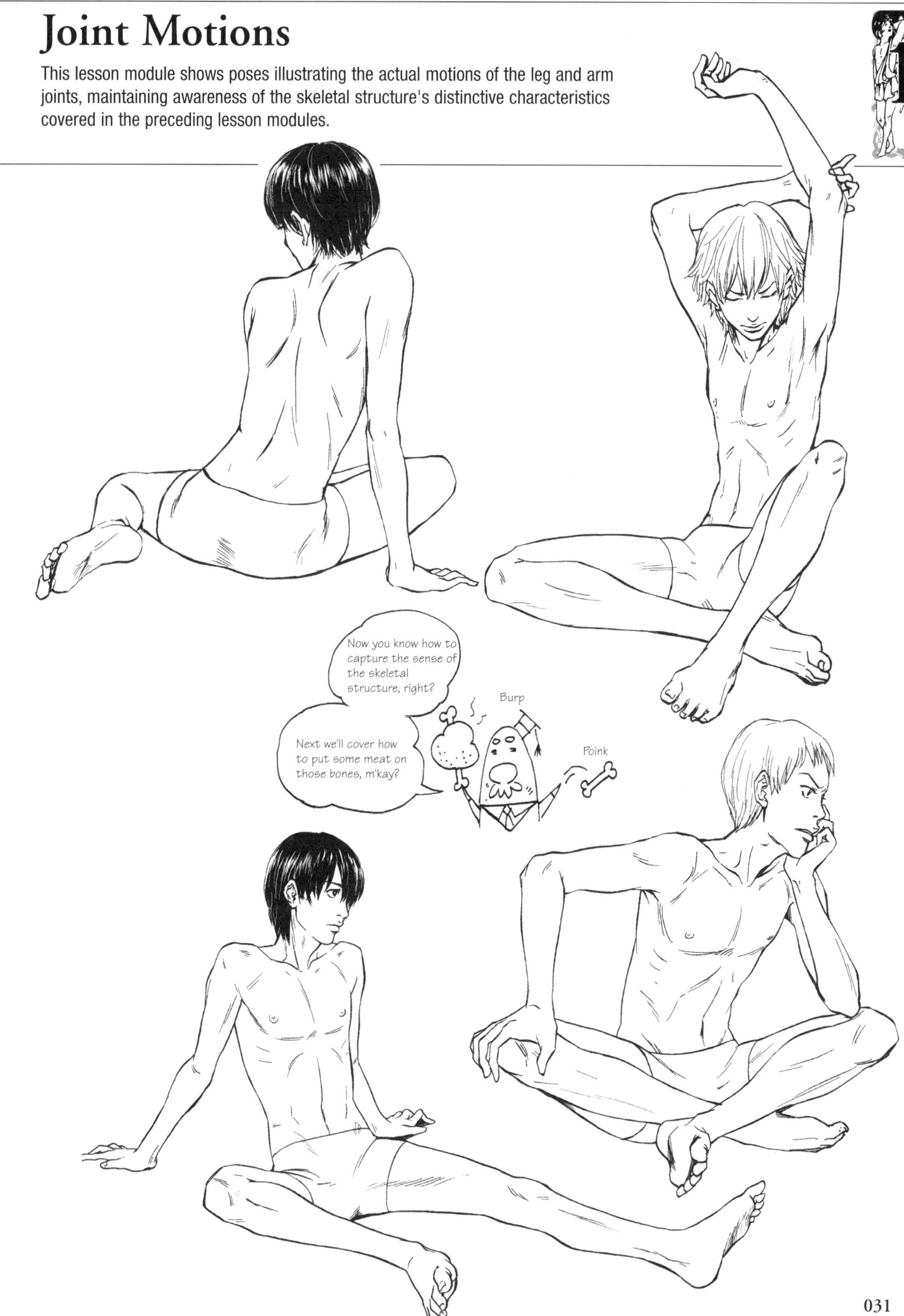

Now you know how to capture the sense of the skeletal structure, right?
Burp
Next we'll cover how to put some meat on those bones, m'kay?
Poink

Drawing Muscles

The musculature in the human body may be divided into approximately 450 parts. There is no way to draw them all, but to omit any hint of musculature results in infantile-looking characters. Shallow but developed sinews are crucial to portraying *bishonen*. There are three styles of abstracting musculature that produce natural results. Make an effort to learn them.

1 Basic Contours

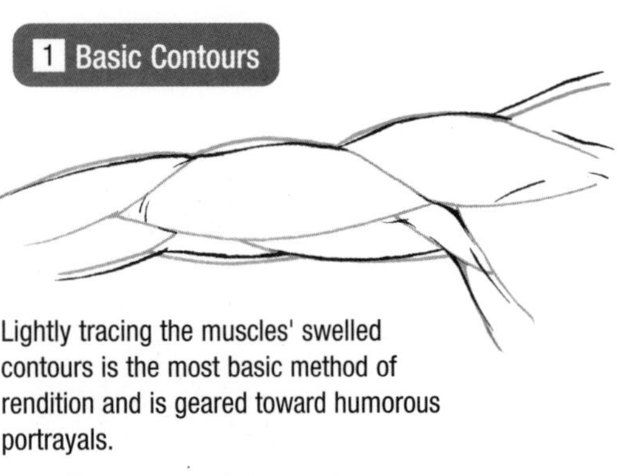

Lightly tracing the muscles' swelled contours is the most basic method of rendition and is geared toward humorous portrayals.

2 Basic Contours + Hatching

This is a more realistic portrayal and gives the muscles a supple appearance.

3 Basic Contours + Crosshatching

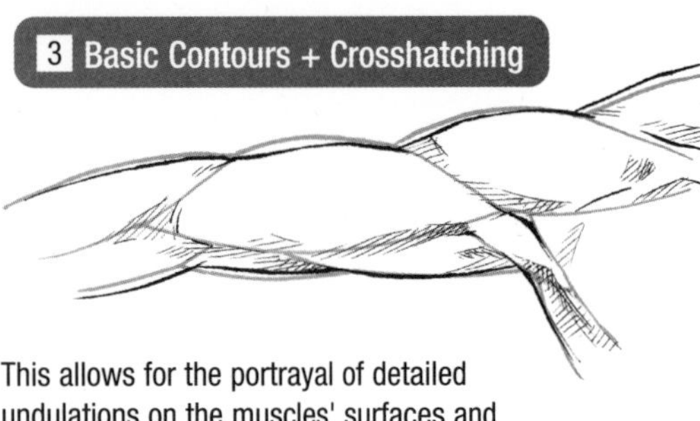

This allows for the portrayal of detailed undulations on the muscles' surfaces and is suited to dramatic *manga*.

Degrees of Abstracted

Musculature should be abstracted from most simplified and abbreviated to most realistic in the following order: "slim build," "average build," and "muscular build."

Musculature Diagram (Front View)

Darker shading indicates higher priority for inclusion.

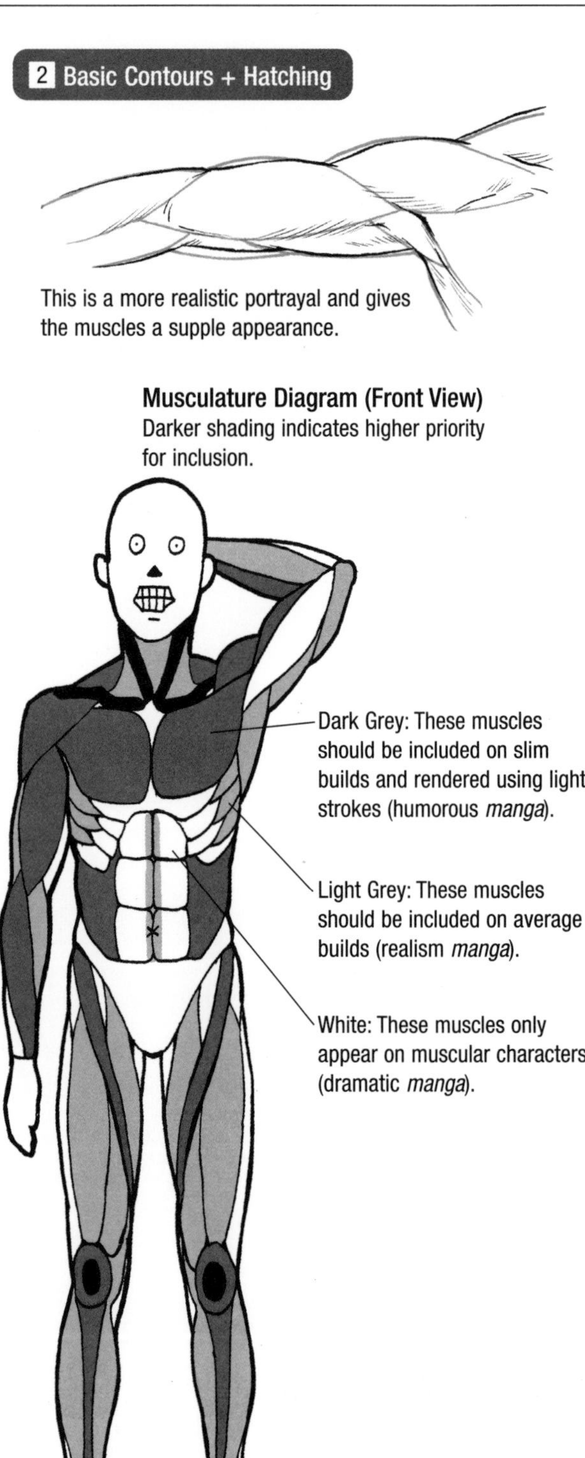

Dark Grey: These muscles should be included on slim builds and rendered using light strokes (humorous *manga*).

Light Grey: These muscles should be included on average builds (realism *manga*).

White: These muscles only appear on muscular characters (dramatic *manga*).

Three Styles of Muscle Portrayal (Front View)

As seen below, the style of musculature portrayal used affects the impression a character projects, even when the build type remains the same.

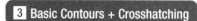

2 Basic Contours + Hatching

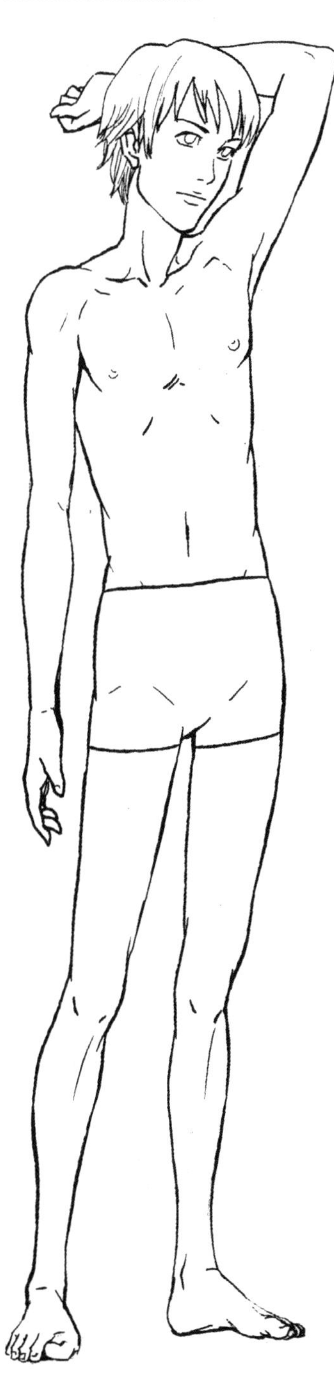

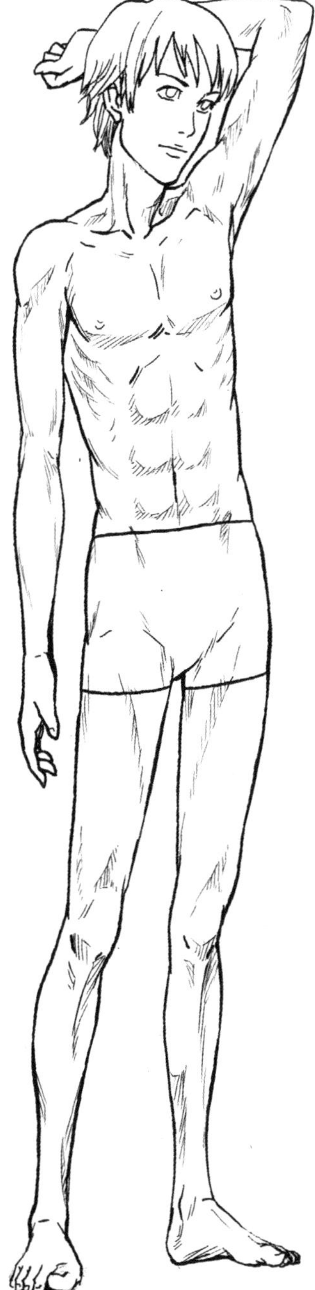

Drawing Muscle Contours

Muscle contours shift as the body moves. This lesson module covers how to draw muscle contours using the light source as primary reference.

1 Basic Contours

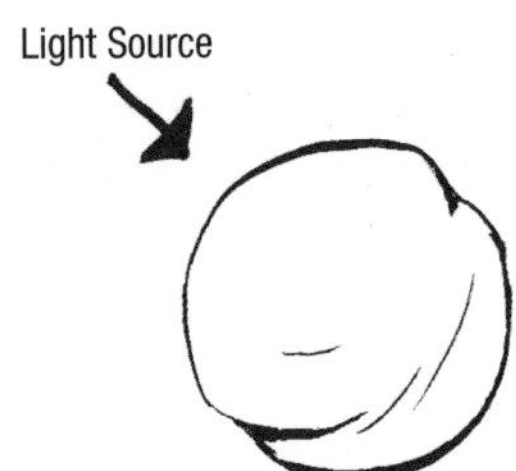

Draw the muscle's curved bulges using light strokes.

2 Basic Contours + Hatching

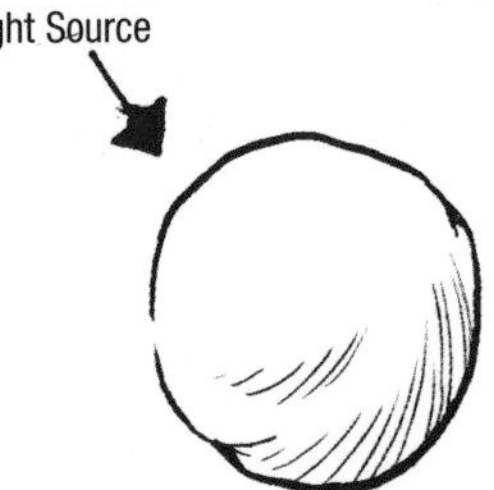

Use a Maru pen to draw fine hatched strokes, adhering to the muscle's curved contours. The trick is to shift the angle in which you draw the strokes to get better results.

3 Basic Contours + Crosshatching

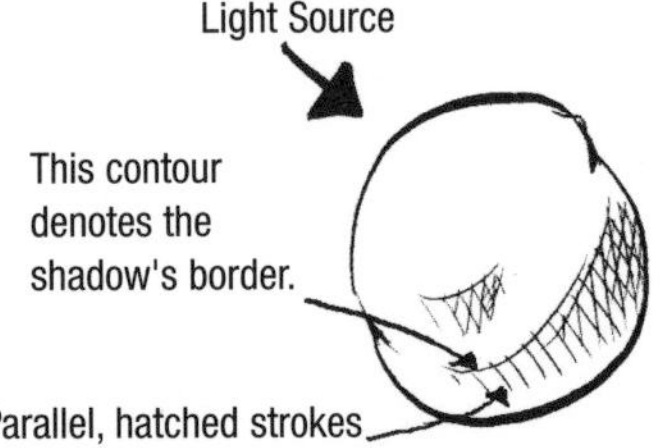

This contour denotes the shadow's border.

Draw basic contours facing the light source and add fine, parallel hatched lines with a Maru or similar pen. Shift angles to crosshatch those regions of the muscle that are the darkest.

Pitfalls

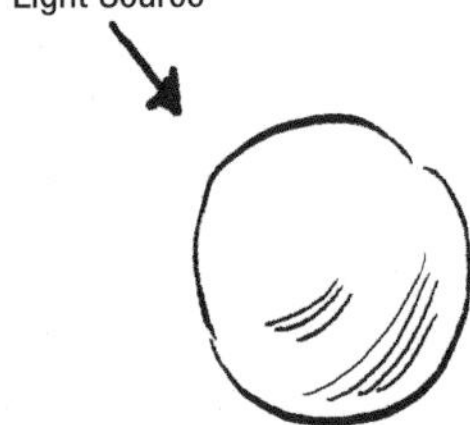

Incorrect Use of Hatching
Evenly spaced lines produce the appearance of fatty tissue rather than shaded muscle.

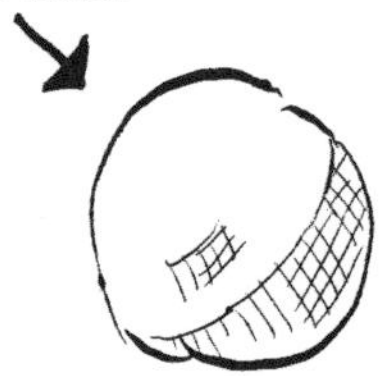

Incorrect Use of Crosshatching
Perpendicular crosshatching does not yield the supple appearance of human flesh.

The crosshatched lines should be drawn at increasing angles, m'kay?
1
2
3

Crosshatching for Muscles
Note that crosshatching used for muscles is different from standard crosshatching.

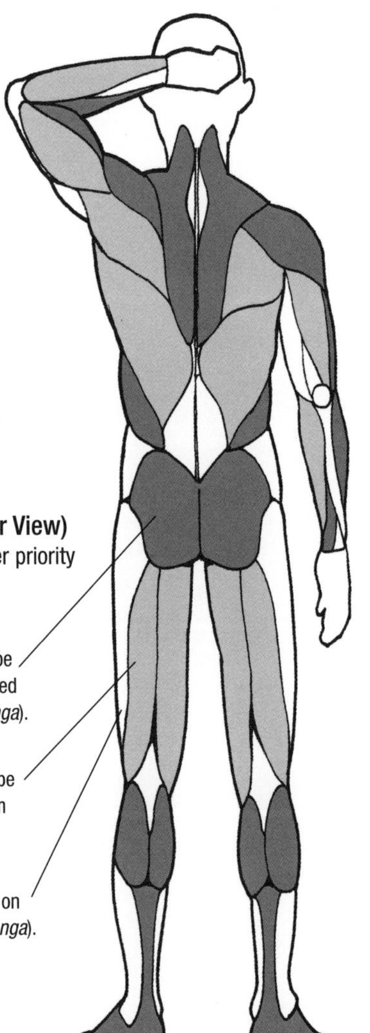

Musculature Diagram (Rear View)
Darker shading indicates higher priority for inclusion.

Dark Grey: These muscles should be included on slim builds and rendered using light strokes (humorous *manga*).

Light Grey: These muscles should be included on average builds (realism *manga*).

White: These muscles only appear on muscular characters (dramatic *manga*).

Three Styles of Muscle Portrayal (Rear View)

As seen below, the style of musculature portrayal used affects the impression a character projects, even when the build type remains the same.

1 Basic Contours

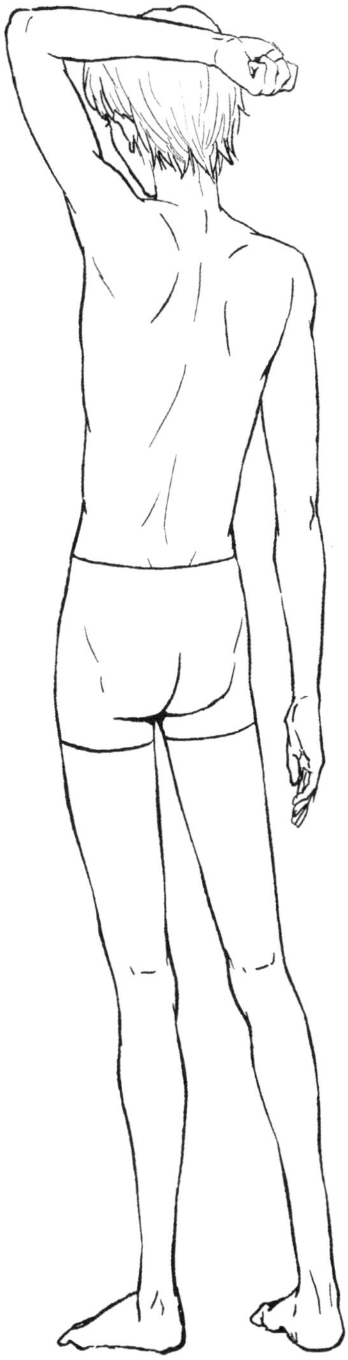

2 Basic Contours + Hatching

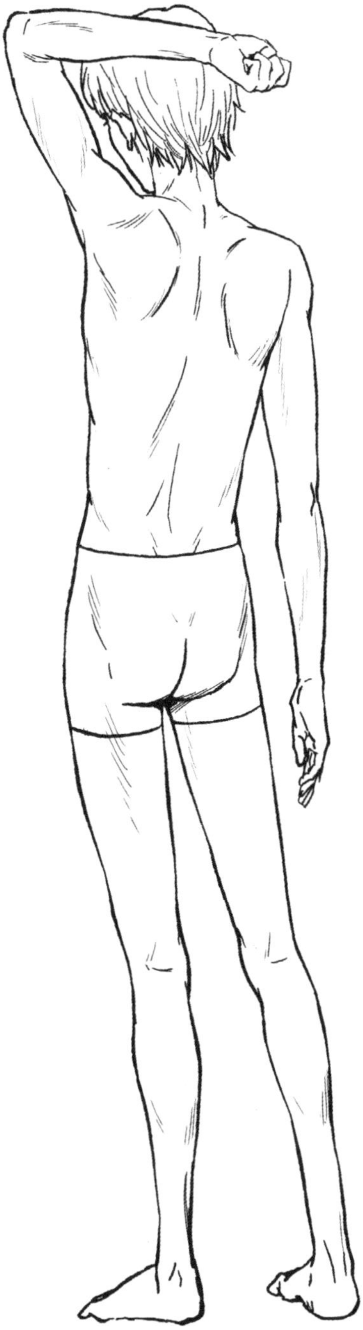

3 Basic Contours + Crosshatching

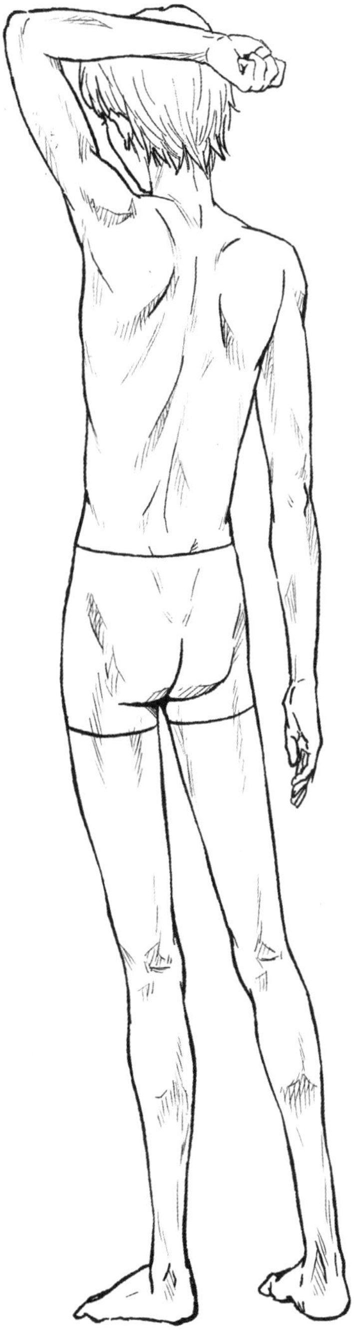

Muscle Extension, Contraction and Torsion

Visualize how the muscles stretch and contract as the body moves when portraying a figure in motion.

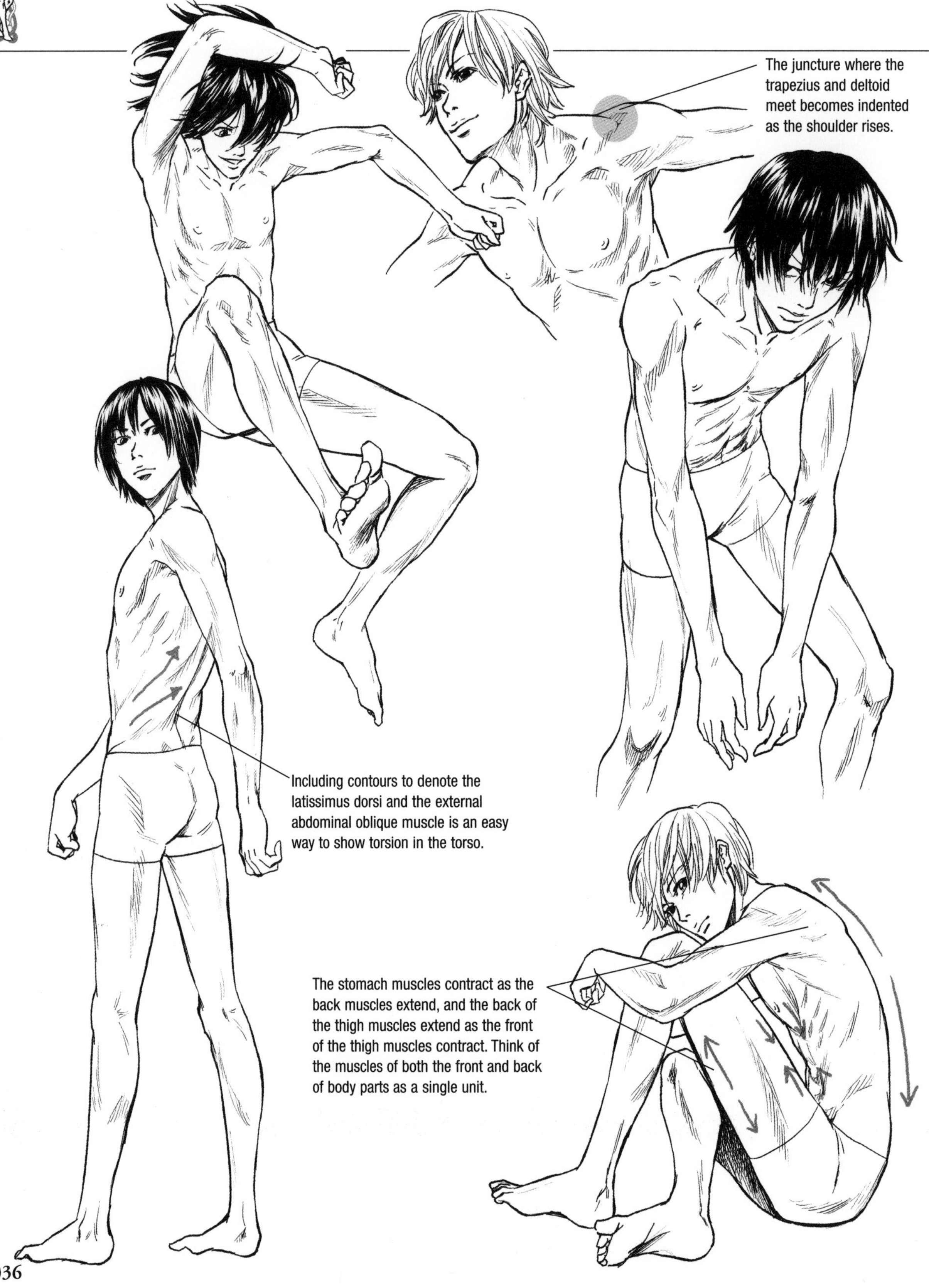

The juncture where the trapezius and deltoid meet becomes indented as the shoulder rises.
Including contours to denote the latissimus dorsi and the external abdominal oblique muscle is an easy way to show torsion in the torso.
The stomach muscles contract as the back muscles extend, and the back of the thigh muscles extend as the front of the thigh muscles contract. Think of the muscles of both the front and back of body parts as a single unit.

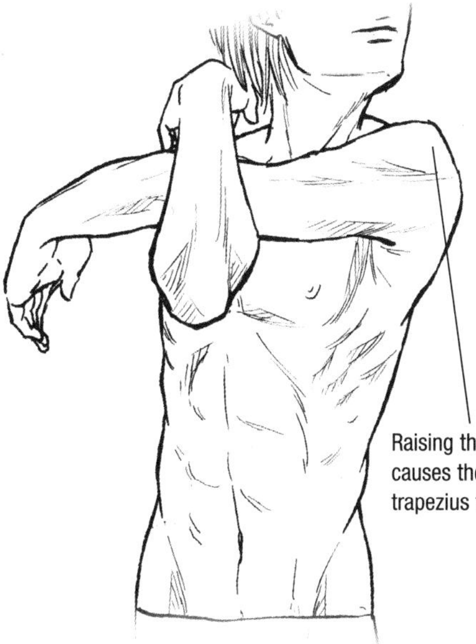

Raising the arm slightly causes the deltoid and trapezius to bulge.

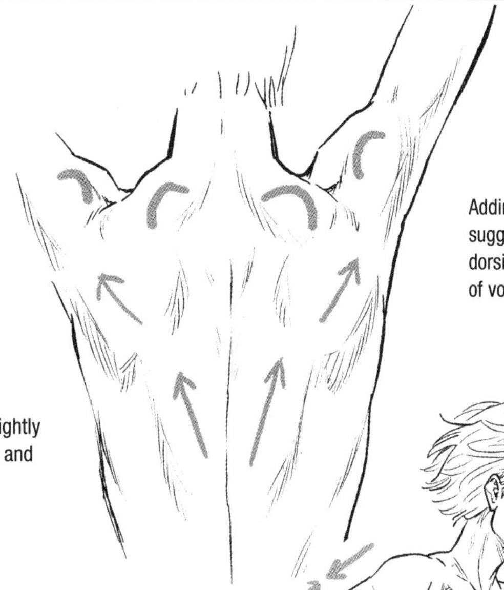

Adding contours that suggest the latissimus dorsi enhances the sense of volume.

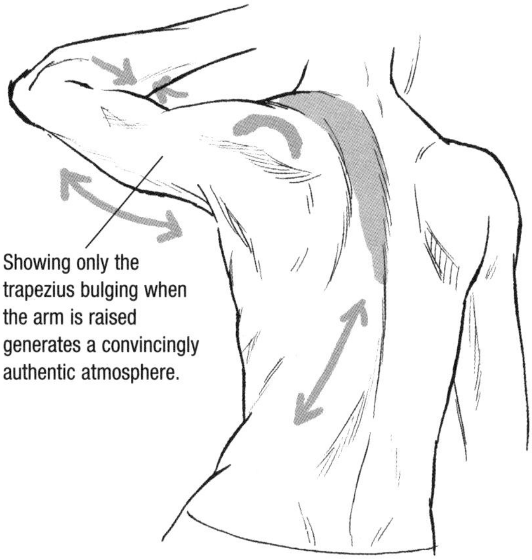

Showing only the trapezius bulging when the arm is raised generates a convincingly authentic atmosphere.

Sketching axial lines, side lines, and section lines will help you identify where the body stretches, contracts, and torques. Being aware of how the axial line appears as it runs from the throat to the navel when the body twists will help the figure maintain a convincing structure.

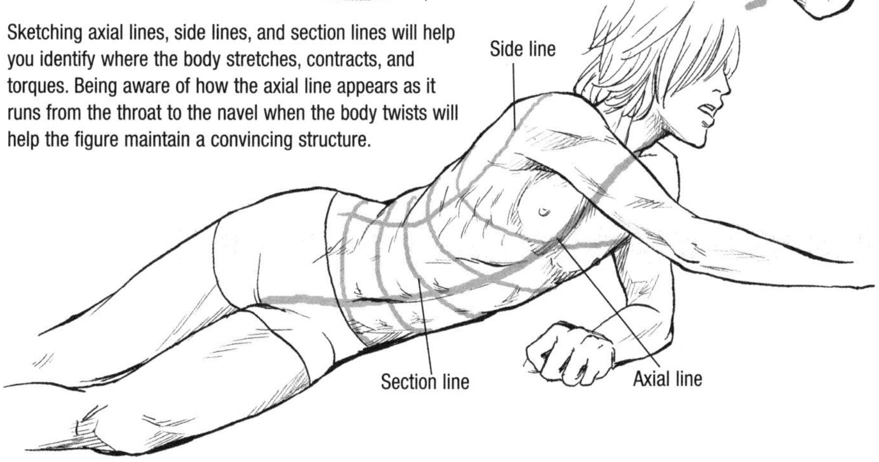

Side line

Section line

Axial line

Practical Application Drawing a Standing Figure

This lesson module allows you to practice drawing a standing figure with Dr. *Bishonen*'s guidance and making use of the skeletal structure and musculature covered previously.

Dr. *Bishonen*: "Get out a sheet of paper and mechanical pencil and get ready to draw, m'kay?"

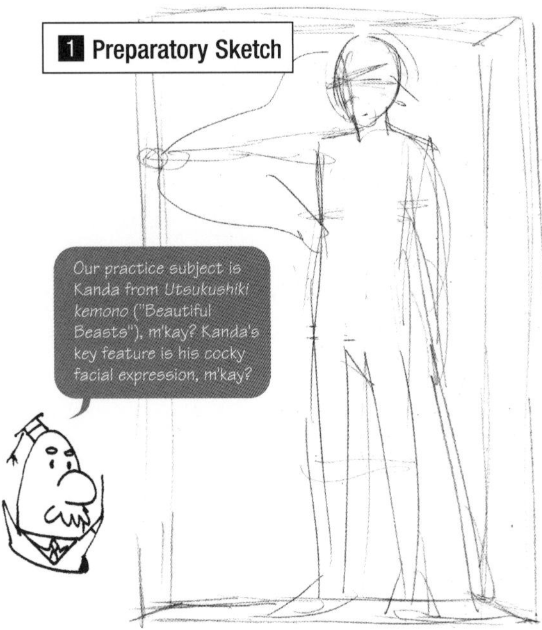

1 Preparatory Sketch
Our practice subject is Kanda from Utsukushiki kemono ("Beautiful Beasts"), m'kay? Kanda's key feature is his cocky facial expression, m'kay?

First, gain a developed visual image of the drawing subject. Imagine his clothing, facial expression, pose, and everything else including his personality in detail. Next, jot out the space occupied by the subject in three dimensions and create a rough sketch of the subject within that three-dimensional space. Avoid producing a careful, detailed drawing at this point, as you might end up having to erase any mistakes you make later down the road. Just produce a quick, rough sketch.

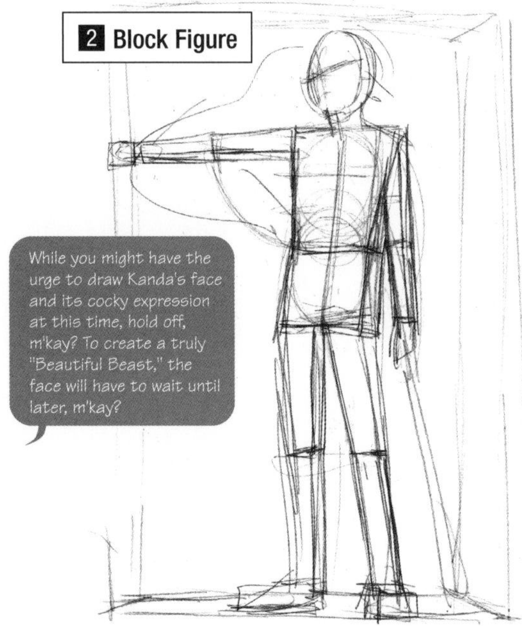

2 Block Figure
While you might have the urge to draw Kanda's face and its cocky expression at this time, hold off, m'kay? To create a truly "Beautiful Beast," the face will have to wait until later, m'kay?

Using the abdominal circle, which was one of the three circles of the torso covered during the skeletal structure discussion (pp. 13 to 15), capture the overall proportioning of the skeletal structure. Identify in which directions the blocks composing the torso, legs, arms, and head should face. While the resulting figure may not look remotely human, you should still have successfully captured the figure as a three-dimensional object at the end of this stage.

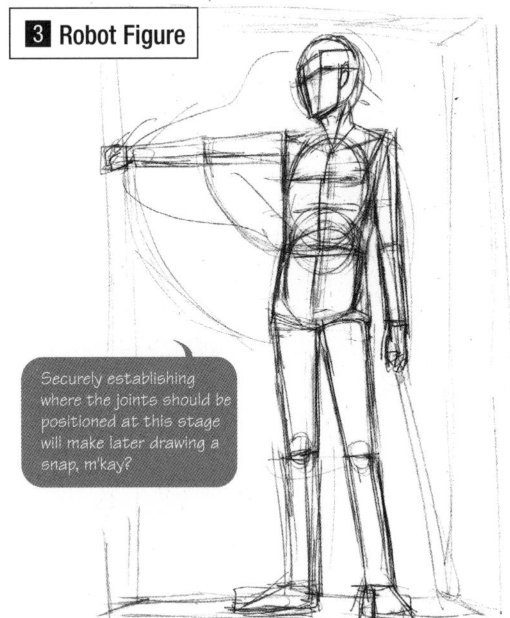

3 Robot Figure
Securely establishing where the joints should be positioned at this stage will make later drawing a snap, m'kay?

Next, give the blocks drawn in step 2 more human detail, while determining where to position the abdominal circle and the joints.

Roughly sketch the figure's exterior contours, hair, and clothing. Adjust the overall proportioning. Lightly jot down the direction in which the fabric creases flow. Imagine that a breeze is blowing to create the flow of the creases. While steps 2 through 4 might seem basic and lackluster, they constitute the absolutely vital sketching stages. If you feel that any portion of your figure is drawn incorrectly, dive in and fix it until you have achieved a form you find satisfying.

5 Detailed Drawing

Looking good!!

This is what you have been waiting for—to draw the figure in detail. At this stage you may draw the facial expression and clothing in as much detail as you like. Go ahead, cast off all restraints and compose Kanda according to your personal taste. Add personal effects and other props. Dr. *Bishonen*'s enthusiasm is getting a little out of control.

6 Inking Primary Lines

If line modulation doesn't seem necessary, you may skip this step, m'kay?

Take the drawing of Kanda completed in step 5 and lay it under a clean sheet. Quickly and using powerful strokes, go over the primary contours, lines indicating roughly the direction in which the hair flows, major fabric creases and front pleats with a wide pen nib (a G pen was used to create the image above). Avoid adding details (hair details, eyes, mouth, detailed fabric creases, muscle contours, etc.). Drawing the primary lines first using wide strokes results in a final drawing with line modulation.

7 Inking the Details

Adding a touch of blood to the mouth gives the character the air of a wild beast, m'kay?

In this stage, use a fine pen nib (a Maru pen was used to create the image above) and carefully add in the details. Make the drawing as detailed as you like. Be as particular about what you want to add and how you want it to look as you feel necessary. The more attention you pay to details, such as the blazer's shoulder seams, the cuff buttons, the manner in which the breast pocket on Kanda's shirt sags, the more heightened the sense of reality will be.

8 Final Image

C'est fini! And now we are ready to admit a new student to our academy and earn a tidy bundle in tuition fees, m'kay?

Apply tone, establishing where the light source is located before determining where to place the shadow.

Practical Application Drawing a Seated Figure

This lesson module introduces drawing a figure seated as an exercise in practical application. Follow Dr. *Bishonen* and Bontaro Hei's guidance as you work. Do you have a paper and mechanical pencil ready?

1 Preparatory Sketch

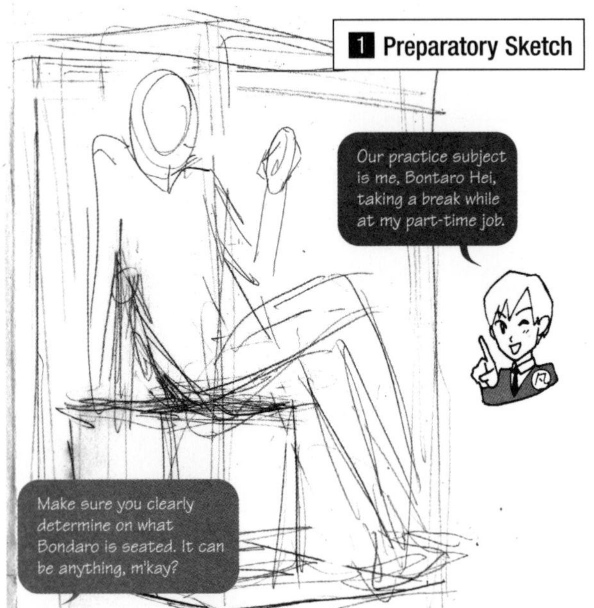

Our practice subject is me, Bontaro Hei, taking a break while at my part-time job.
Make sure you clearly determine on what Bondaro is seated. It can be anything, m'kay?

As with the drawing of Kanda, first, gain a developed visual image of the subject. Capture the space occupied by the subject in three dimensions and create a rough sketch of the subject within that three-dimensional space. Avoid adding details at this juncture. Be certain that you firmly establish how high the seated figure will be.

2 Block Figure

It is difficult to draw one thigh resting on top of another like this. However, if you compose the legs as one block laying over the other, then the pose becomes a piece of cake to draw.

Is that a fact?

Using the abdominal circle, which was one of the three circles of the torso covered during the skeletal structure discussion (pp. 13 to 15), capture the overall proportioning of the skeletal structure. Identify in which directions the blocks composing the torso, legs, arms, and head face. Pay careful attention to ensure that the right and left legs are relatively equal in length both above and below the knee. The right thigh will appear somewhat shorter than the left thigh, as it is viewed obliquely from the left, crossed over the other thigh.

3 Robot Figure

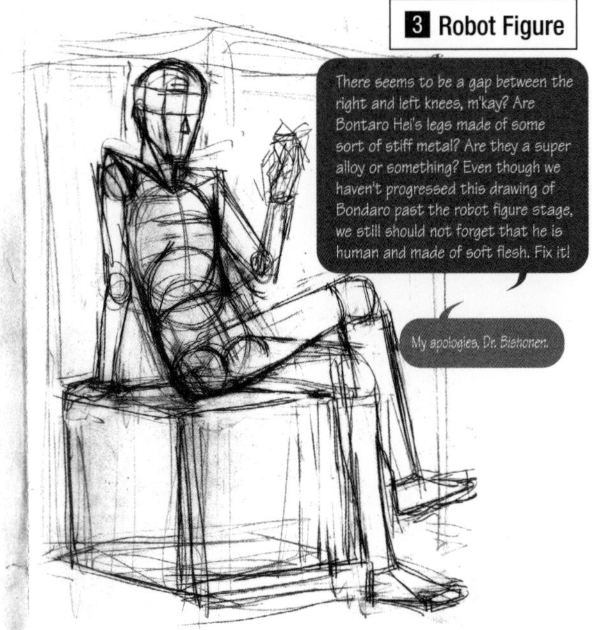

There seems to be a gap between the right and left knees, m'kay? Are Bontaro Hei's legs made of some sort of stiff metal? Are they a super alloy or something? Even though we haven't progressed this drawing of Bondaro past the robot figure stage, we still should not forget that he is human and made of soft flesh. Fix it!
My apologies, Dr. Bishonen.

Next, give the blocks drawn in step 2 more human detail, while determining where to position the abdominal circle and the joints.

4 Rough Sketch

My left knee still looks like it's suspended in air. But, I guess we did manage to progress this far.
This is still nothing more than an under drawing. Don't hesitate to erase all of it, even if it looks finished. Clinging to an incorrectly composed sketch just because you've completed it is amateurish, m'kay?

Roughly sketch the figure's exterior contours, hair, and clothing. Adjust the overall proportioning. Lightly jot down the direction in which the fabric creases flow. Large fabric creases should appear in the scrunched up sleeves of the hooded sweatshirt. You may need to draw difficult poses over and over again until you get them right.

1

5 Detailed Drawing

Looking good!!
Bontaro, the only personal effects you have are a cell phone and an apron. How ordinary can you get?

This is what you have been waiting for—to draw the figure in detail. At this stage you may draw the facial expression and clothing in as much detail as you like. Go ahead, cast off all restraints and compose Bondaro according to your personal taste. Add personal effects and other props and develop Bondaro's narcissistic personality.

6 Inking Primary Lines

My, my, don't I have a spectacular face?
I don't know if I'd go that far.

Take the drawing of Bontaro Hei completed in step 5 and lay it under a clean sheet. Quickly and using powerful strokes, go over the primary contours, lines indicating roughly the direction in which the hair flows, major fabric creases and pleats with a wide pen nib (a G pen was used to create the image above). Avoid adding details (hair details, eyes, mouth, detailed fabric creases, muscle contours, etc.). Using thick strokes to draw Bondaro's crossed legs and sitting surface evokes the sense of a person seated.

7 Inking the Details

Check it out! I'm sitting on the emergency fire escape ladder.
Get off it already!

In this stage, use a fine pen nib (a Maru pen was used to create the image above) and carefully add in the details. Make the drawing as detailed as you like. Be as particular about what you want to add and how you want it to look as you feel necessary. In this stage you should imbue the clothing with a sense of texture. The more details you add, the more heightened the sense of reality Bontaro Hei projects will be.

8 Final Image

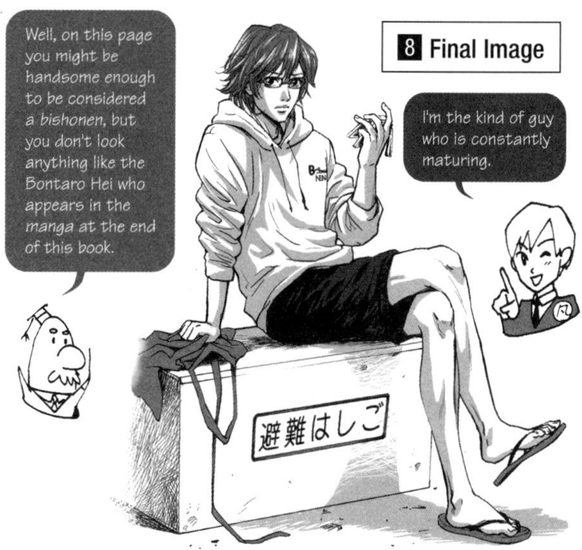

Well, on this page you might be handsome enough to be considered a bishonen, but you don't look anything like the Bontaro Hei who appears in the manga at the end of this book.
I'm the kind of guy who is constantly maturing.

Apply tone, establishing where the light source is located before determining where to place the shadow.

Musculature Reference Diagram

As with the skeletal structure, you must maintain awareness of how the muscles connect and flow to produce a human figure with a sense of three-dimensionality. Use the musculature diagram below as reference.

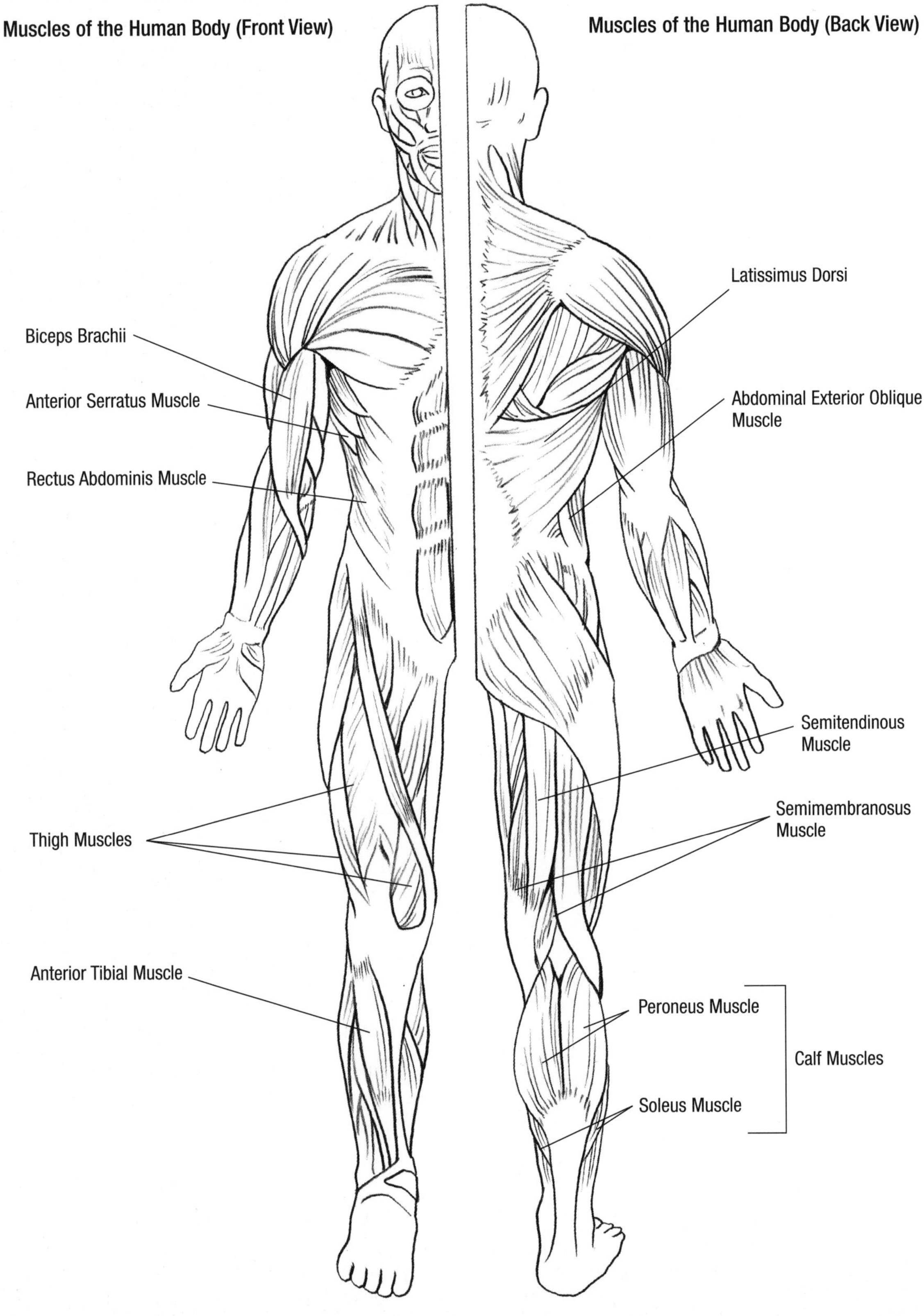

Muscles of the Human Body (Front View)

Muscles of the Human Body (Back View)

Latissimus Dorsi

Biceps Brachii

Anterior Serratus Muscle

Abdominal Exterior Oblique Muscle

Rectus Abdominis Muscle

Semitendinous Muscle

Semimembranosus Muscle

Thigh Muscles

Anterior Tibial Muscle

Peroneus Muscle

Calf Muscles

Soleus Muscle

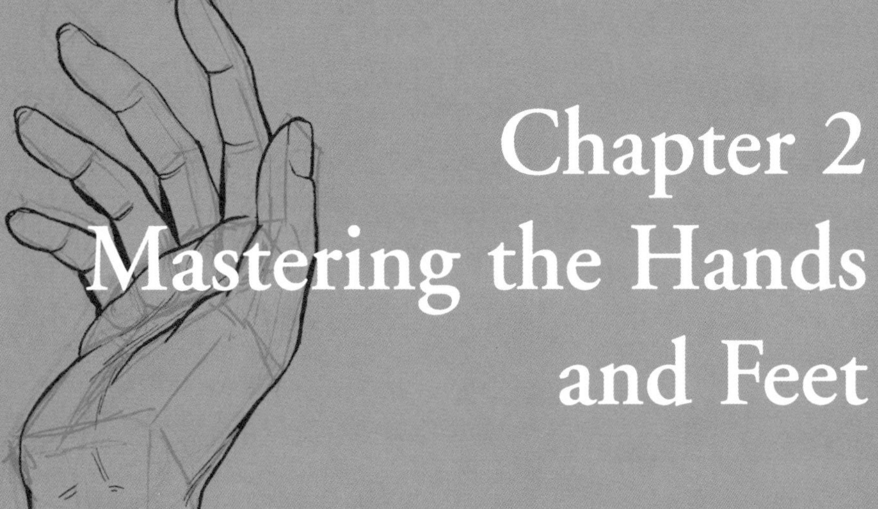

Chapter 2 Mastering the Hands and Feet

How to Draw the Hand The Elusive Third Joint

Everyone recognizes the first and second joints in the average human finger. However, the finger's third joint, the knuckle, tends to become lost in the hand itself. Draw the region shown below in grey as part of the fingers.

Structure of the Hand

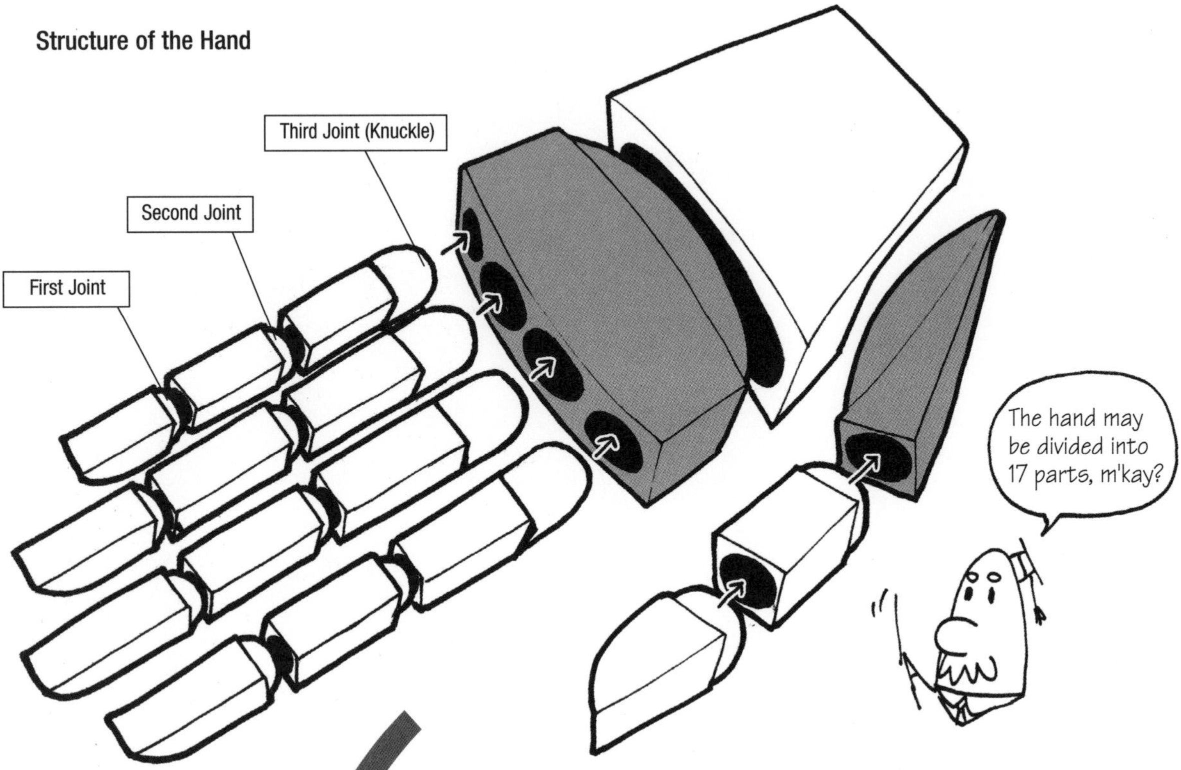

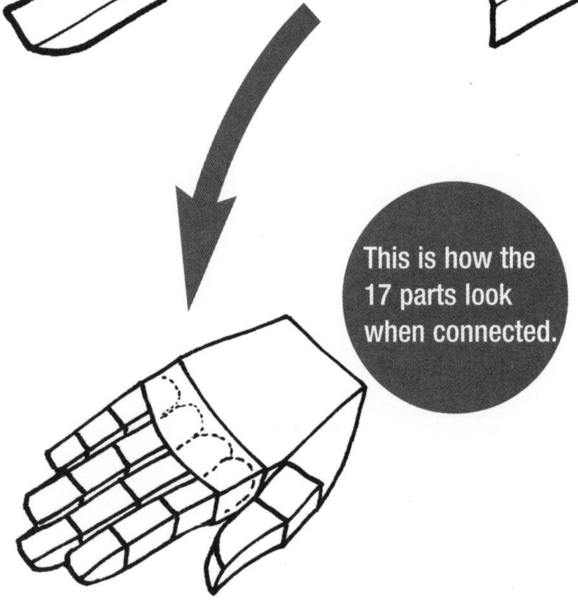

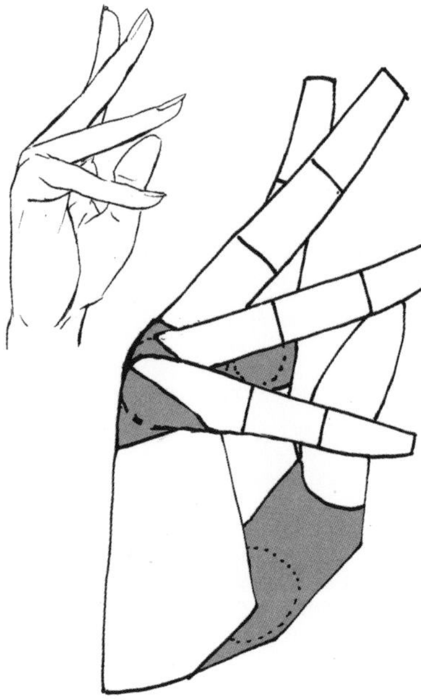

Part of the hand itself is connected to the fingers. The knuckles take on a variety of forms as the fingers move.

Special Characteristics of the Hand

An attractive hand results when the joints and fingers are properly aligned.

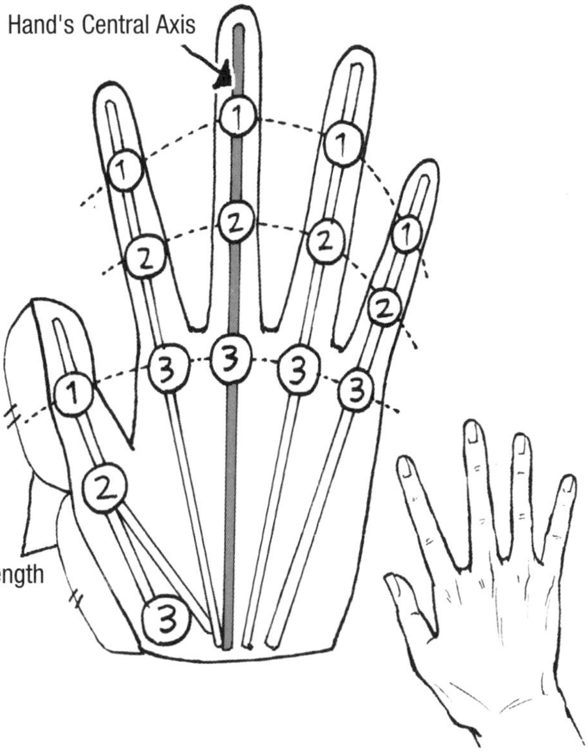

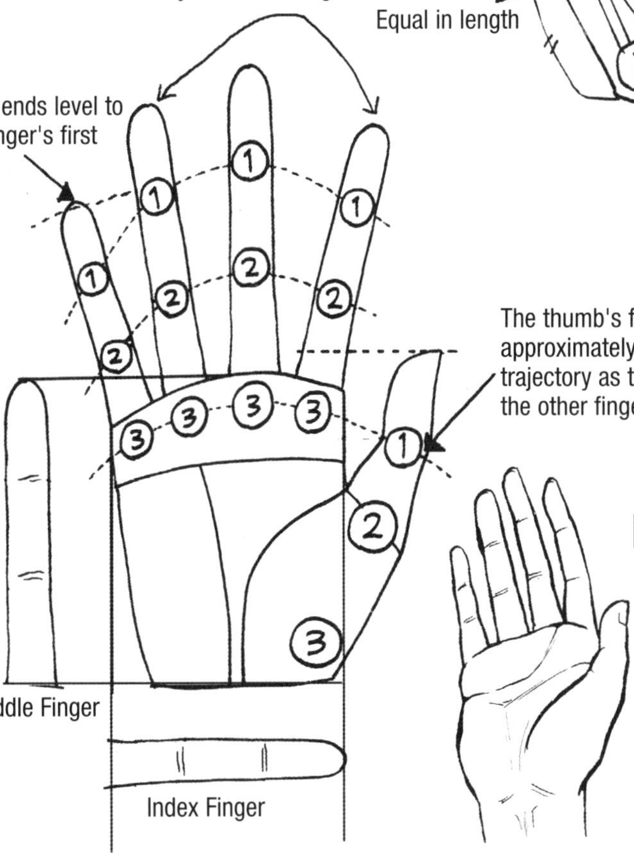

Special Characteristics of Each Part of the Hand

The hand itself changes in shape according to how the third joints move.

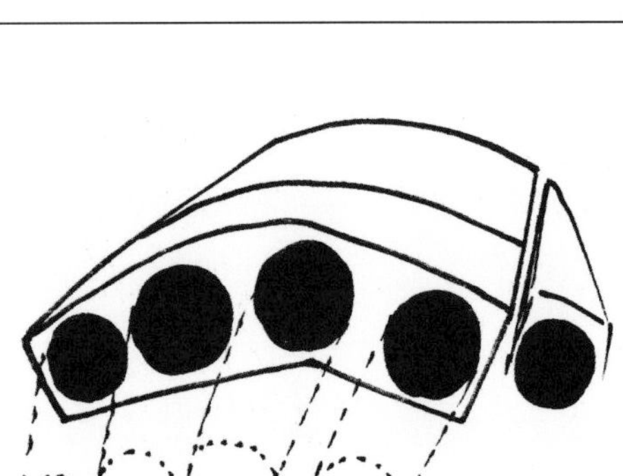

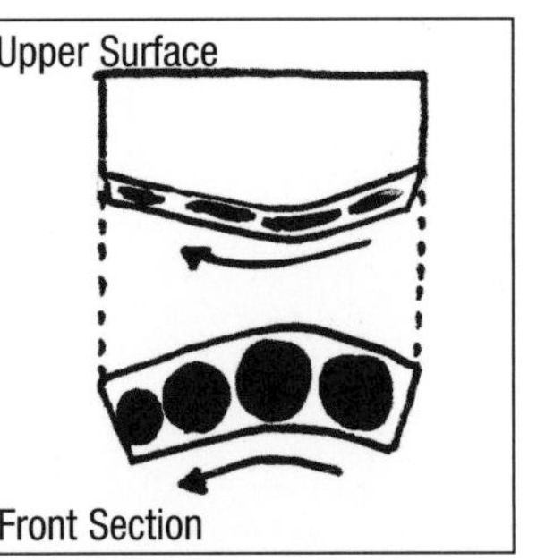

When the hand is in a resting position, the third joints (the knuckles) form a gentle, inverted "V".

When the hand is contracted, the inverted "V" becomes more acute.

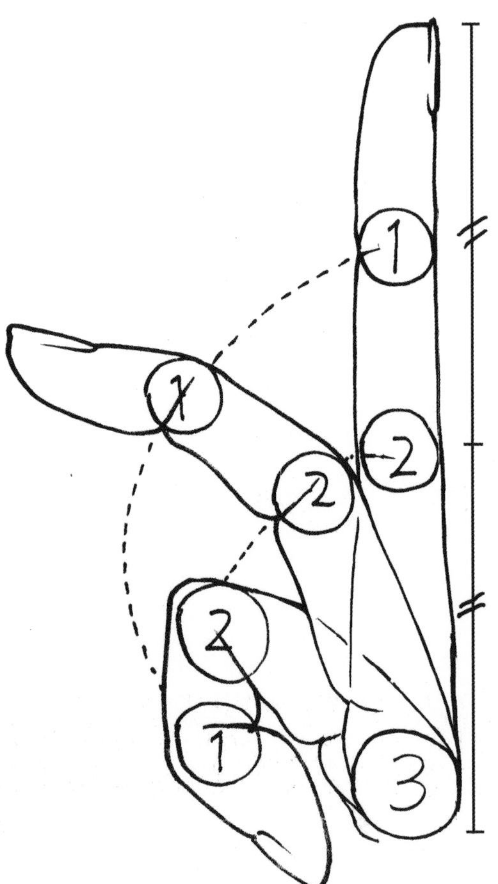

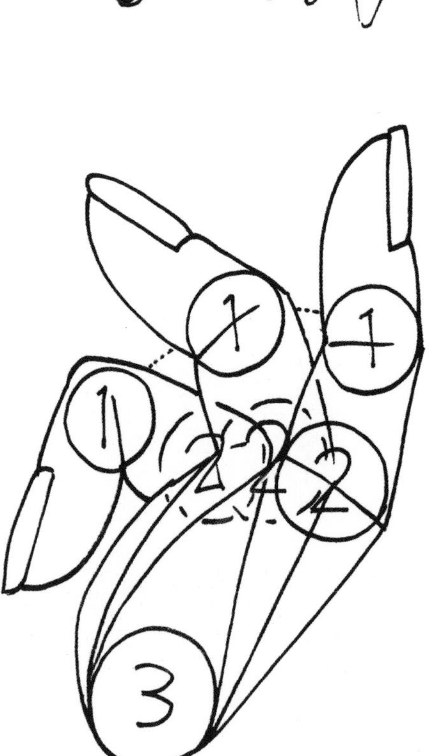

Fingers' Range of Motion

The fingers, from the index finger to the pinky, move dexterously upwards and downwards. They are not able to move much to the right and left. While the index finger, middle finger, ring finger, and pinky have different lengths, they share the same ranges of motion. (I.e. the pinky is the middle finger in miniature.)

Thumb's Range of Motion

The thumb has a broad range of motion and is able to move freely up and down and from left to right.

The Three Steps in Drawing the Hand

This lesson module covers the steps involved in actually drawing the hand. The key point is to use straight lines and compose the hand in block form in the under drawing.

1 First, draw the wrist and the palm.

2 Next, establish the palm's angle and the general positions of the fingers.

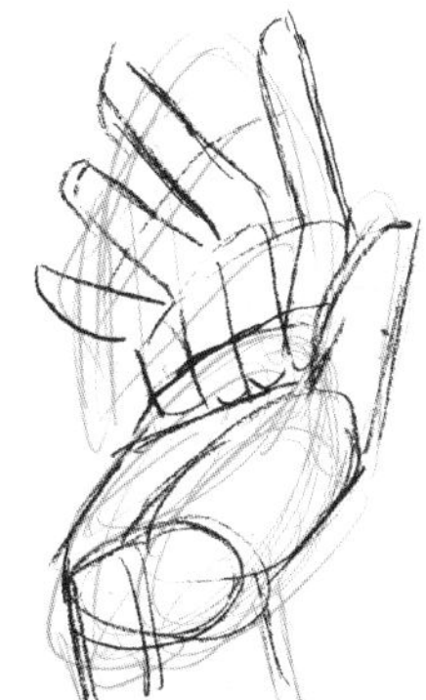

3 Delineate the positions of the fingers more precisely.

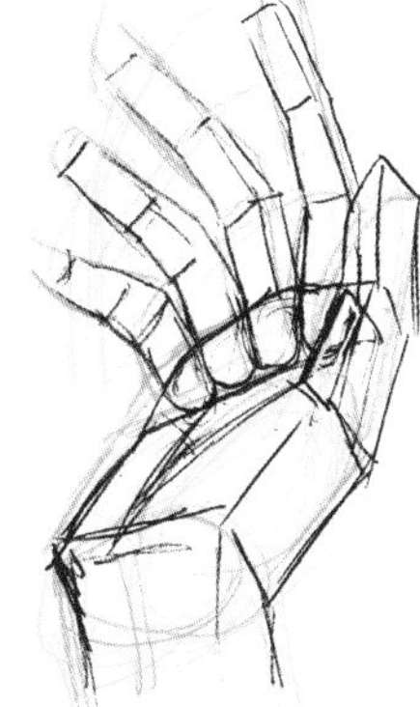

4 Divide the entire hand into the 17 partsÅ

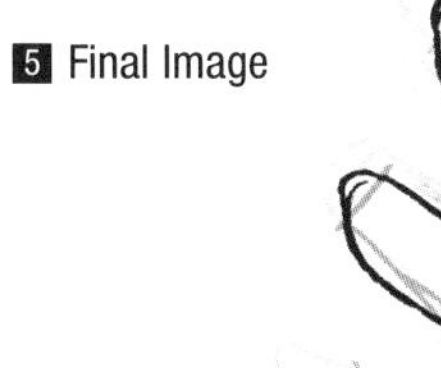

5 Final Image

Pay careful attention to dividing the hand into its 17 parts when producing the under drawing, m'kay?

POINT

Portraying the Nails

Drawing the nails' contours in full will make the nails stand out too much visually and destroy the fingers' shapes. Instead, leave a portion of each nail's contours open to achieve a cleaner look.

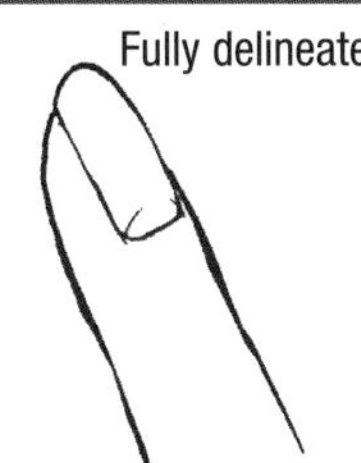

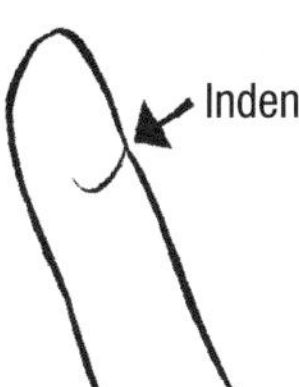

Portraying a Hand Held Naturally

Proper hand portrayal plays a key role in drawing *manga*. Regardless of how well-formed the hand might be, a hand without a sense of movement has only half the appeal as one that does. This lesson module covers everything from how to portray a hand held naturally to an array of hand movements.

The Roles of Each Digit

When we hold an object, each of our fingers plays a different role that affects how it moves.

Thumb: Provides Gripping Power
The thumb is the only digit on the hand able to move in a direction opposite the others. Without the thumb, we would not be able to hold an object.

Index Finger: Provides Gripping Power
The index finger works as a team with the thumb in handling objects.

Middle Finger: Assists the Thumb and the Index Finger
Because the middle finger forms the hand's central axis, it is able to perform multiple functions.

Ring Finger: Assists the Middle Finger
The ring finger moves as a pair either with the middle finger or the pinky. It does not move independently.

Pinky: Assists the Ring Finger
The yakuza have a penchant for severing this finger when attempting to drive a point home, demonstrating that the human hand is able to function perfectly fine without the pinky. A raised pinky evokes a delicate, sophisticated air.

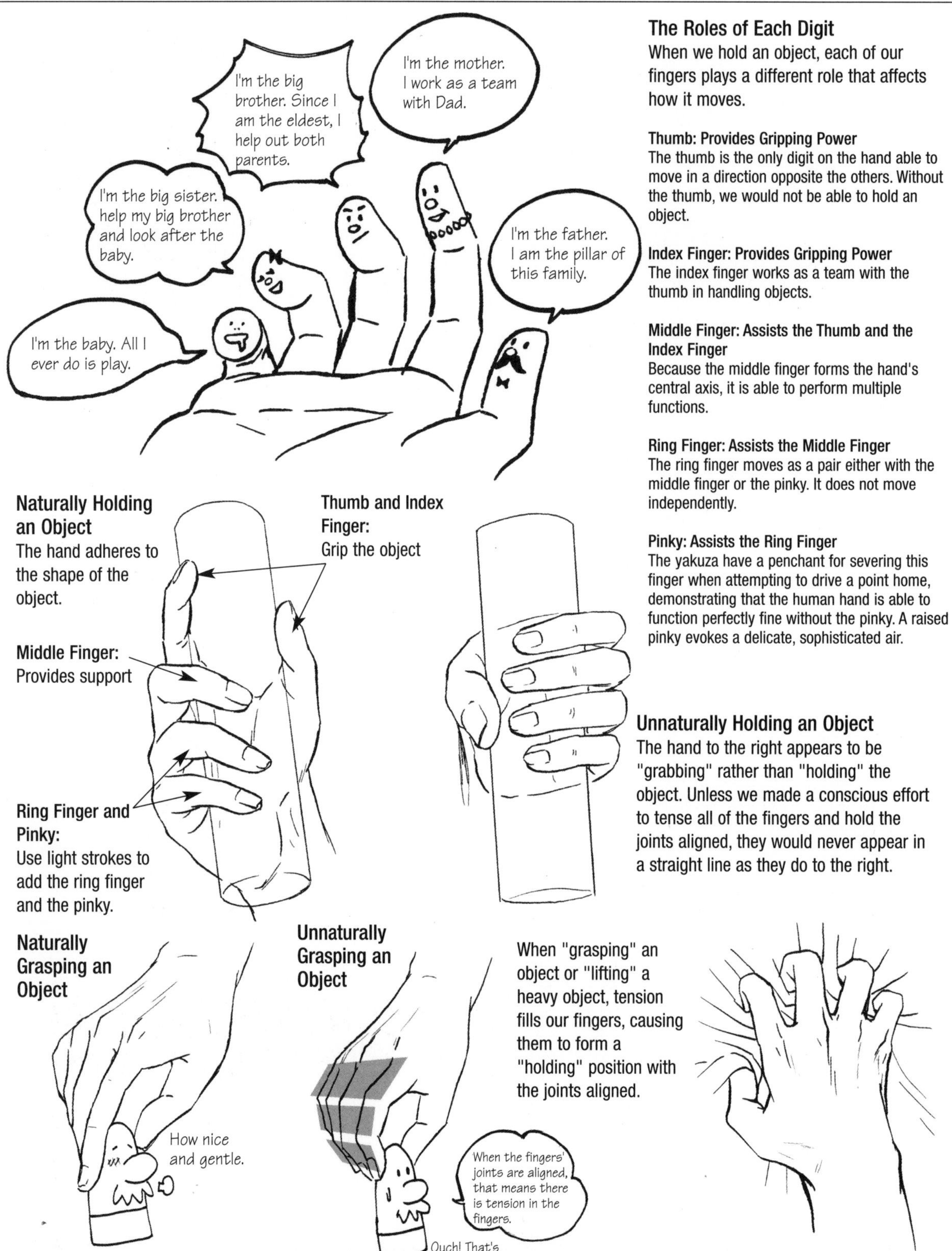

I'm the big brother. Since I am the eldest, I help out both parents.
I'm the mother. I work as a team with Dad.
I'm the big sister. I help my big brother and look after the baby.
I'm the father. I am the pillar of this family.
I'm the baby. All I ever do is play.
Naturally Holding an Object
The hand adheres to the shape of the object.
Thumb and Index Finger:
Grip the object
Middle Finger:
Provides support
Ring Finger and Pinky:
Use light strokes to add the ring finger and the pinky.
Unnaturally Holding an Object
The hand to the right appears to be "grabbing" rather than "holding" the object. Unless we made a conscious effort to tense all of the fingers and hold the joints aligned, they would never appear in a straight line as they do to the right.
Naturally Grasping an Object
How nice and gentle.
Unnaturally Grasping an Object
When the fingers' joints are aligned, that means there is tension in the fingers.
Ouch! That's tight!
When "grasping" an object or "lifting" a heavy object, tension fills our fingers, causing them to form a "holding" position with the joints aligned.

Drawing an Empty Hand

A relaxed, empty hand has a gently flowing shape as the eye moves from the index finger to the pinky.

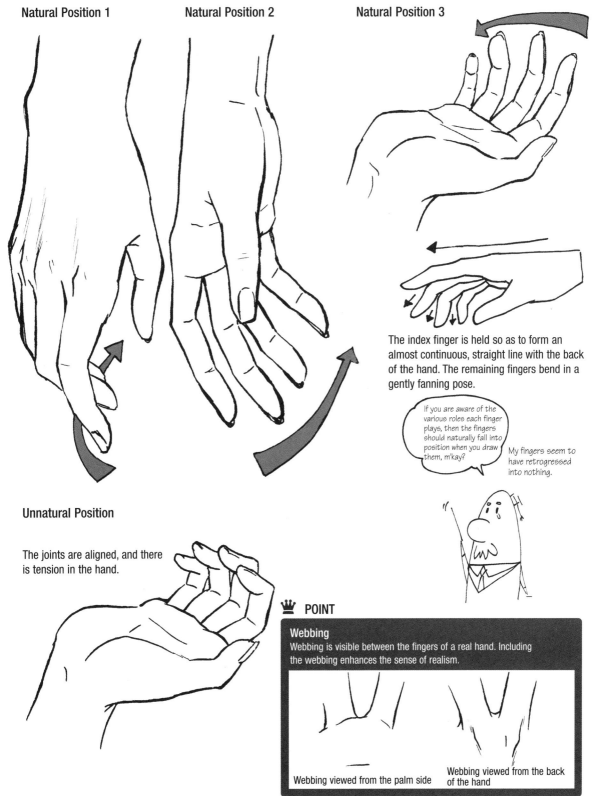

Natural Position 1

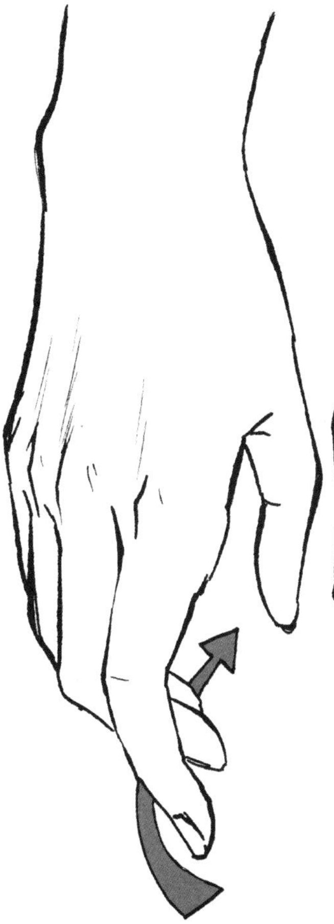

Natural Position 2

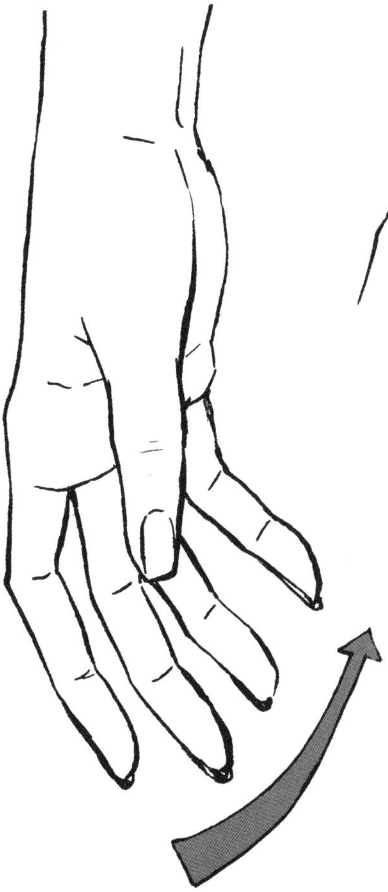

Natural Position 3

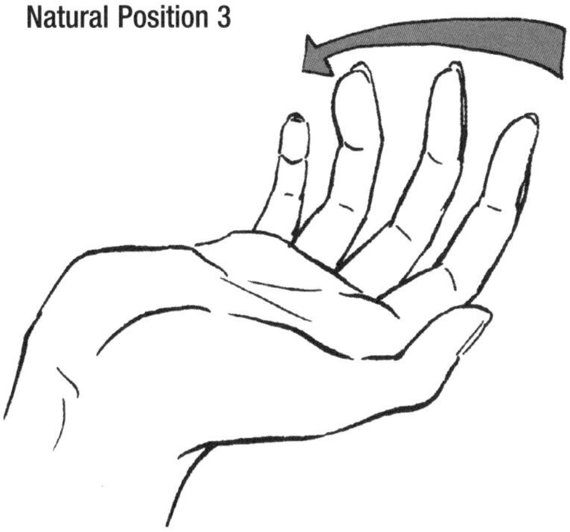

The index finger is held so as to form an almost continuous, straight line with the back of the hand. The remaining fingers bend in a gently fanning pose.

If you are aware of the various roles each finger plays, then the fingers should naturally fall into position when you draw them, m'kay?

My fingers seem to have retrogressed into nothing.

Unnatural Position

The joints are aligned, and there is tension in the hand.

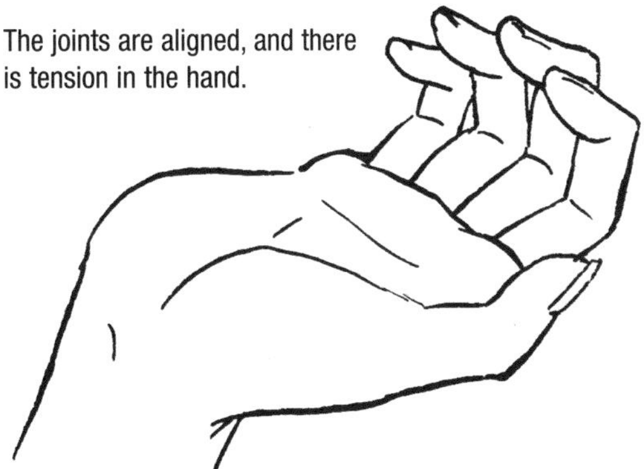

POINT

Webbing

Webbing is visible between the fingers of a real hand. Including the webbing enhances the sense of realism.

Webbing viewed from the palm side

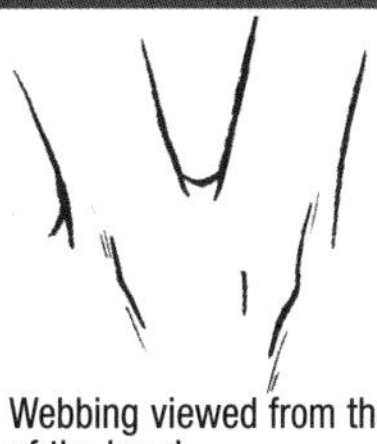

Webbing viewed from the back of the hand

Assorted Portrayals

Practice drawing the hand in various positions and from an array of angles. Use the steps learnt on page 45.

Fist

1 Sketch the fist as a single unit.

2 Divide the hand into its parts.

3 Add in the details.

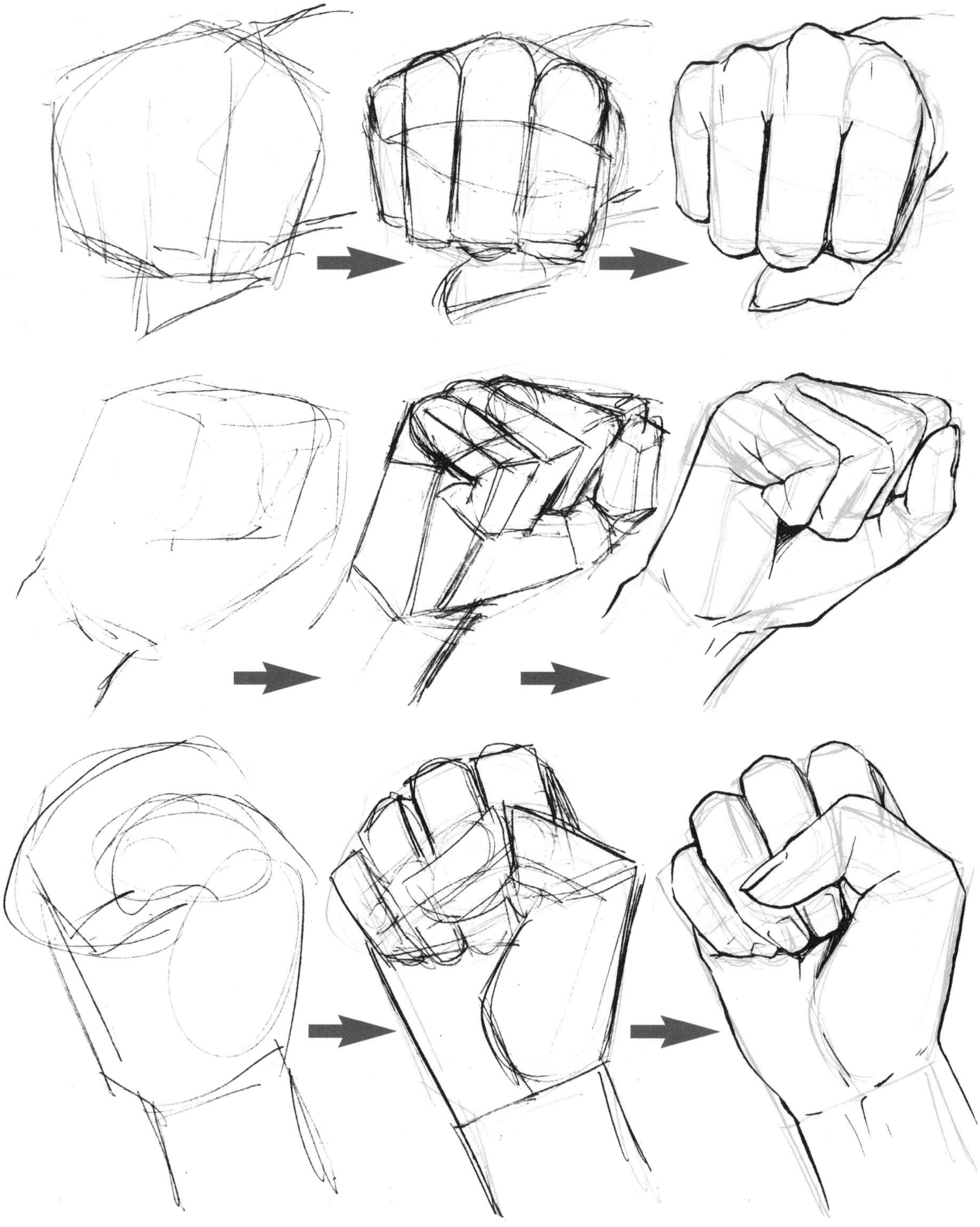

Open Hand

1 Sketch the hand as a single unit.

2 Divide the hand into its parts.

3 Add in the details.

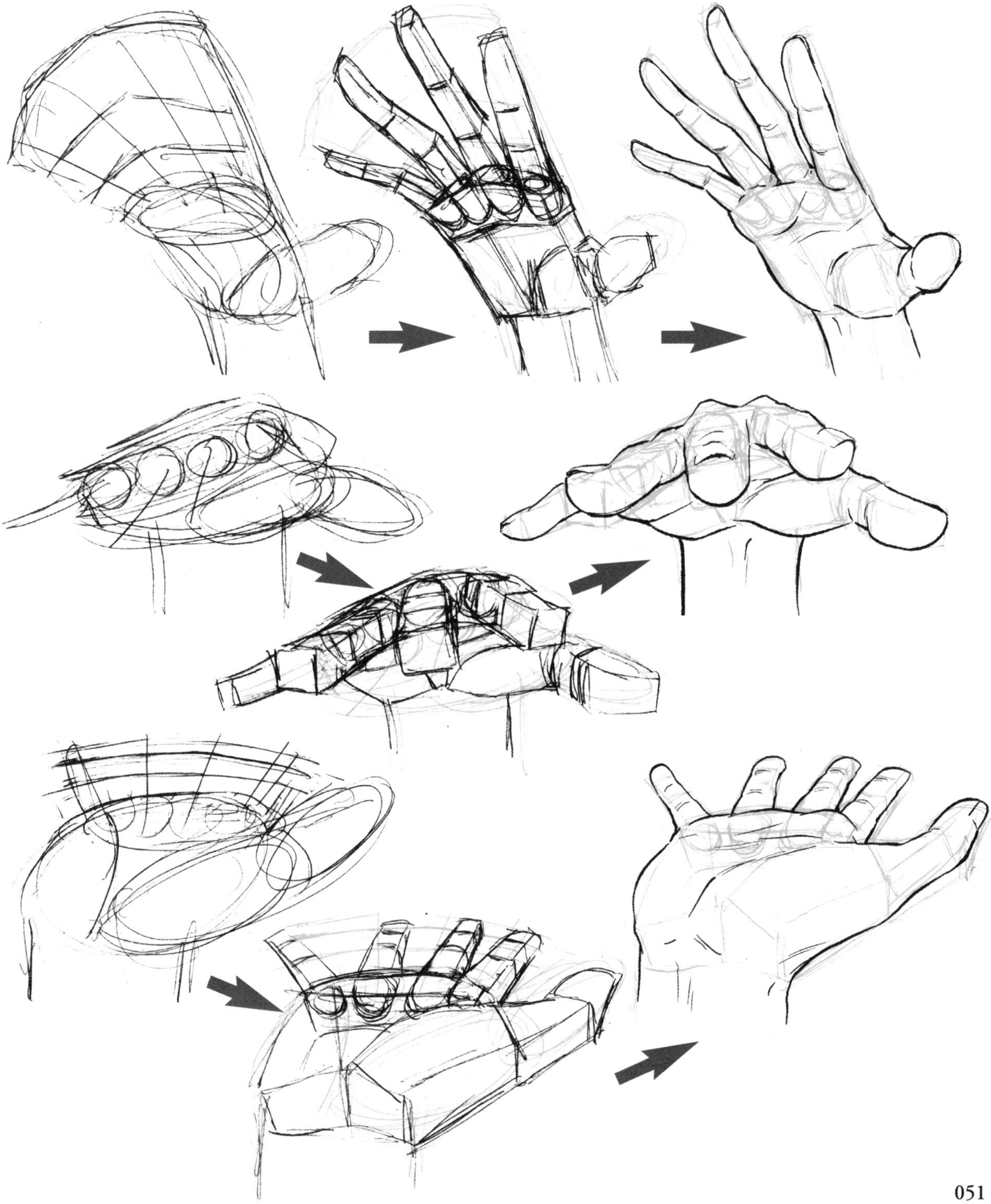

Pointing with a Finger

1 Sketch the fist as a single unit.

2 Divide the hand into its parts.

3 Add in the details.

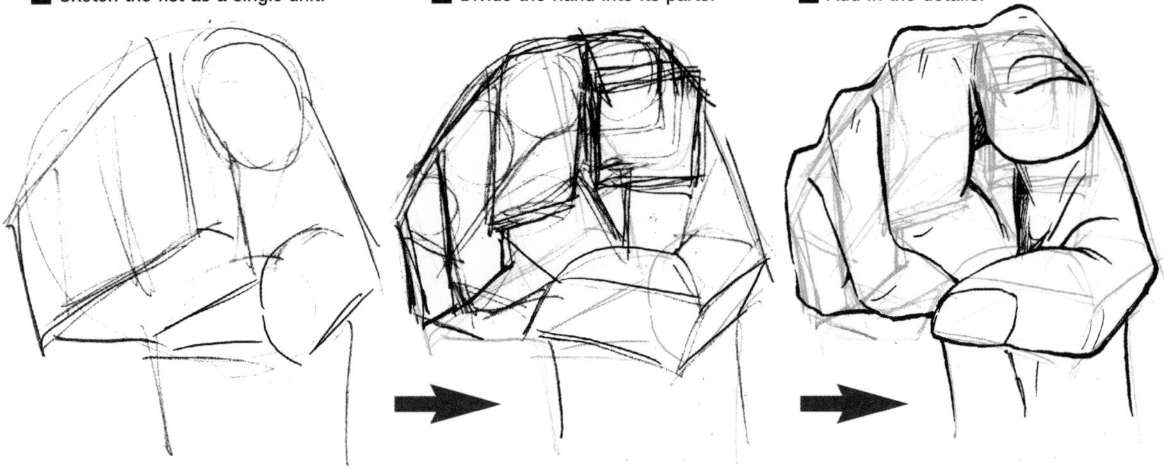

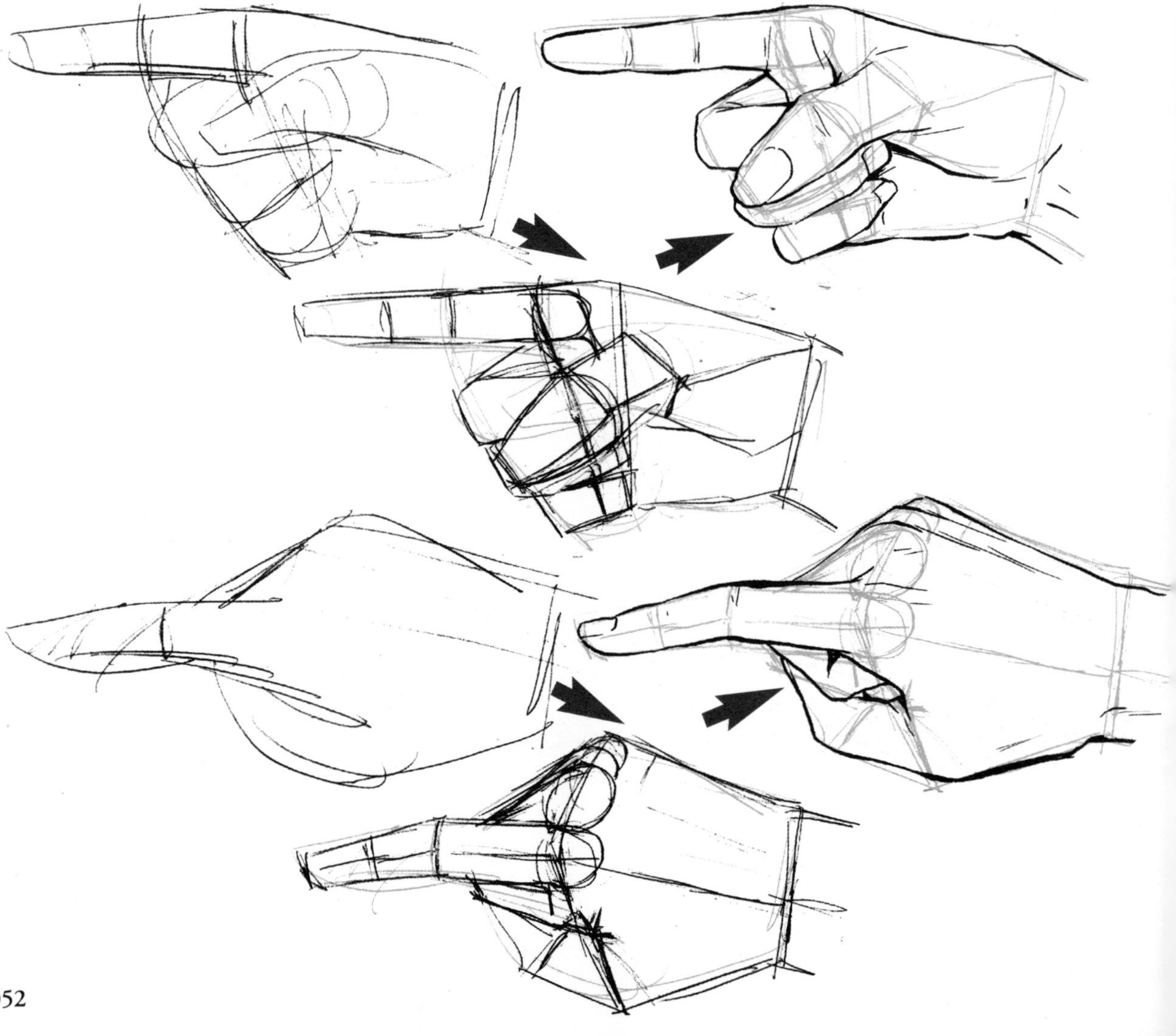

Holding a Cigarette

1 Sketch the fist as a single unit.

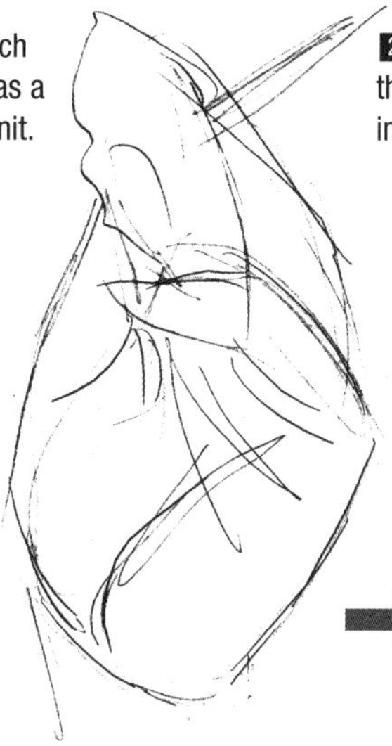

2 Divide the hand into its parts.

3 Add in the details.

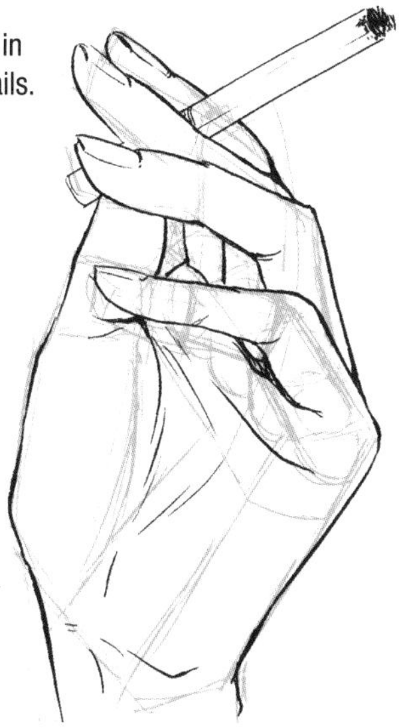

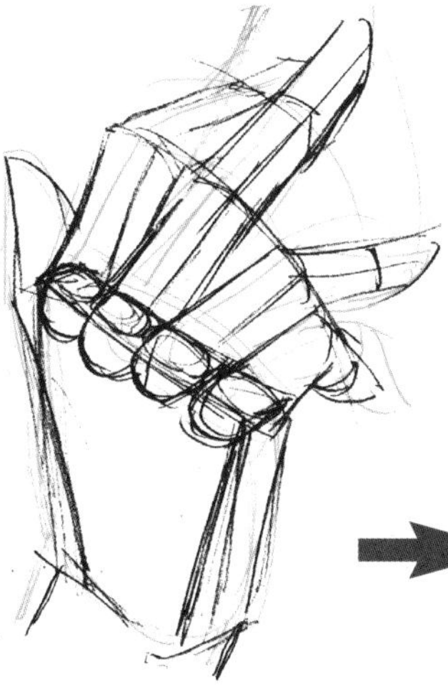

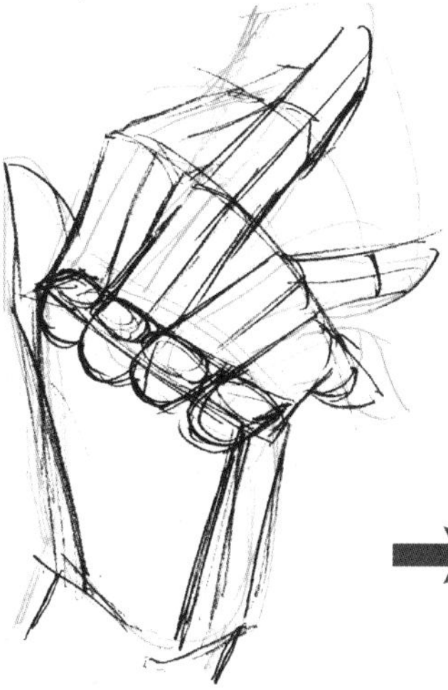

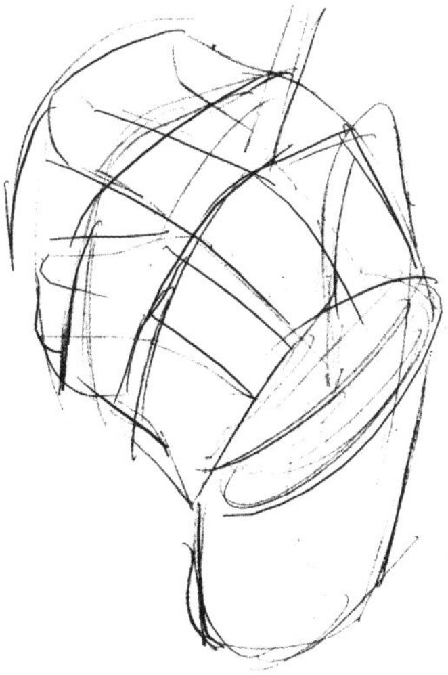

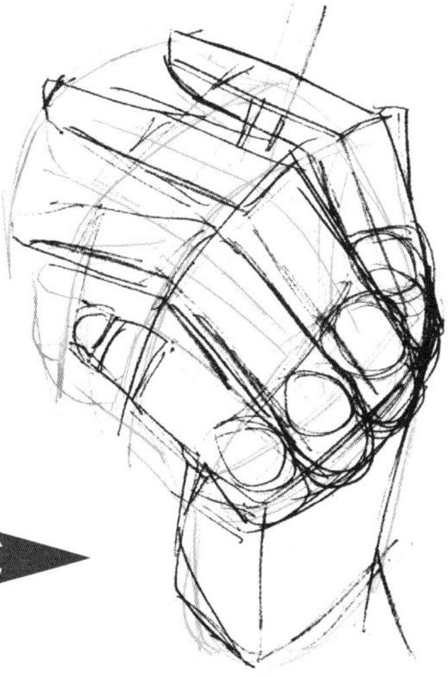

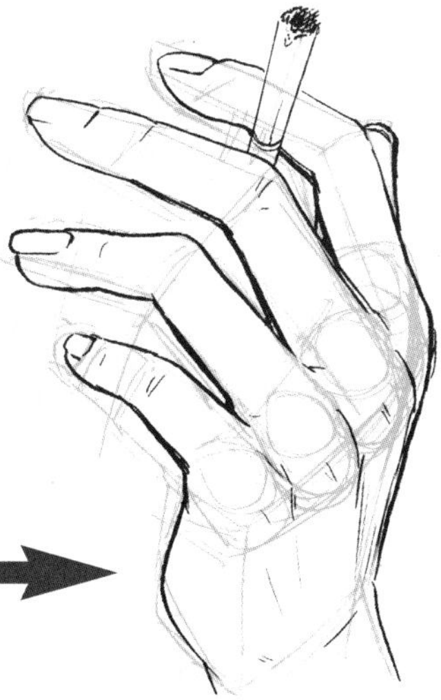

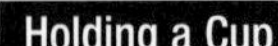

Holding a Cup

1 Sketch the fist as a single unit.

2 Divide the hand into its parts.

3 Add in the details.

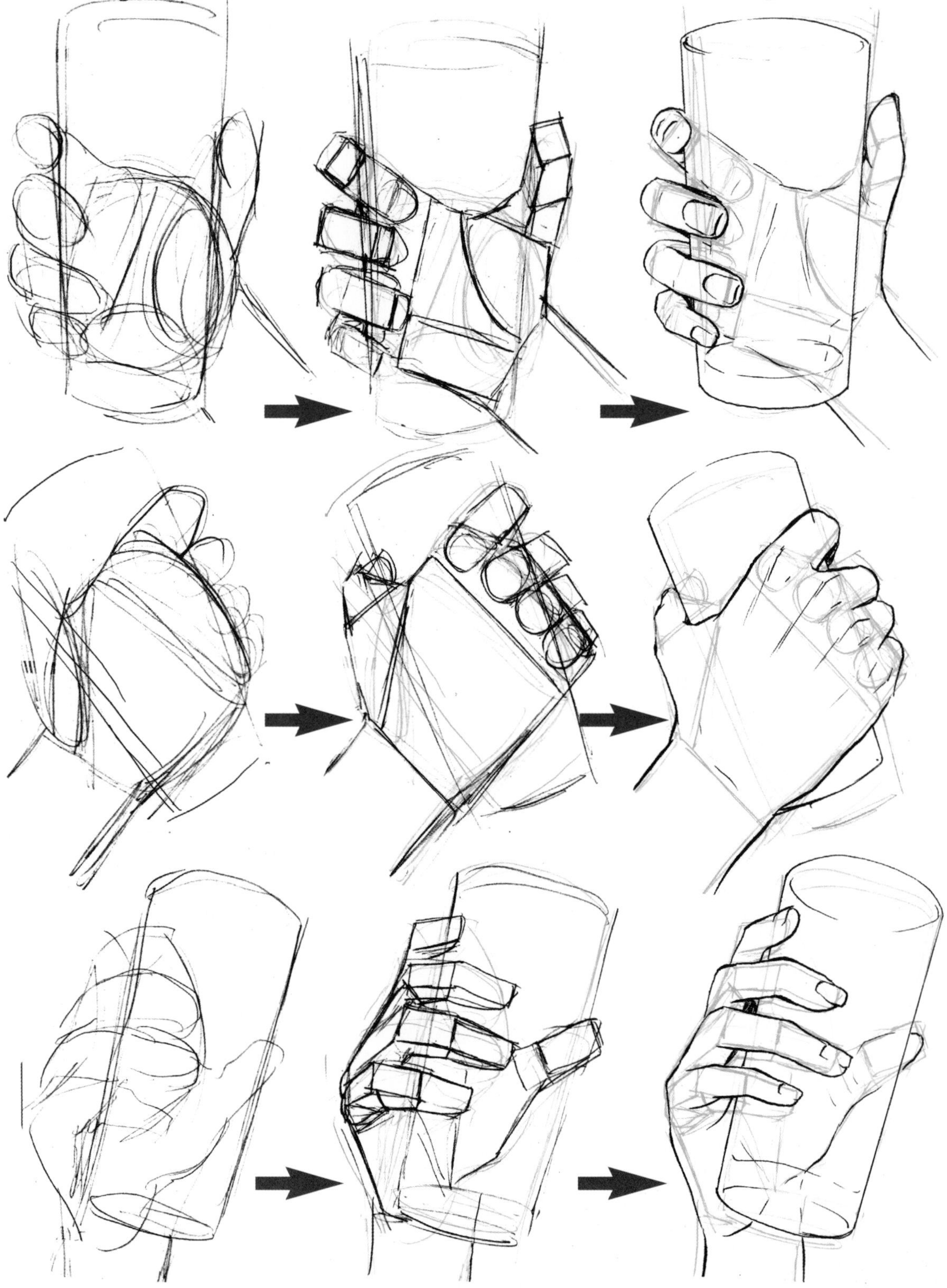

Holding a Pen

1 Sketch the fist as a single unit.

2 Divide the hand into its parts.

3 Add in the details.

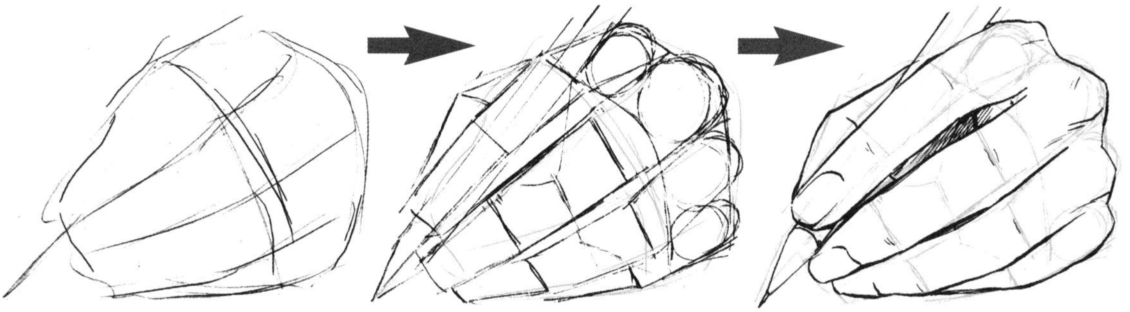

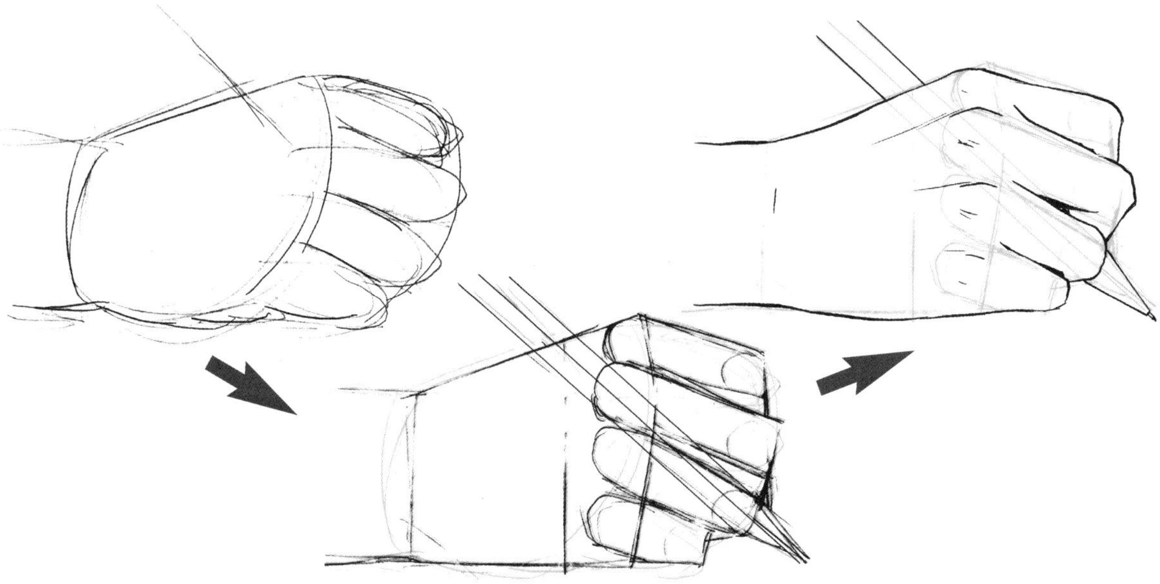

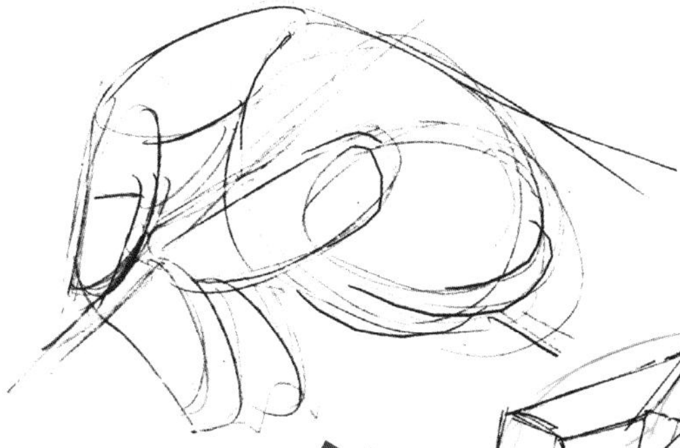

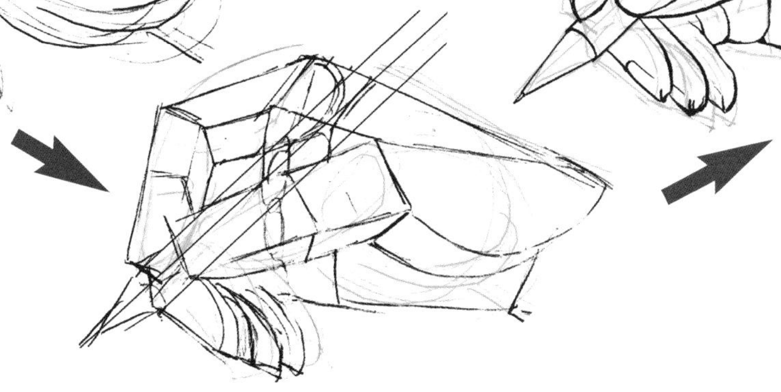

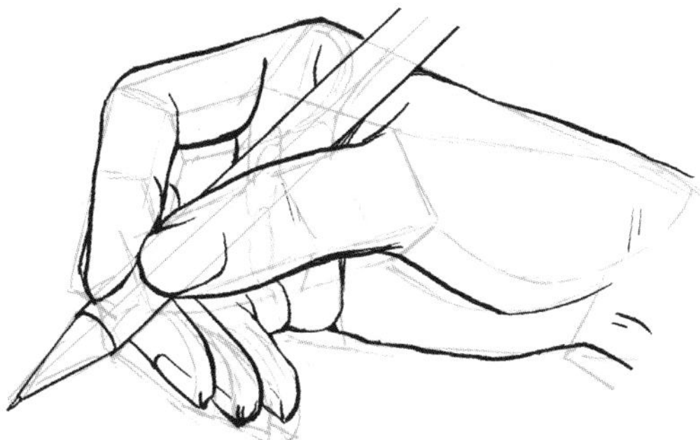

Firing a Gun

1 Sketch the fist as a single unit.

2 Divide the hand into its parts.

3 Add in the details.

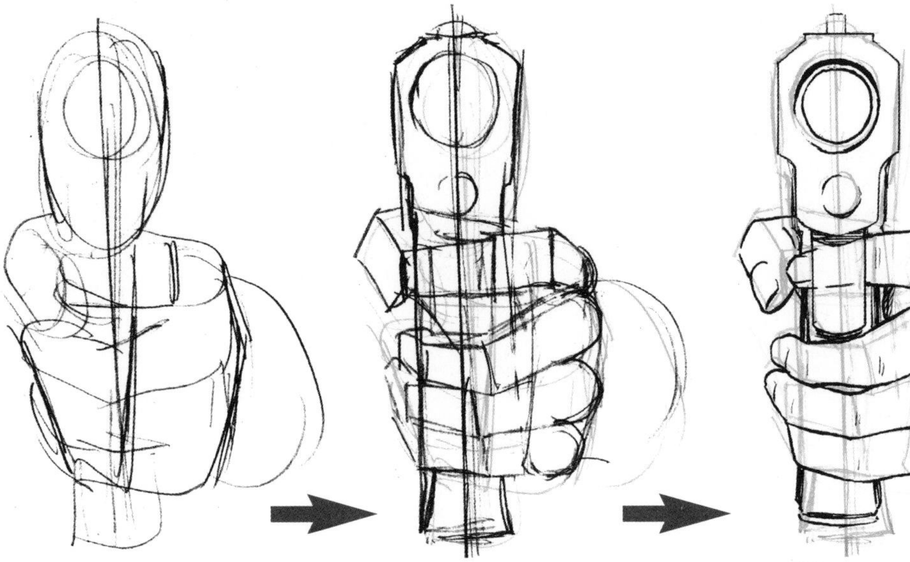

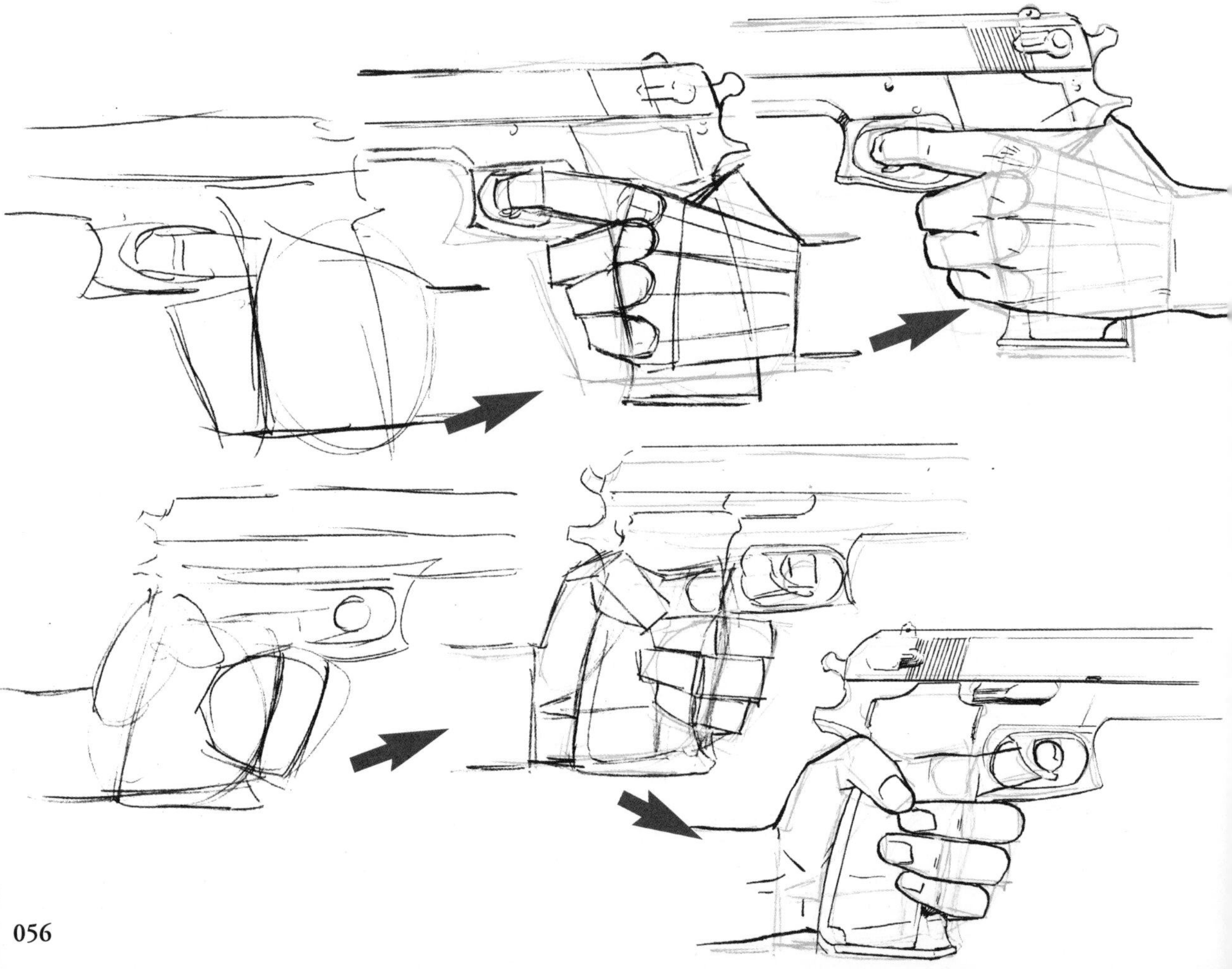

Holding a Cell Phone

1 Sketch the fist as a single unit.

2 Divide the hand into its parts.

3 Add in the details.

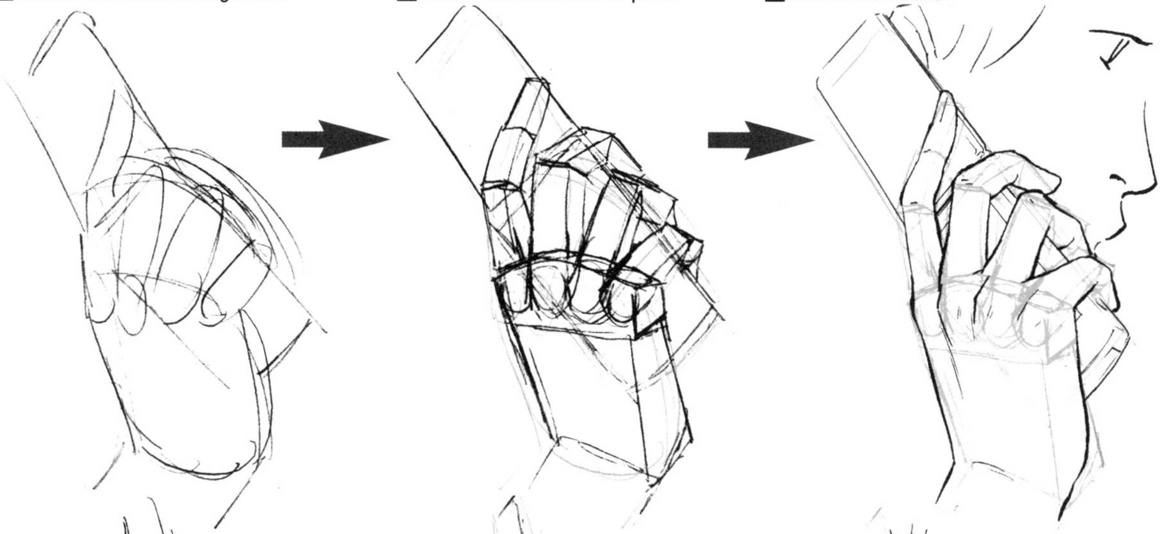

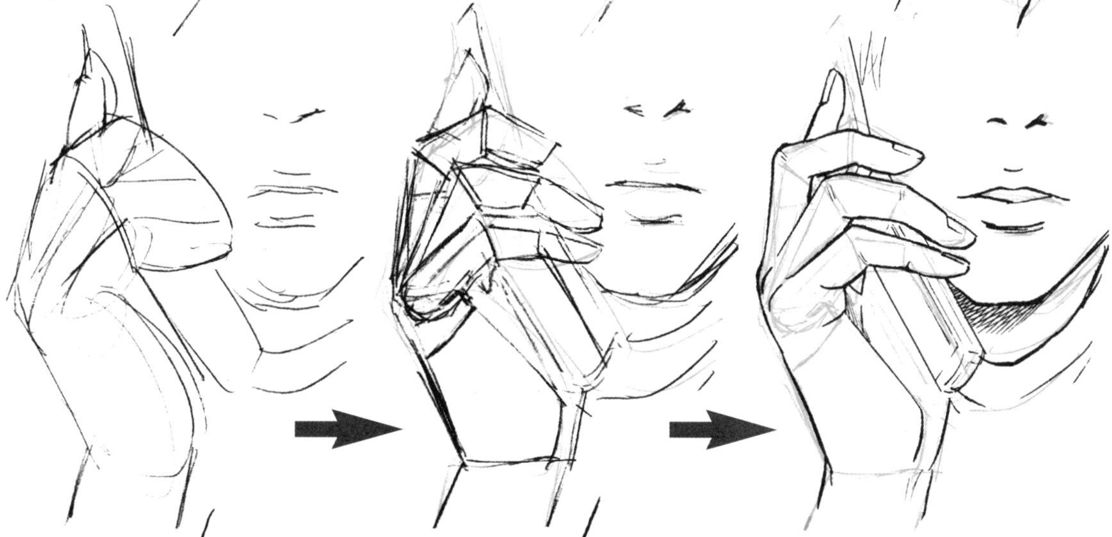

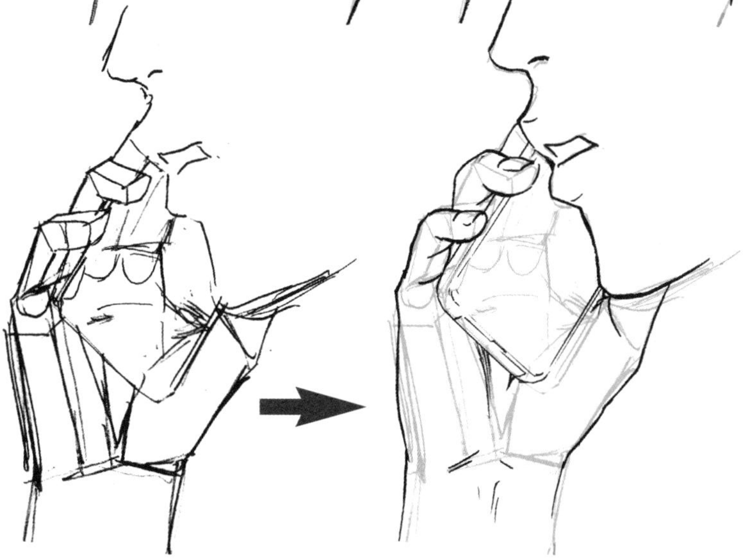

The image below illustrates the standard positions the fingers occupy when holding a cell phone.

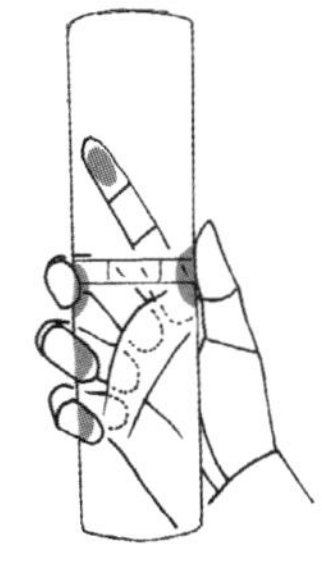

Interlocking the Hands

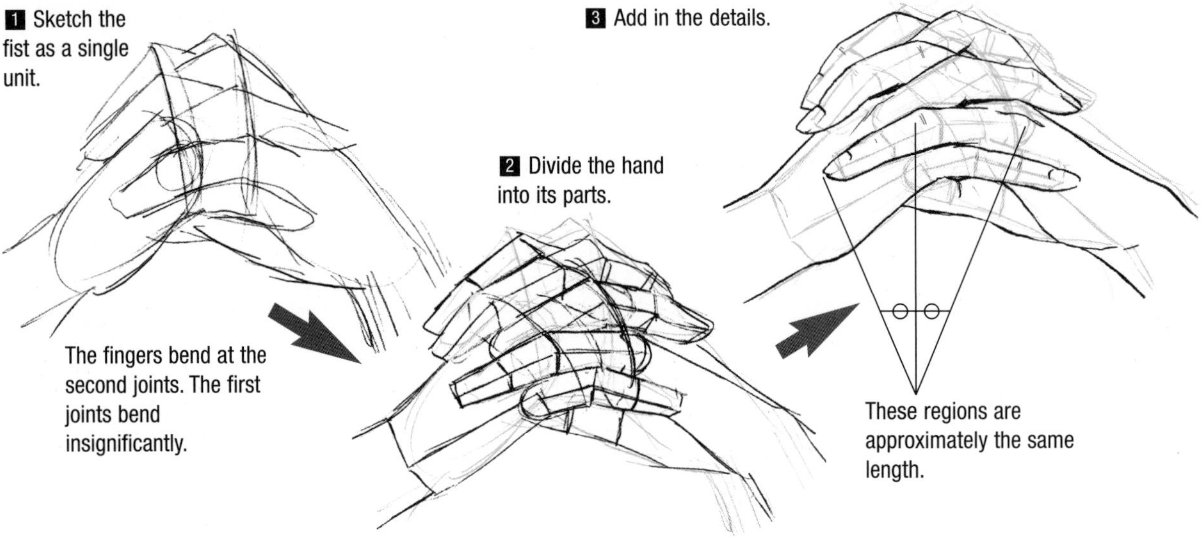

1 Sketch the fist as a single unit.

The fingers bend at the second joints. The first joints bend insignificantly.

2 Divide the hand into its parts.

3 Add in the details.

These regions are approximately the same length.

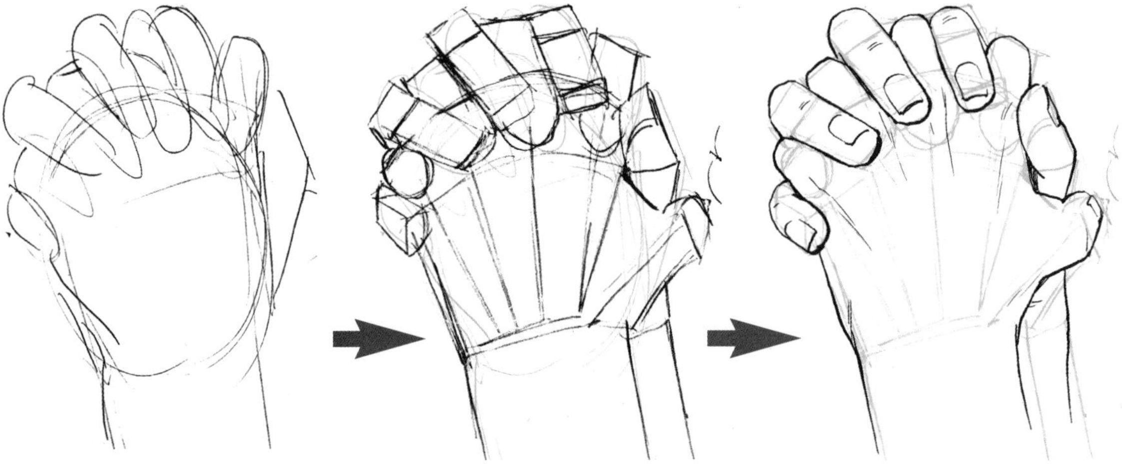

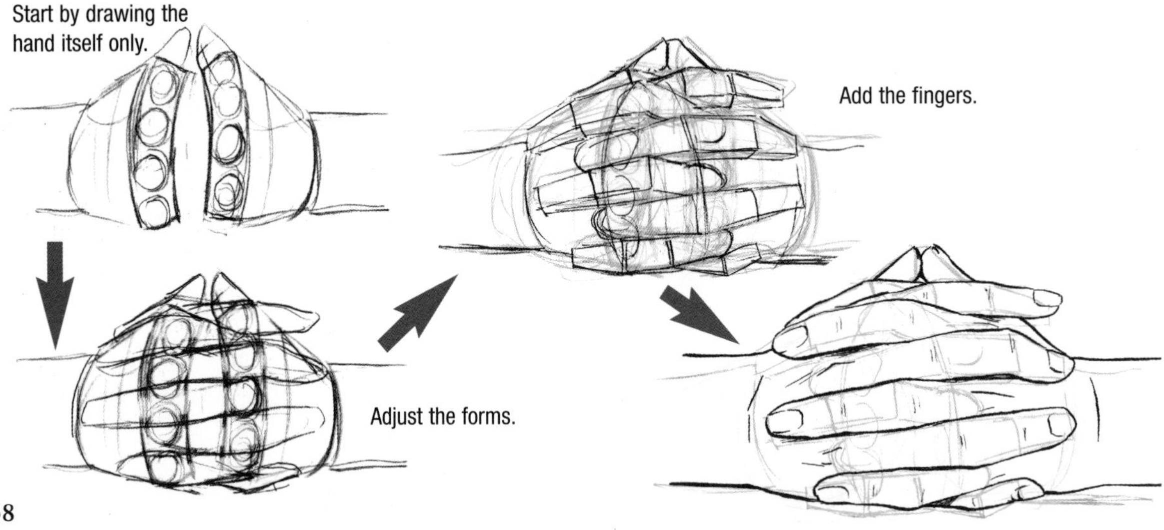

Start by drawing the hand itself only.

Adjust the forms.

Add the fingers.

Pushing up Eyeglasses

Take extra care balancing the sizes of the hand versus the face. The open palm should be large enough to cover the face.

Hands Inserted in Pockets

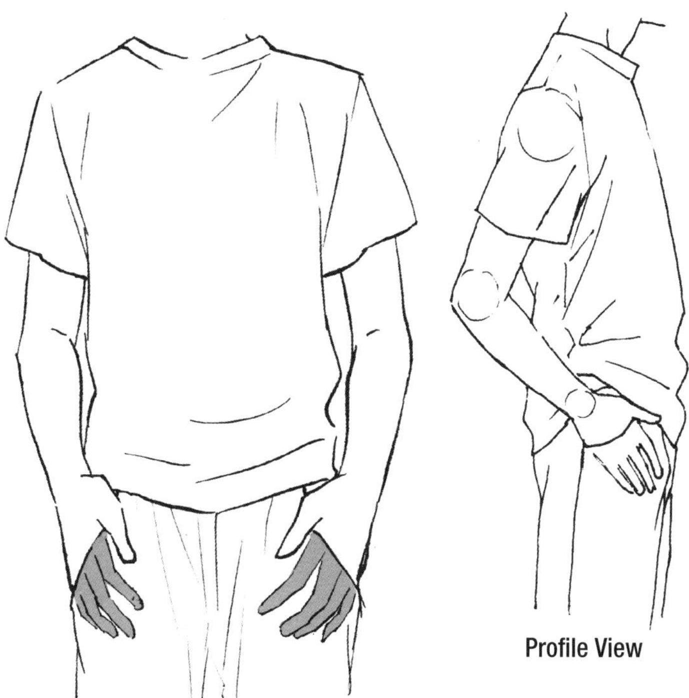

Profile View

Correct
The arms are pulled back, as can be seen in the profile view.

Incorrect
The elbows should not jut out to the side like this.

Gloved Hands

When drawing a gloved hand, make distinctions in the types and degree of creases, the texture, and the thickness resulting from the material. Making a careful study of gloves by trying them on your own hands or looking at examples in magazines and on the Internet will facilitate the drawing process. Gloves come in an array of designs and colors. This lesson module features a few common designs.

Gloves come in a wide variety.

Try putting gloves of assorted textures on the same model's hands and take careful note of how the gloves' fabrics differ in texture, and how and where the different fabrics cause creases to form, m'kay?

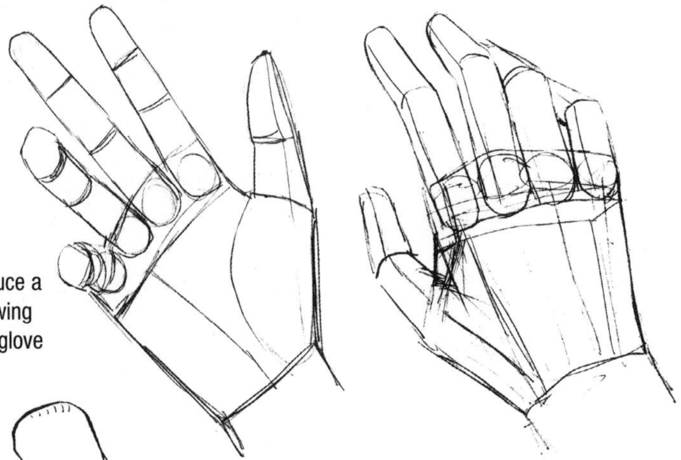

Before drawing a glove, produce a carefully rendered under drawing of a hand and then draw the glove on top of the hand.

Cotton Work Gloves, Woolen Gloves, and Other Gloves with Rough Weaves

- Avoid adding fine creases. Instead draw large creases to suggest a coarse texture.
- The tips of the fingers on cotton work gloves should be somewhat flat.

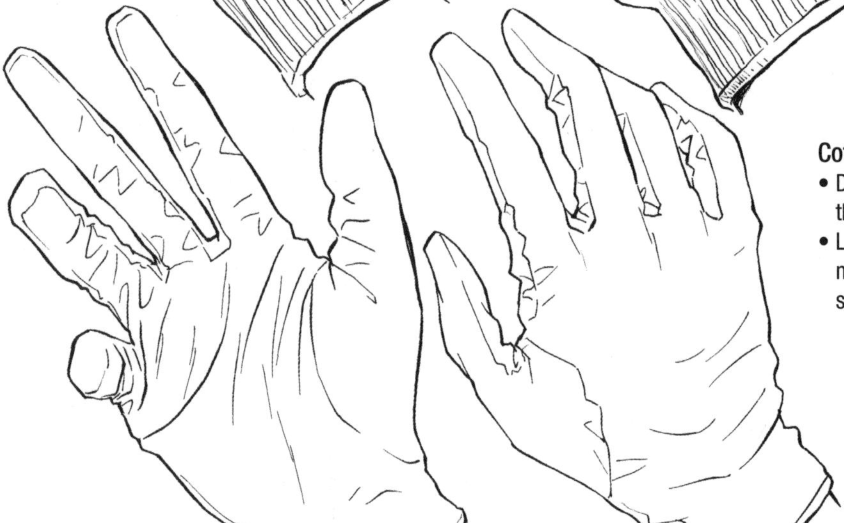

Cotton and Other Thin Gloves

- Draw fine creases to suggest a thin fabric.
- Lines denoting creases should not be straight but rather should undulate.

Leather Gloves

- Avoid drawing fine creases. Instead, draw large creases to suggest a rough texture.

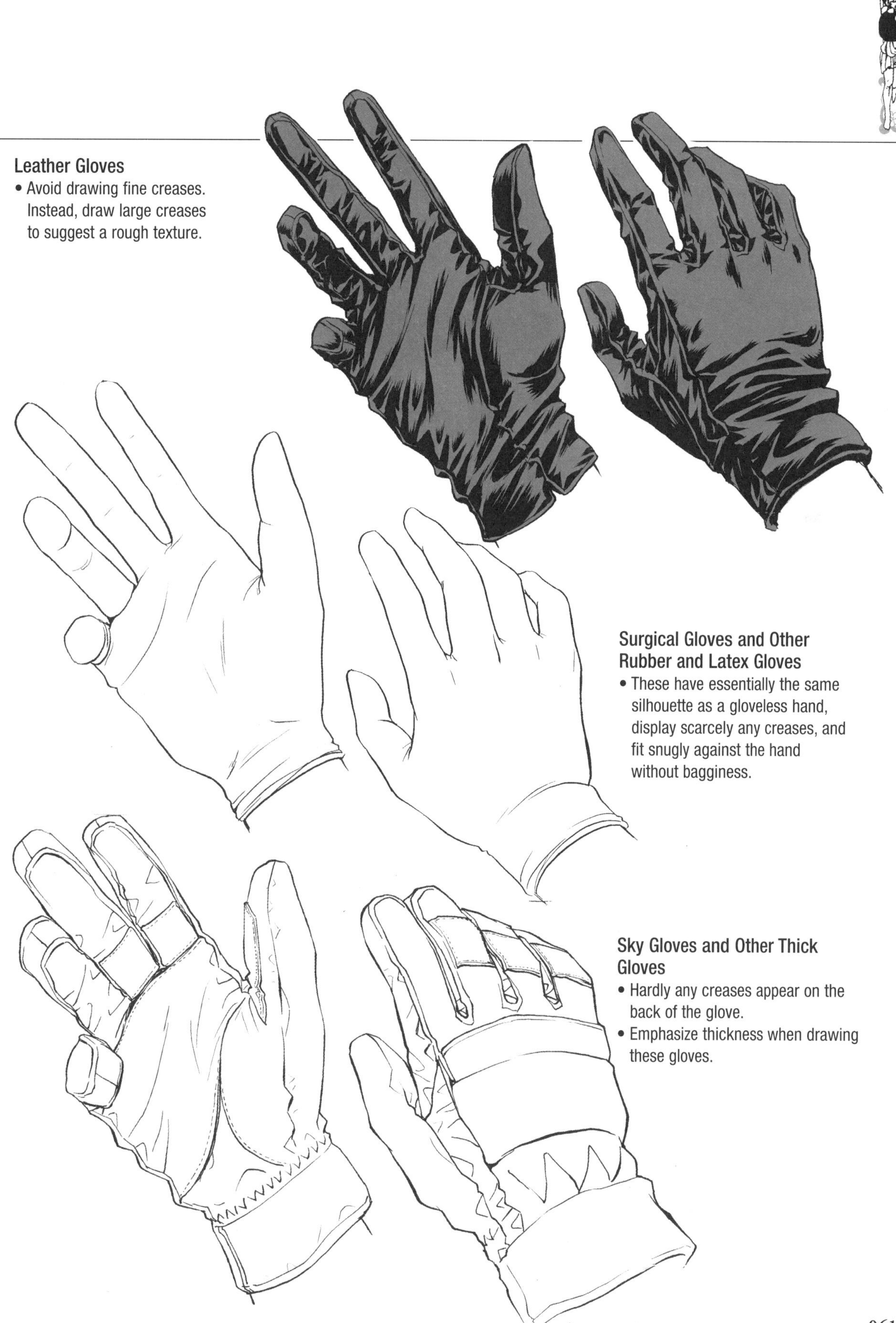

Surgical Gloves and Other Rubber and Latex Gloves

- These have essentially the same silhouette as a gloveless hand, display scarcely any creases, and fit snugly against the hand without bagginess.

Sky Gloves and Other Thick Gloves

- Hardly any creases appear on the back of the glove.
- Emphasize thickness when drawing these gloves.

How to Draw the Foot

Render the top of the foot as a curve. (The bones actually composing the top of the foot form an arch.) The ankle and the shaded regions in the diagrams depicted below are capable of motion. As with the hand, the toes' third joints are attached to the foot itself, making them somewhat imperceptible. Note that unlike the thumb, the big toe only contains two joints.

Structure of the Foot

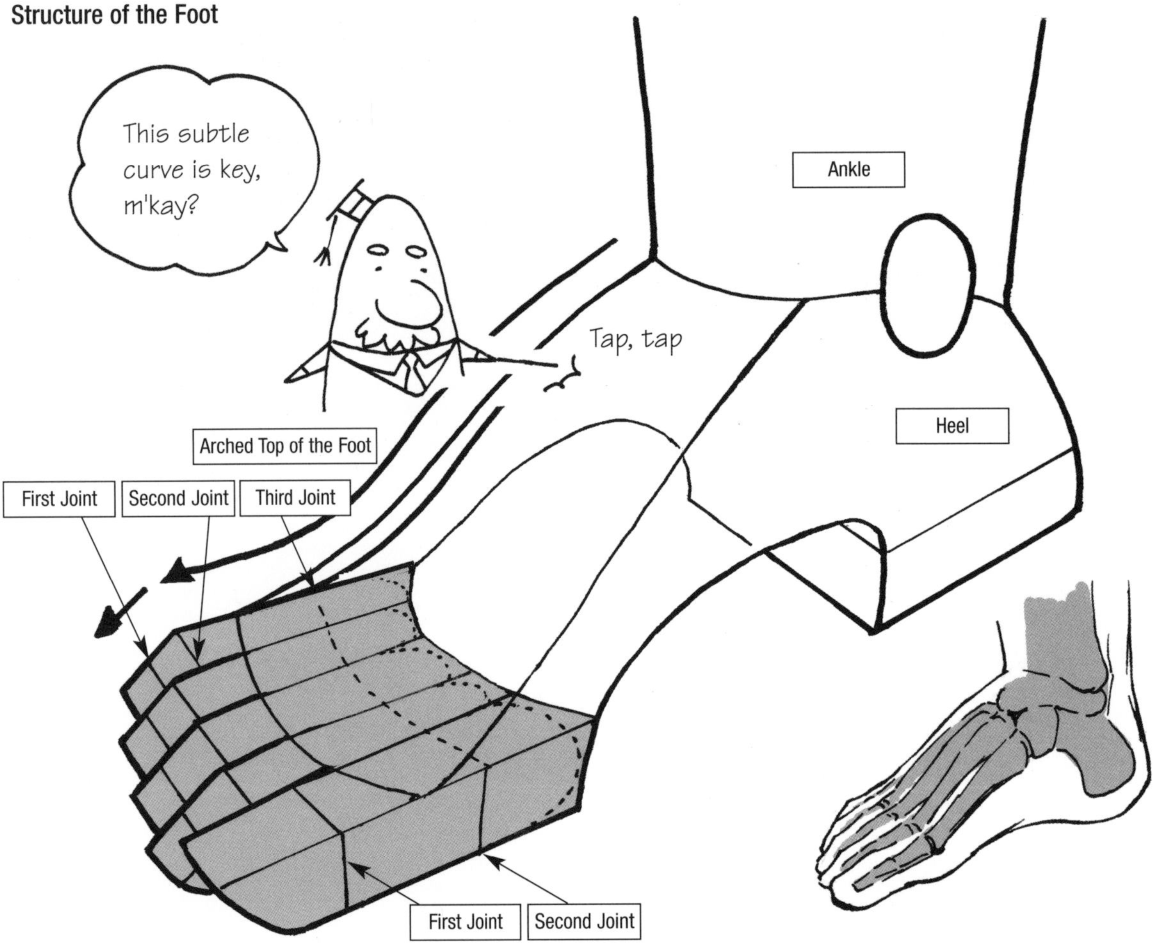

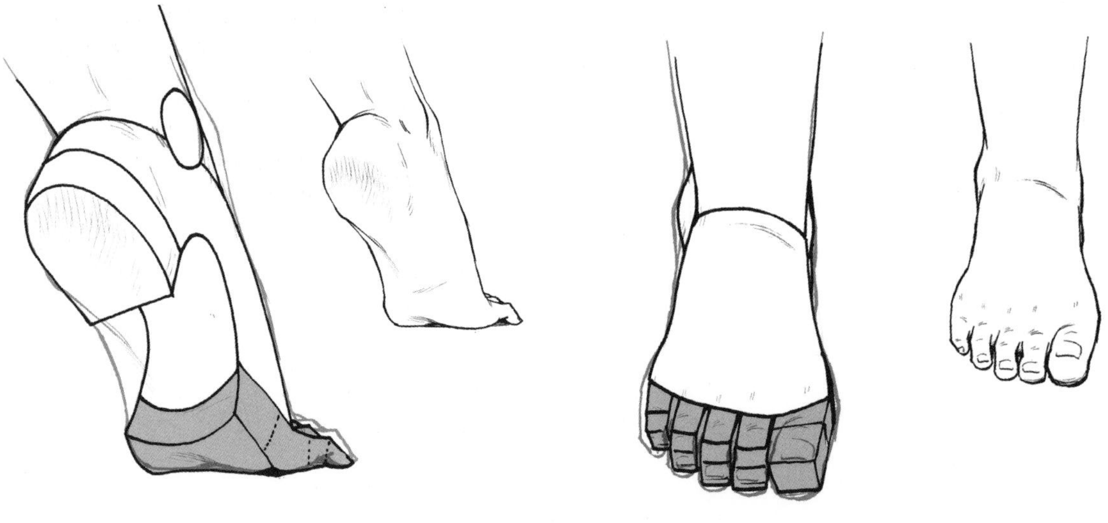

Top and Underside of the Foot

The majority of the outside of the foot (the little toe's side) touches the ground. Incidentally, the foot's length should be approximately the same as the face's.

Top of the Foot

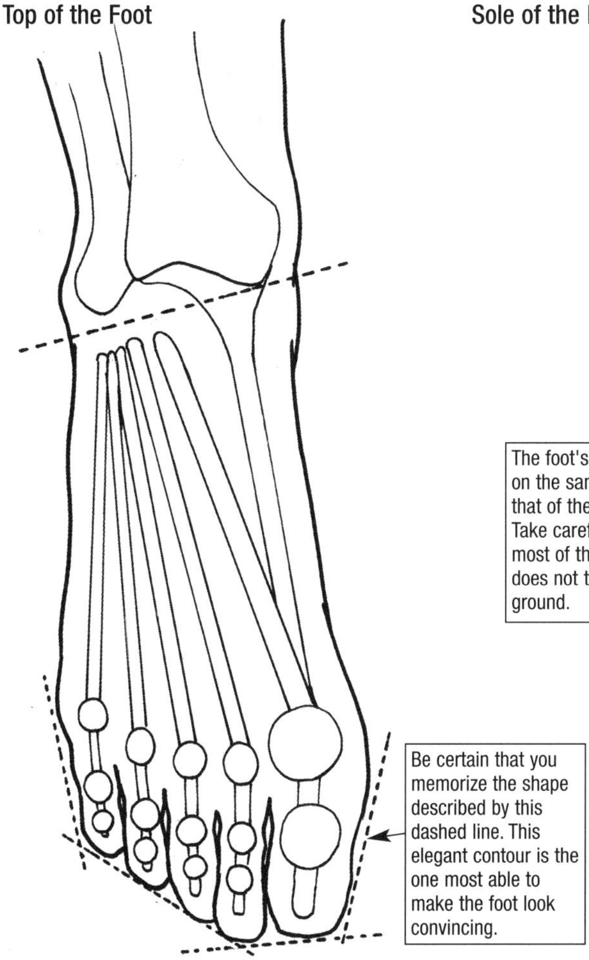

Be certain that you memorize the shape described by this dashed line. This elegant contour is the one most able to make the foot look convincing.

Sole of the Foot

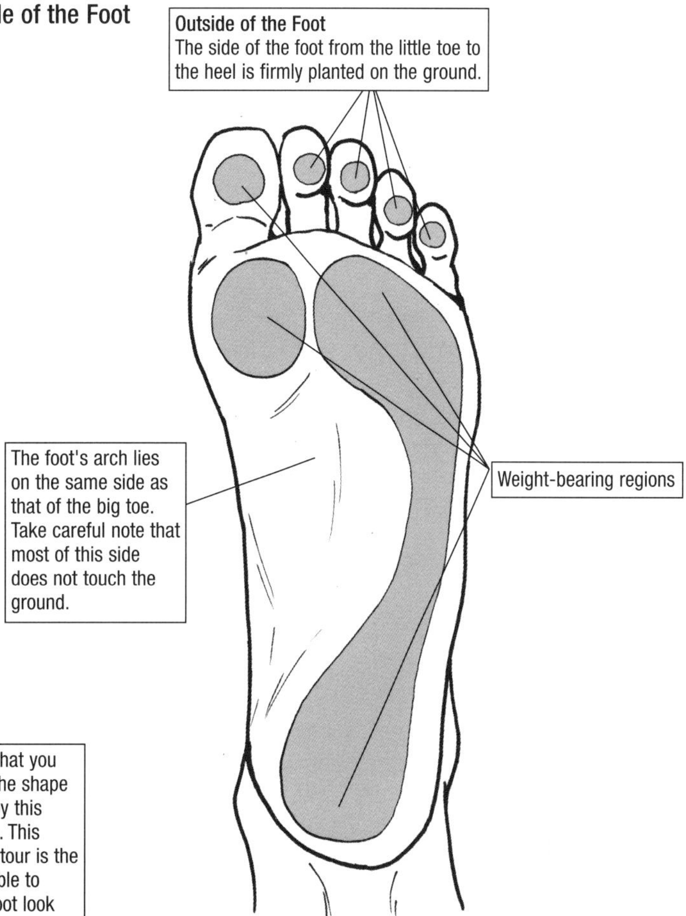

Outside of the Foot
The side of the foot from the little toe to the heel is firmly planted on the ground.

The foot's arch lies on the same side as that of the big toe. Take careful note that most of this side does not touch the ground.

Weight-bearing regions

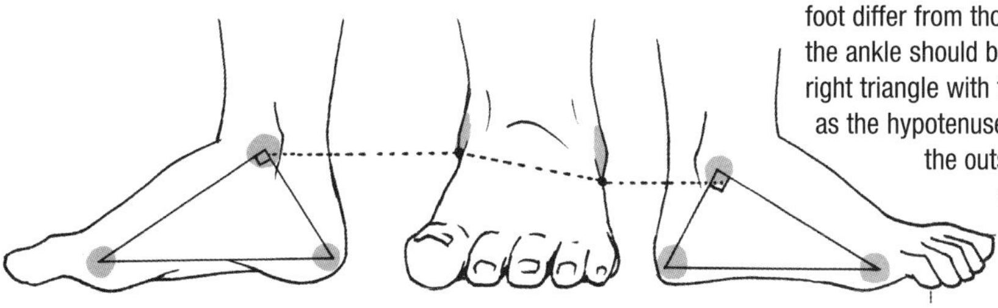

The position and height of the ankle on the inside of the foot differ from those on the outside. To pinpoint where the ankle should be on the inside of the foot, draw a right triangle with the heel to the big toe's second joint as the hypotenuse and the ankle at the right angle. For the outside of the foot, draw a right angle with the heel to the little toe's third joint as the hypotenuse and the ankle at the right angle.

Do not draw the tips of the toes aligned.

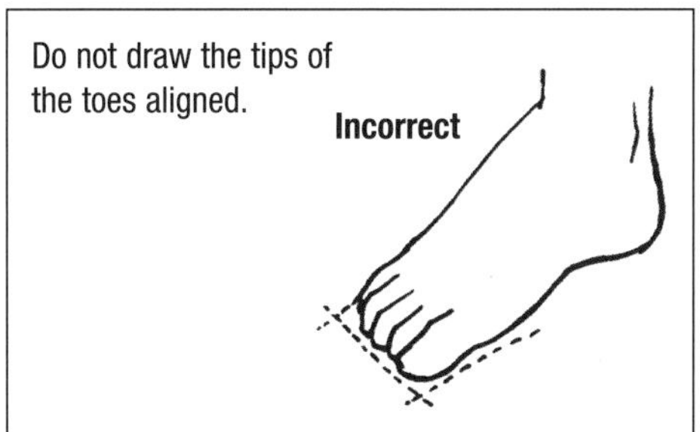

Ankle's Range of Motion
The ankle is limited to up and down motions to the extent depicted to the right. The range of motion is approximately 100° with the ankle at the center. The ankle is surprisingly restricted in its ability to bend. If the ankle is forced to bend any further either up or down, it will break, so avoid drawing the ankle at a dramatic angle.

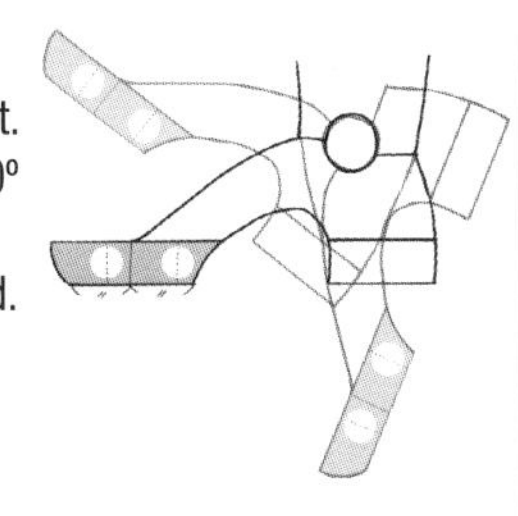

The Top of the Foot, the Heel, and Joints

When drawing a front view of the top of the foot, maintain awareness of the three surfaces of the foot that are visible. This will elicit the feel of a solid, curved object. Also, be sure to observe carefully the appearance of the Achilles tendon and joints.

Top of the Foot Divided into Its Surfaces

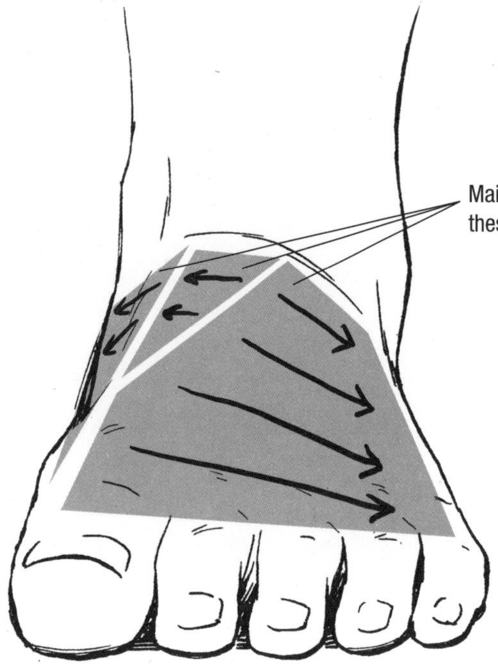

Heel

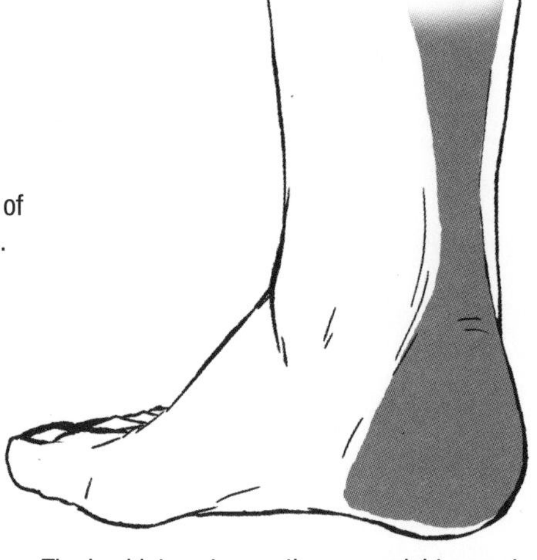

The heel juts out more than one might expect. Draw the Achilles tendon extending from the heel and show the foot tapering at the ankle.

Special Characteristics of the Toes (Excluding the Big Toe)

The toes trace a steep incline from the second joint to the ground.

The toes have large, broad, flat tips.

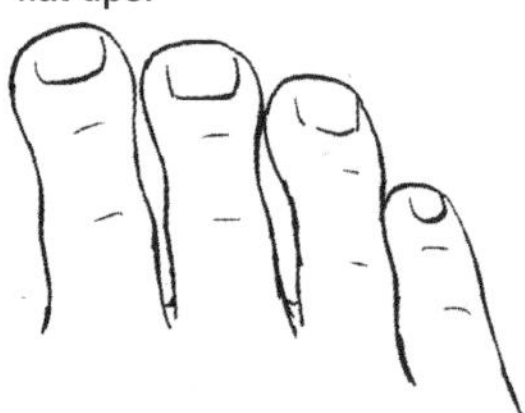

Like the hand, the foot's digits have three joints.

When standing, the first joint bends inward.

Special Characteristics of the Big Toe

The big toe lies relatively flat against the ground.

The big toe boasts about twice the width of the other toes with the base of the nail being the broadest region.

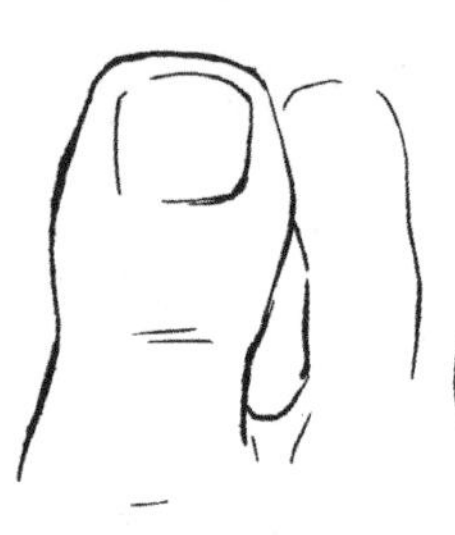

Unlike the other toes, the big toe only has two joints and has a narrow range of motion.

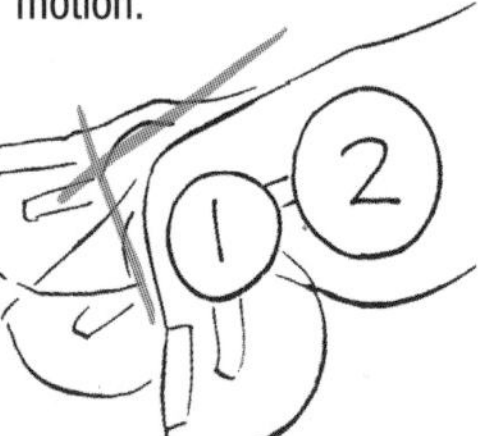

Conceive of the big toe as a separate entity from the other toes when drawing.
Keep 'em separate

The Steps in Drawing the Foot

This lesson module covers the actual drawing of the foot. First, capture the foot as a single unit. Next, establish the positions of the various parts composing the foot. And, finally, gradually build the detail on the foot's surfaces.

1 Capture the Foot as a Solid
Sketch the foot as if it were a toy building block, capturing only the foot's height and size.

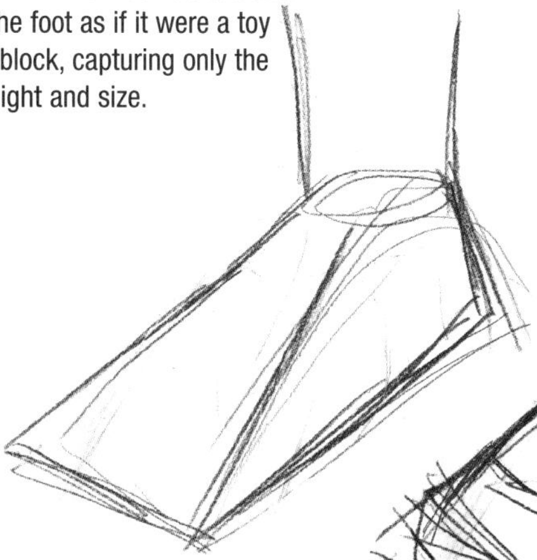

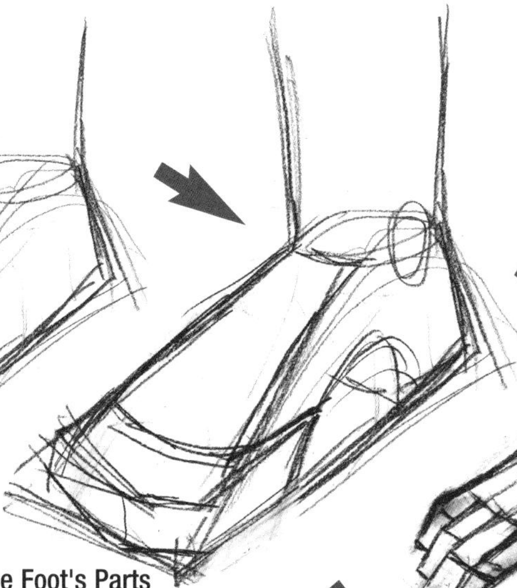

2 Establish the Positions of the Foot's Parts
Determine how the distinctive curve of the top of the foot should appear, the proportioning of the toes to the foot itself, and where the toes should end.

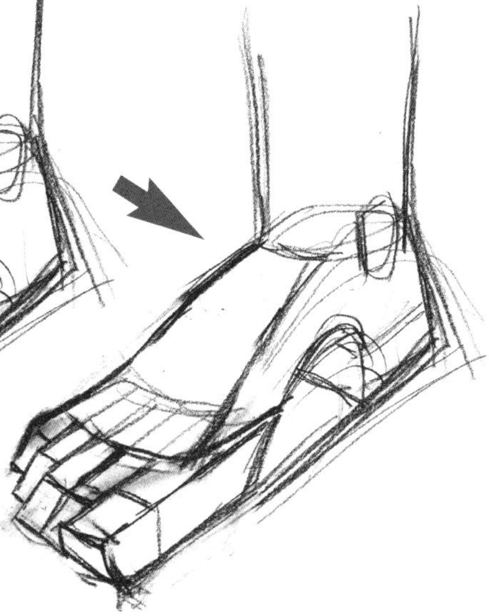

3 Determine the Positions of the Toes and Their Joints
Pay careful attention to the differences between the big toe and the smaller toes.

4 Build the Details
Soften the contour lines and draw toenails and other details.

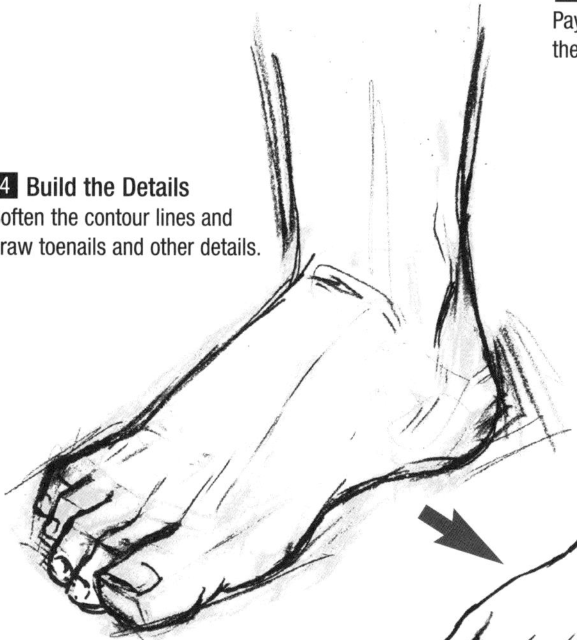

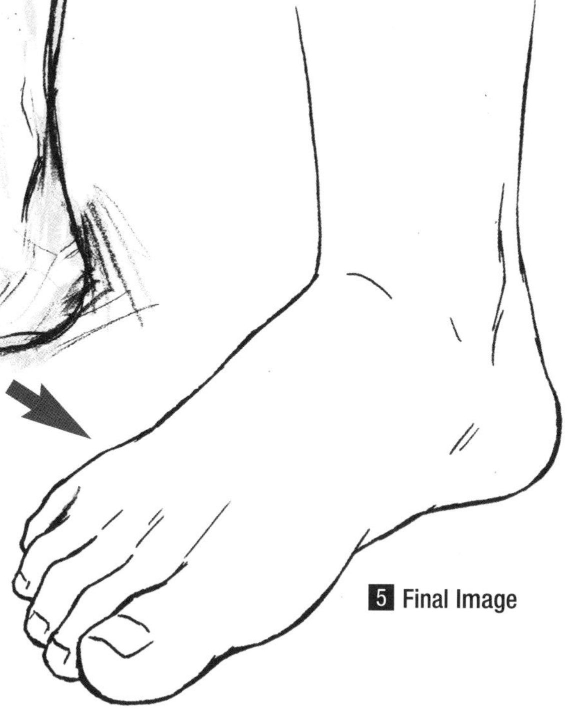

5 Final Image

How the Toes Move

Unlike the fingers, the toes are not capable of highly complex movement. Furthermore, the five toes comprise two units: the big toe and the smaller toes, and the smaller toes are only capable of the same movements. It would be, consequently, no exaggeration to say that the toes are only capable of the six movements illustrated below. This makes drawing mighty easy for artists!

Relaxed Position

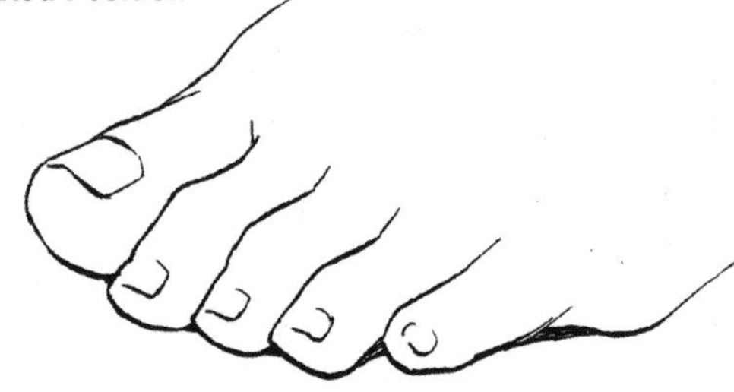

1 Toes Pushed against the Ground

This is how our toes appear when we lift something heavy or exert ourselves in some manner. Note how the smaller toes are staggered.

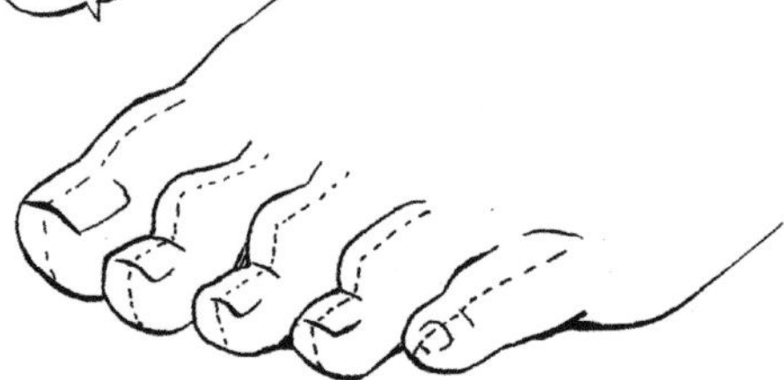

2 Raised Toes

This is how the foot appears with the toes lifted off the ground. Note that the toes will cramp if held in this position for too long.

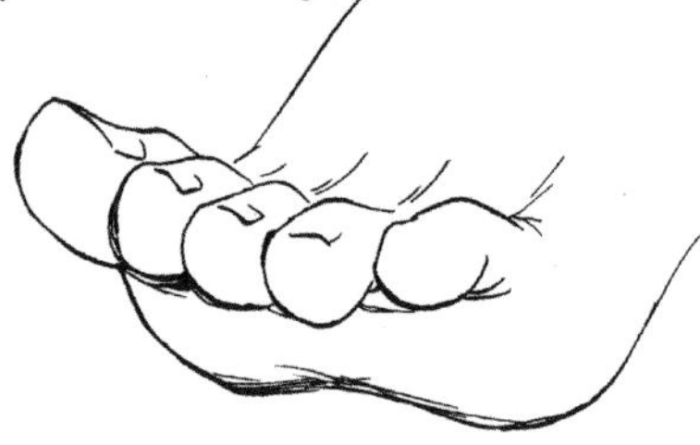

3 Curled Toes

This is how our feet might appear when we use them to lift an object. It is not the most well-mannered pose a foot could adopt. Since the big toe only has two joints, it is unable to curl in the same manner as the smaller toes.

4 Lowered Big Toe (Raised Smaller Toes)

Lowering the big toe causes the smaller toes to rise. Conversely, the big toe cannot be lowered without raising the smaller toes.

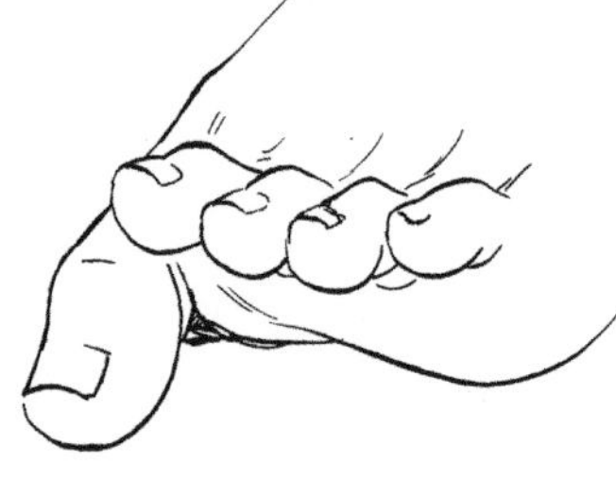

5 Raised Big Toe (Lowered Smaller Toes)

As with 4, raising the big toe causes the smaller toes to lower.

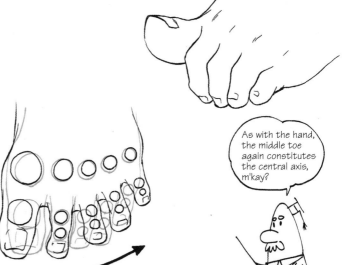

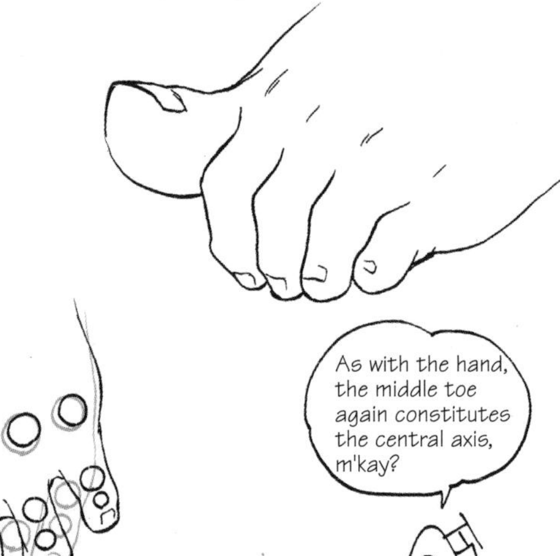

As with the hand, the middle toe again constitutes the central axis, m'kay?

The big toe is a maverick, m'kay?

6 Spread Toes

The Sole

The balls of the feet may be divided into three general groups: the second joint of the big toe, the third joints of the smaller toes, and the heel. The balls of the feet stretch and contract according to how the toes move.

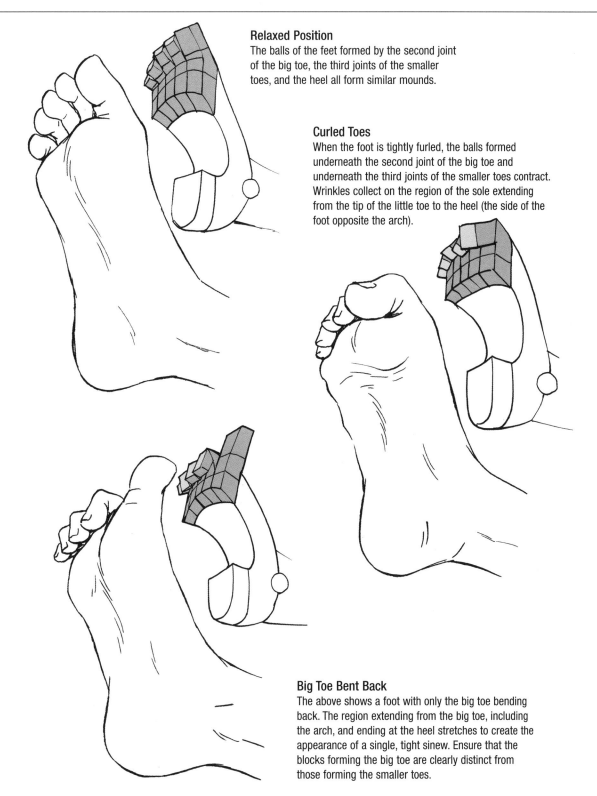

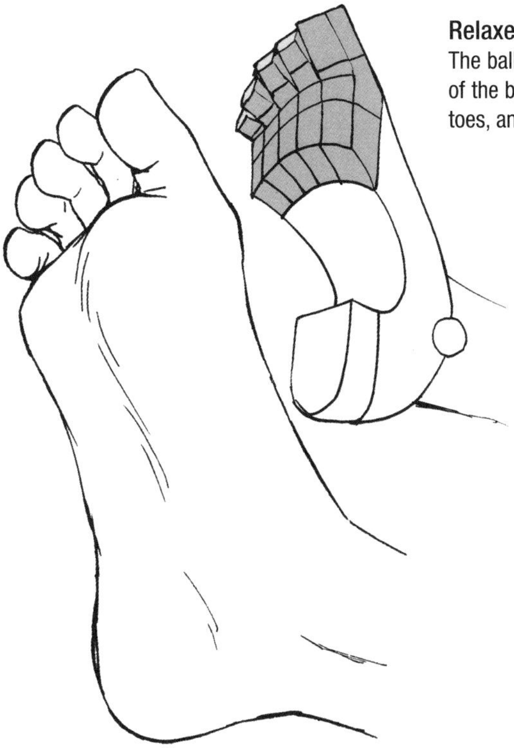

Relaxed Position
The balls of the feet formed by the second joint of the big toe, the third joints of the smaller toes, and the heel all form similar mounds.

Curled Toes
When the foot is tightly furled, the balls formed underneath the second joint of the big toe and underneath the third joints of the smaller toes contract. Wrinkles collect on the region of the sole extending from the tip of the little toe to the heel (the side of the foot opposite the arch).

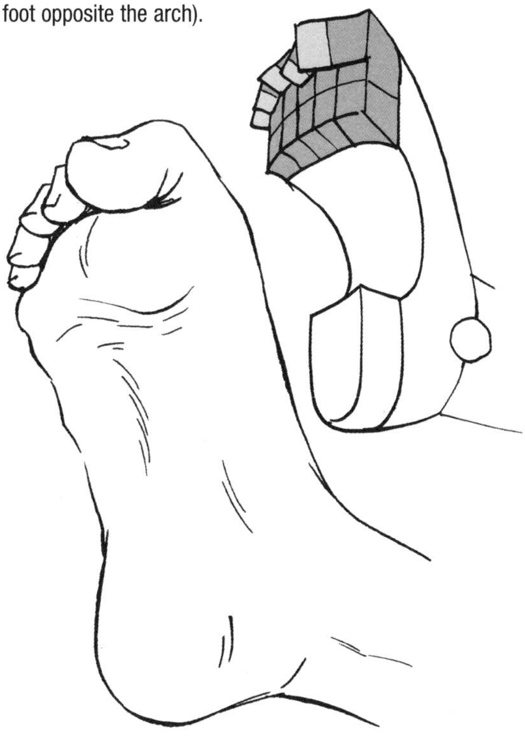

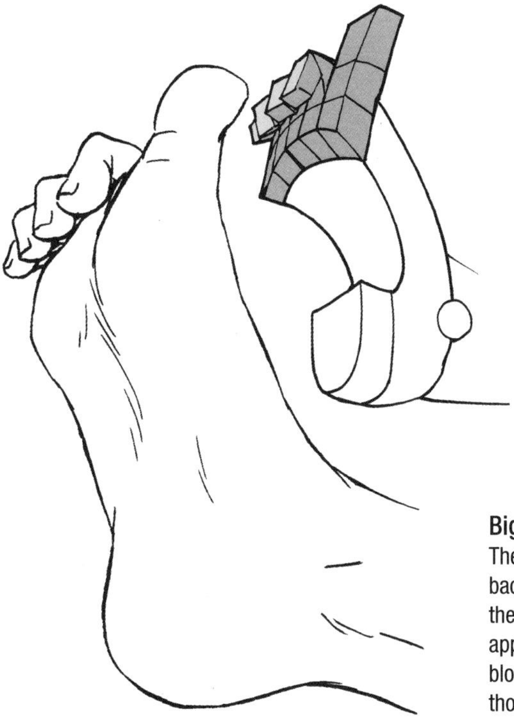

Big Toe Bent Back
The above shows a foot with only the big toe bending back. The region extending from the big toe, including the arch, and ending at the heel stretches to create the appearance of a single, tight sinew. Ensure that the blocks forming the big toe are clearly distinct from those forming the smaller toes.

Assorted Portrayals

Practice drawing the foot in various positions and from an array of angles. Use the steps learnt on page 63.

Natural Position

1. Sketch the fist as a single unit.
2. Divide the hand into its parts.
3. Add in the details.

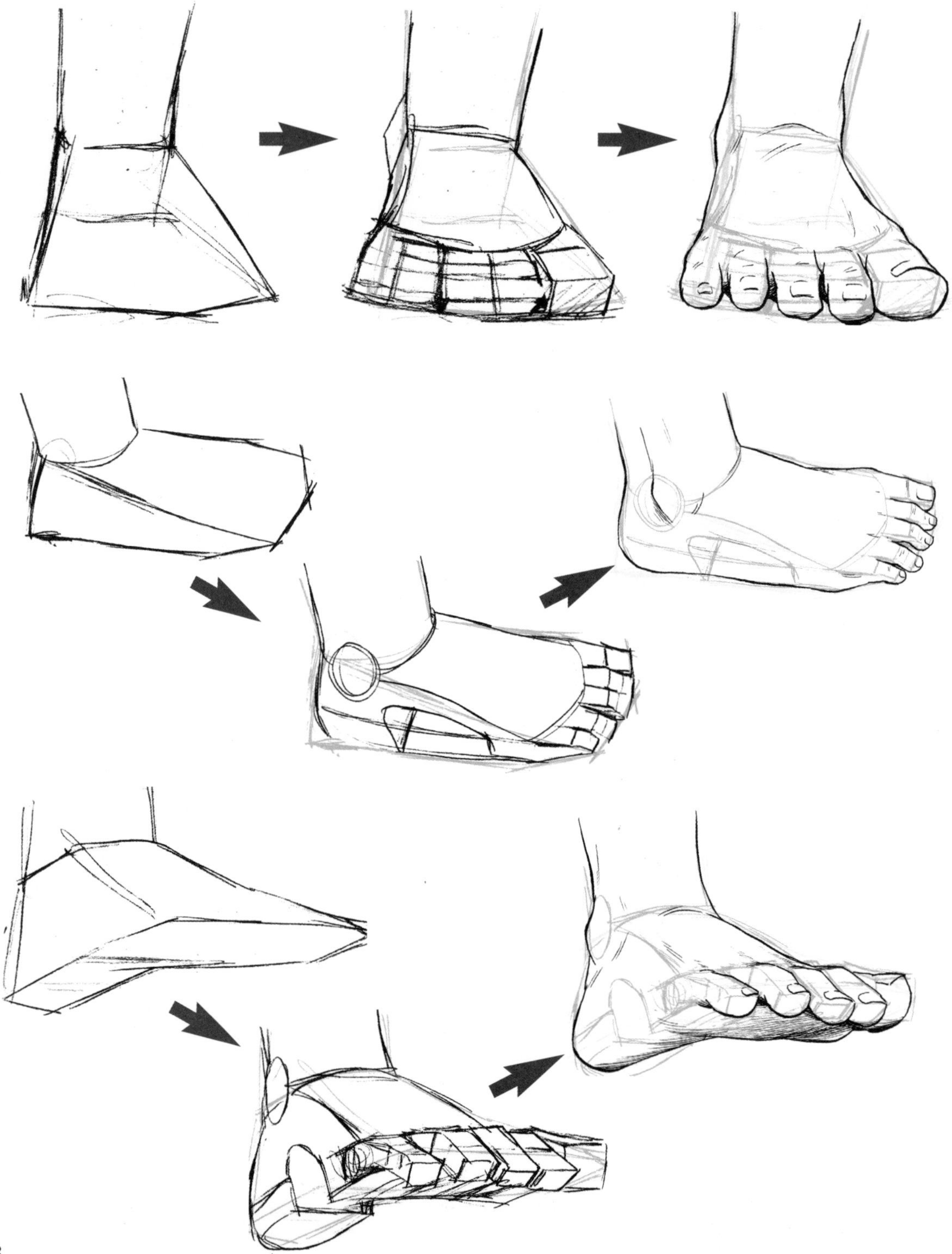

Poised on the Toes

1 Sketch the fist as a single unit.

2 Divide the hand into its parts.

3 Add in the details.

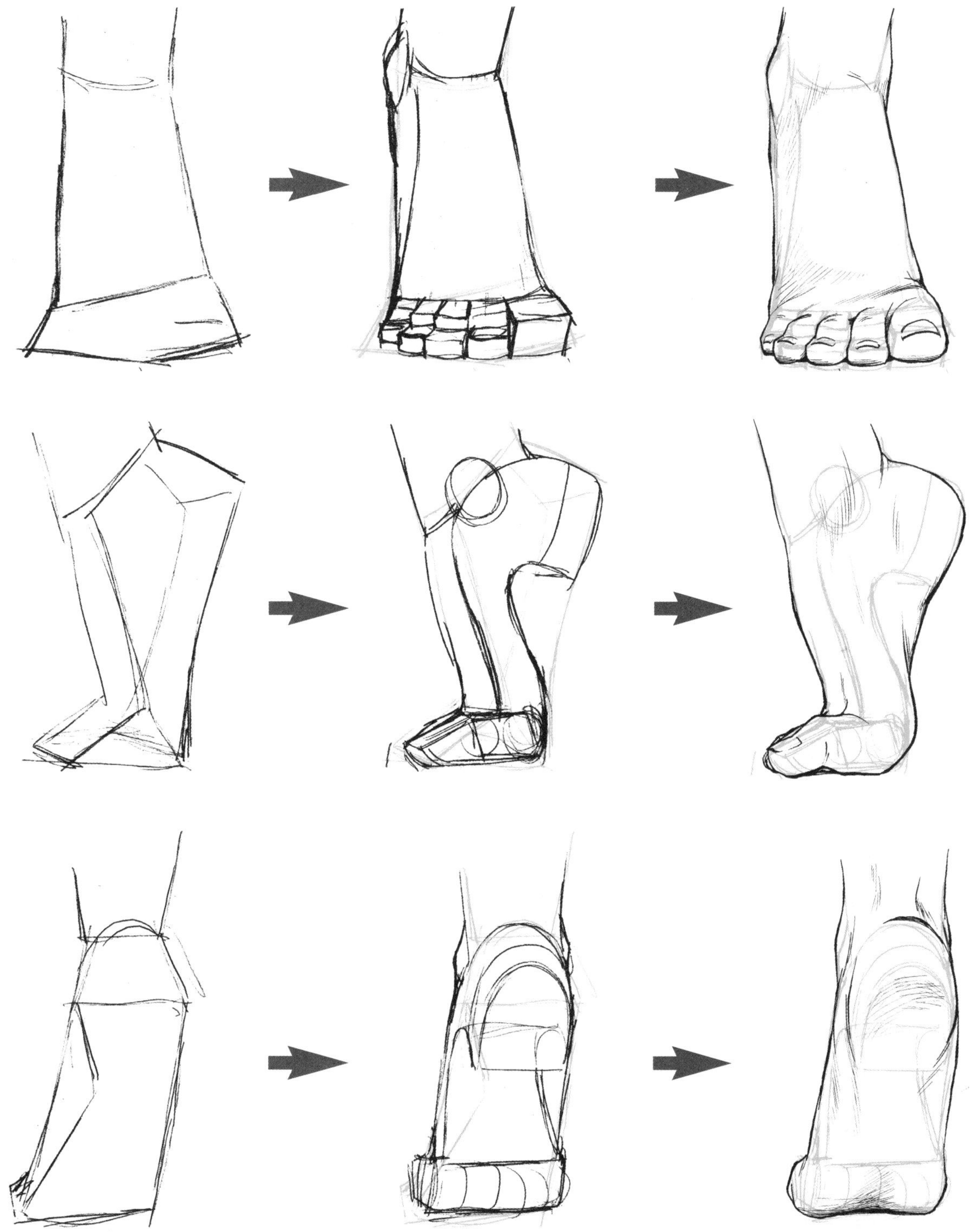

Grasping an Object with the Toes

1 Sketch the fist as a single unit.

2 Divide the hand into its parts.

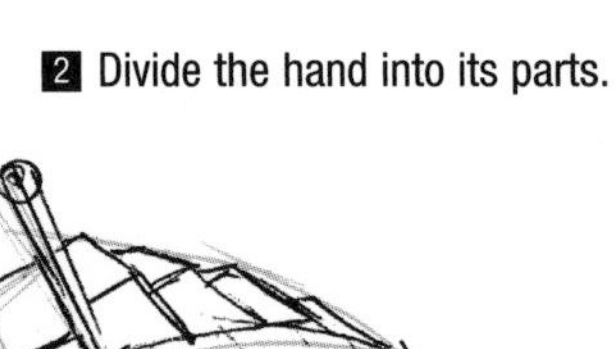

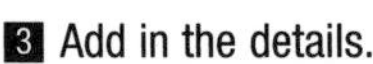

3 Add in the details.

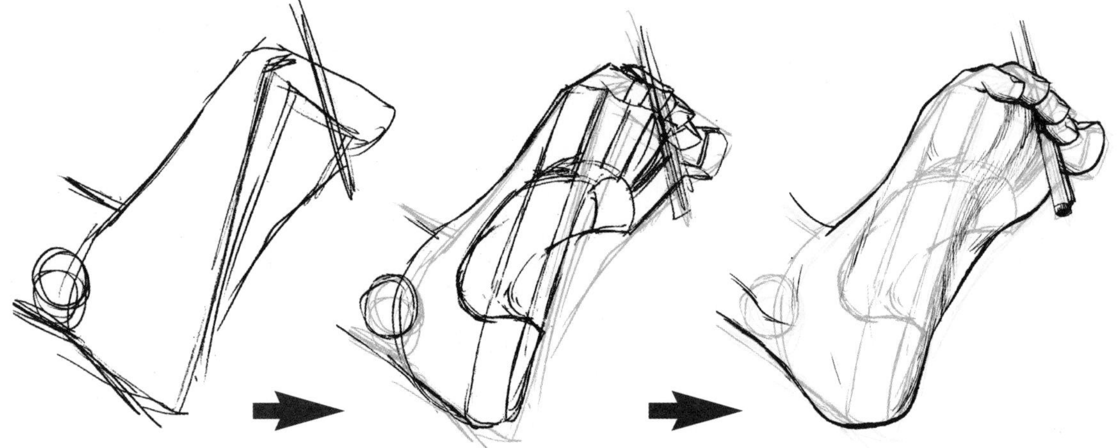

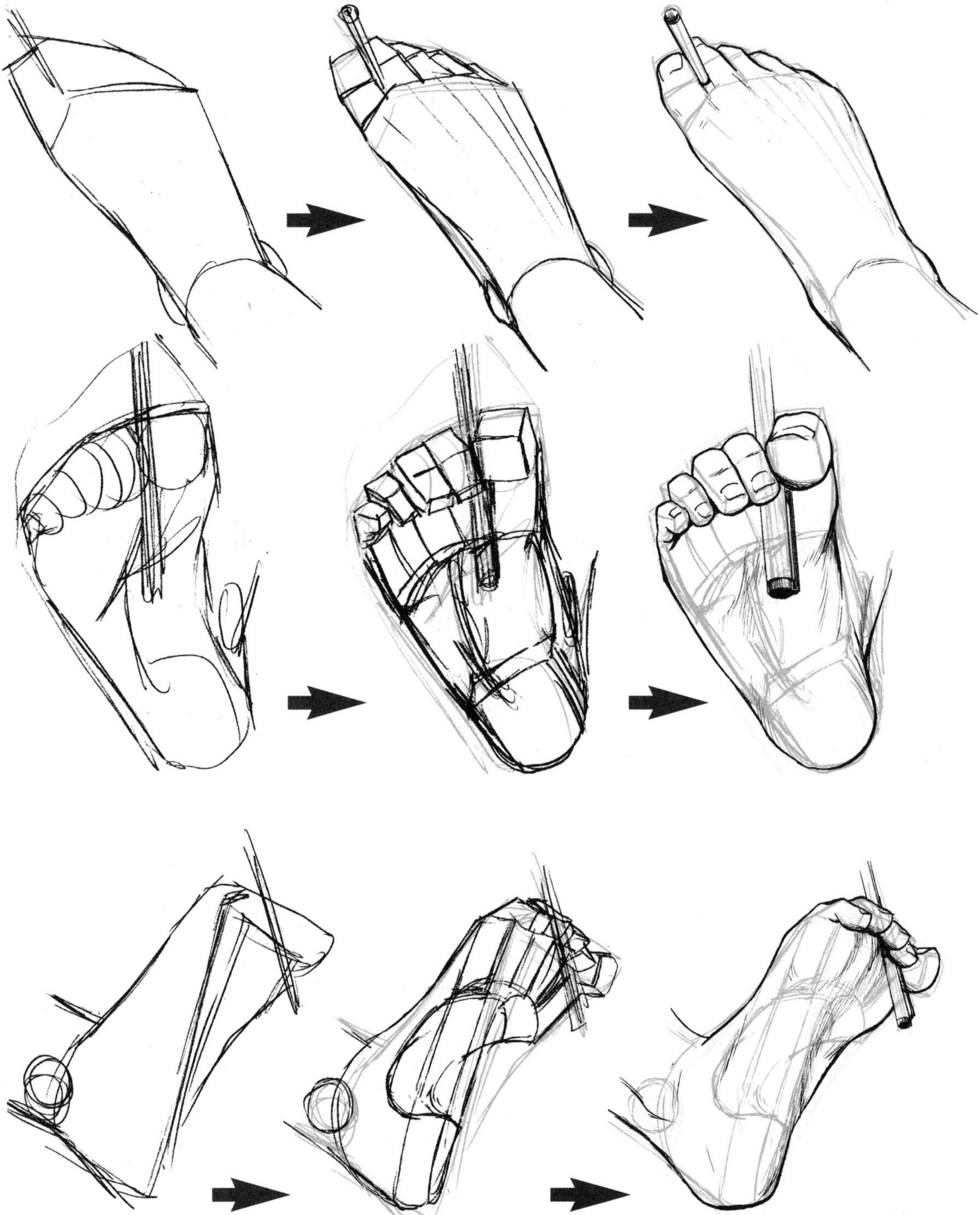

Spreading the Toes

1 Sketch the fist as a single unit.

2 Divide the hand into its parts.

3 Add in the details.

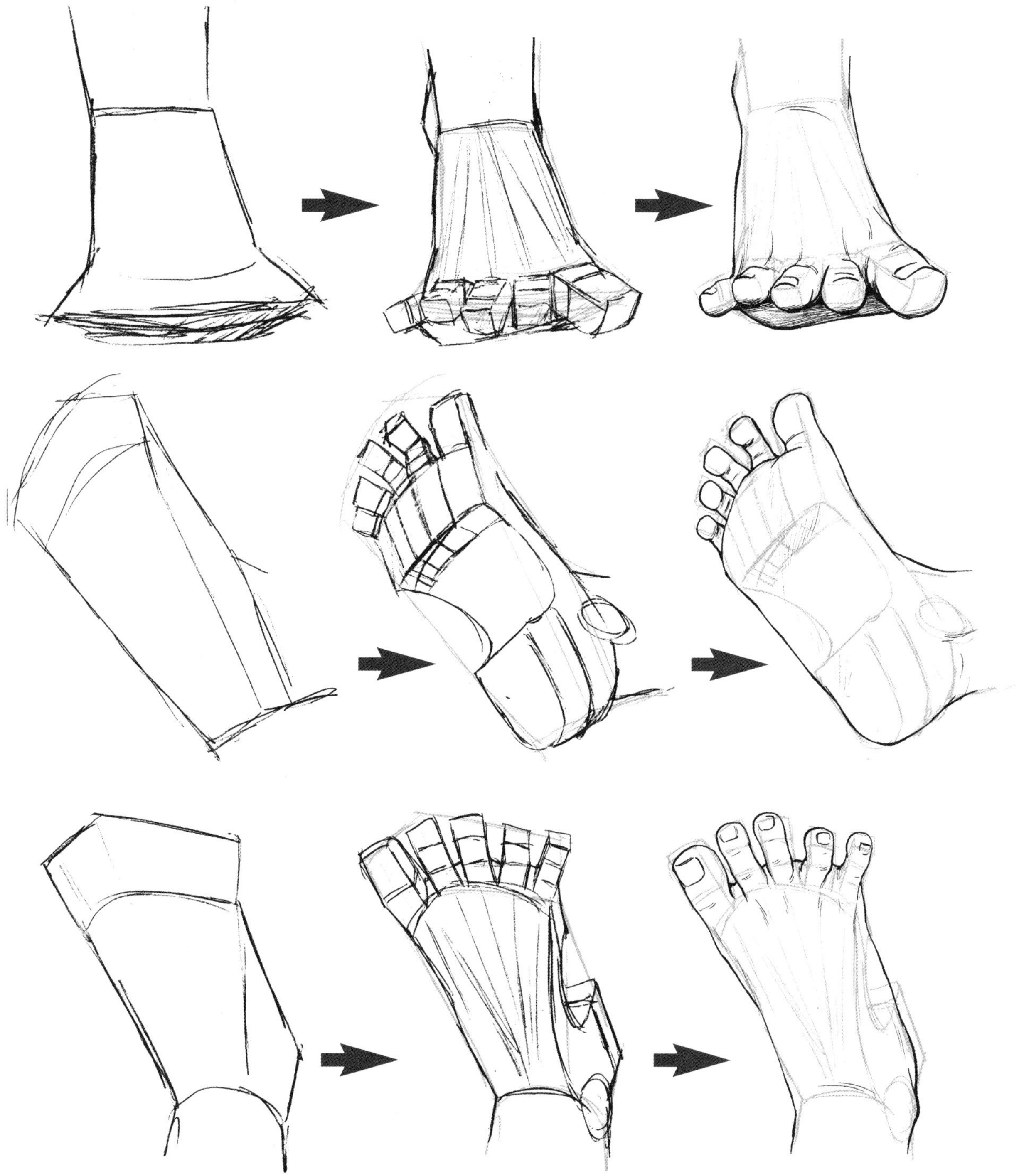

Curling the Toes

1. Sketch the fist as a single unit.
2. Divide the hand into its parts.
3. Add in the details.

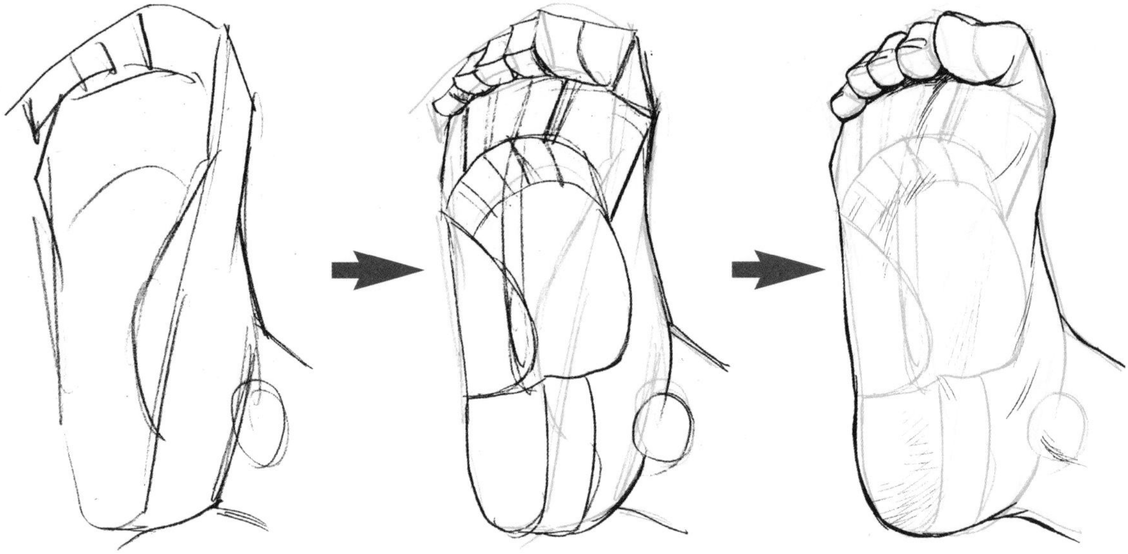

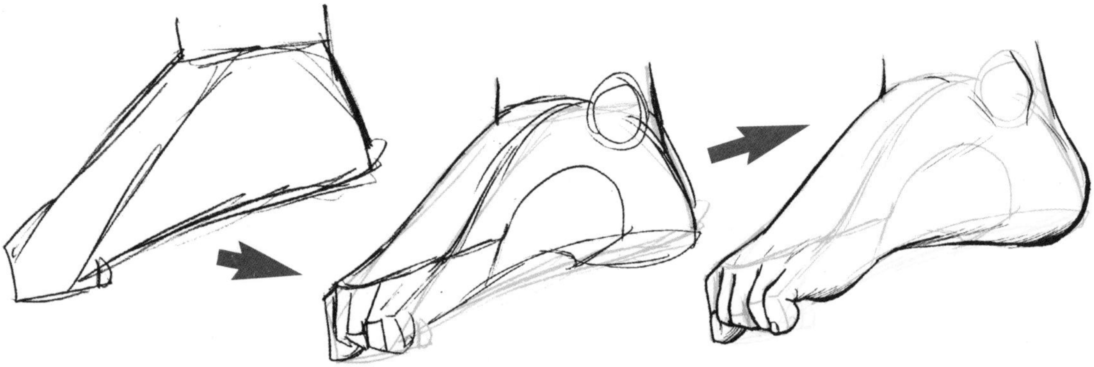

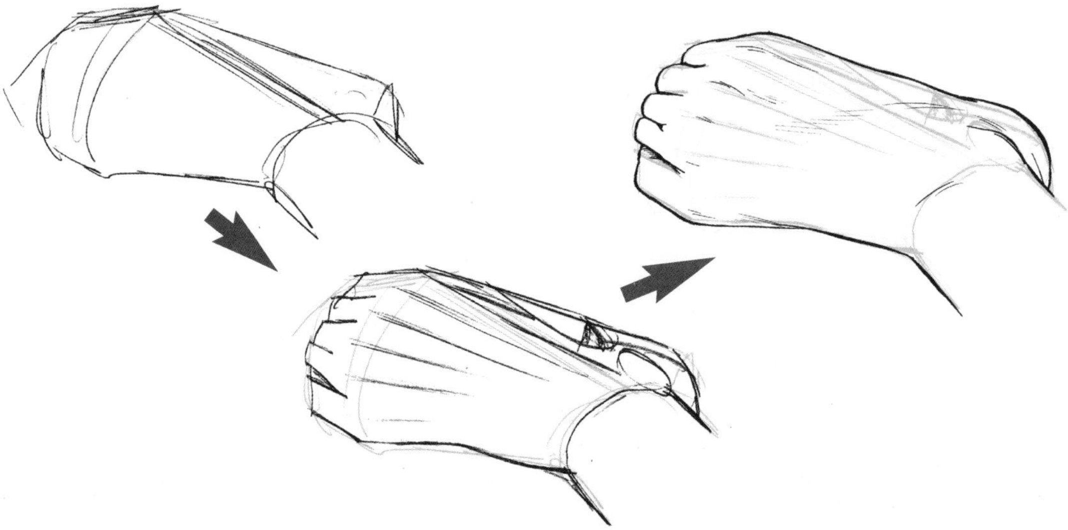

Bending the Foot Inward

1 Sketch the fist as a single unit.

2 Divide the hand into its parts.

3 Add in the details.

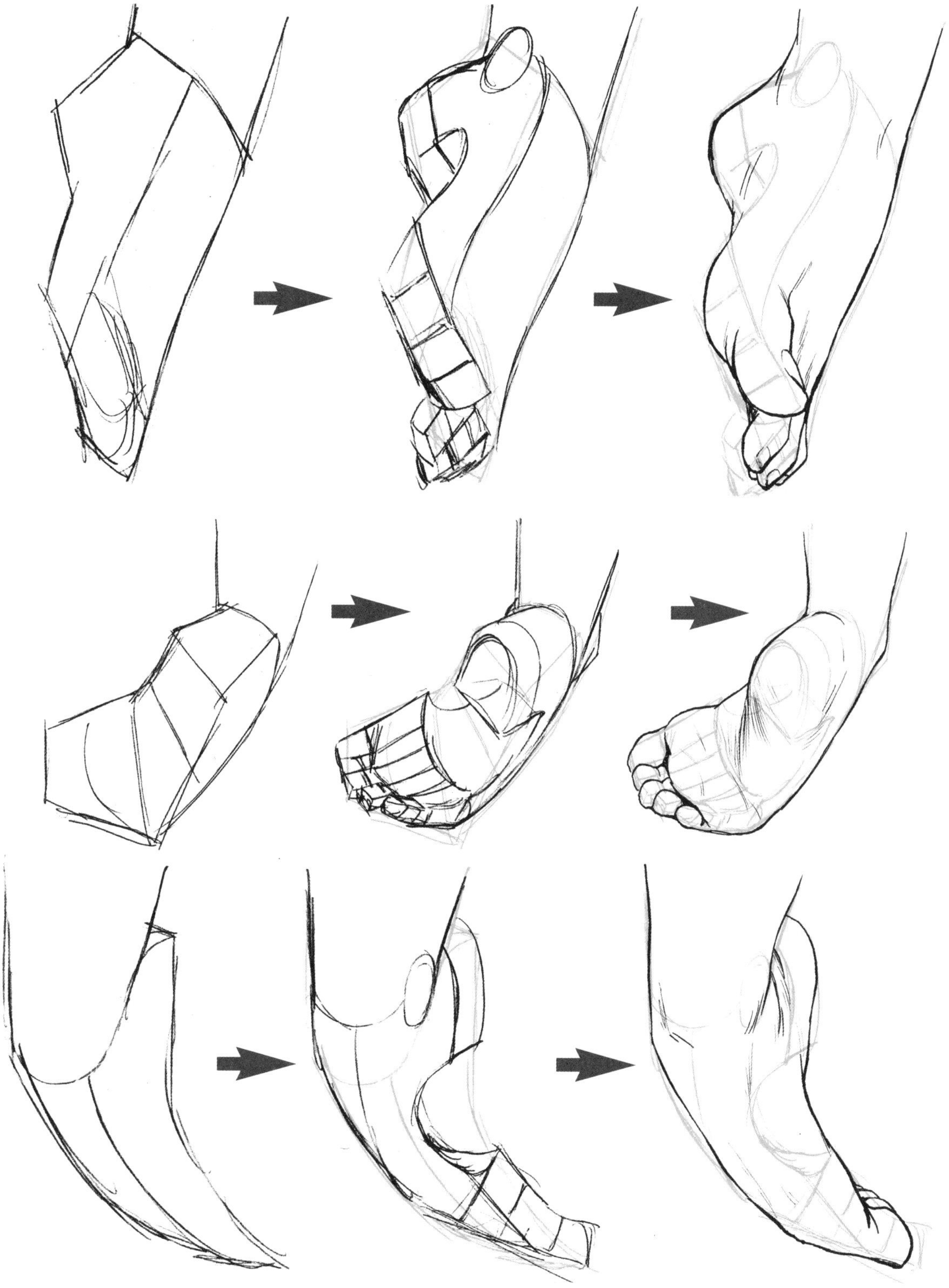

The Toes Held in Various Positions

1 Sketch the fist as a single unit.

2 Divide the hand into its parts.

3 Add in the details.

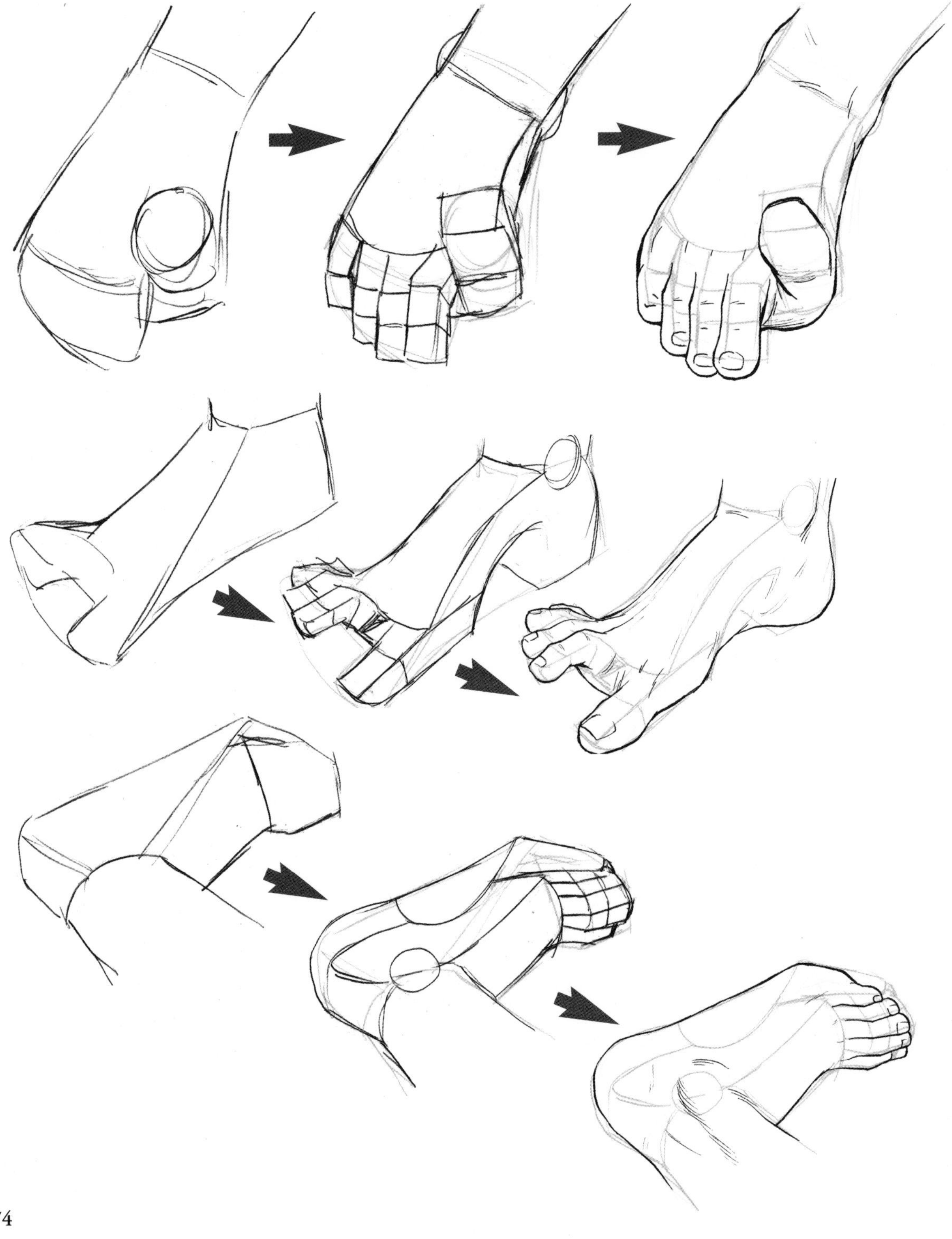

The Close and Yet Distant Relationship between the Foot and the Shoe

As mentioned in the previous lesson module, grey areas indicate the foot's load-bearing regions. These regions become critical when drawing a shoe.

Dashed Line
All shoes bend at this line only.

Left of the Dashed Line
The shoe's upper surface rises as it approaches the toe. Because the shoe's shape changes greatly depending on the style of shoe or the materials, this is the area where the shoe's form is most distinct.

Right of the Dashed Line
All styles of shoe share this basic form.

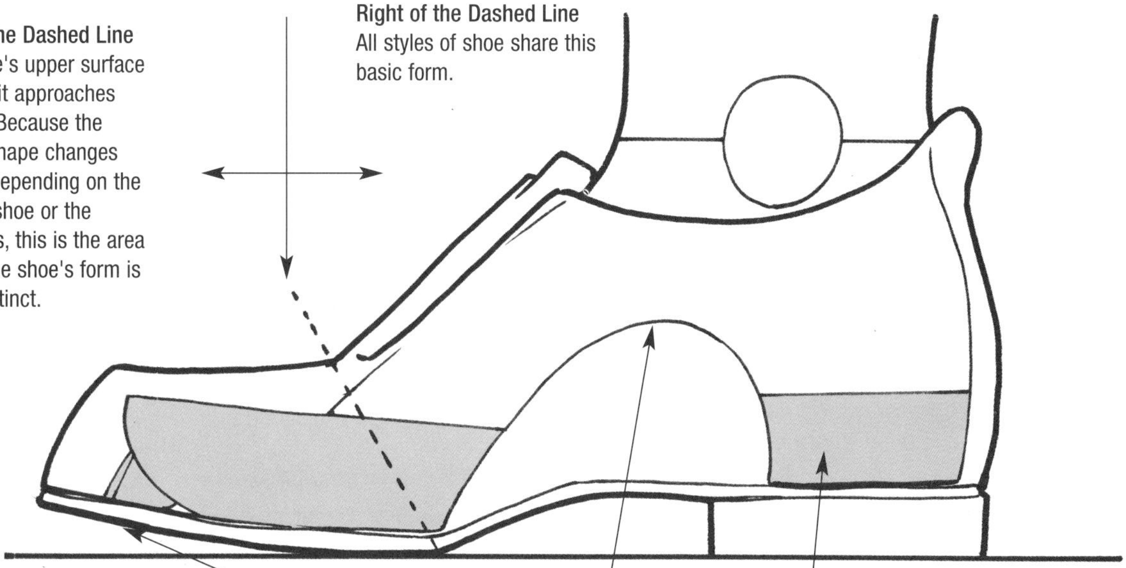

Toe
There tends to be a larger gap between the foot and the toe of the shoe than the foot and the back of the shoe. Consequently, an under drawing of a foot wearing a shoe should be larger than the under drawing of the same foot bare.

Arch
The inside of the foot (big toe's side) indents at the arch.

Heel
The foot's heel should appear firmly planted against the shoe's heel.

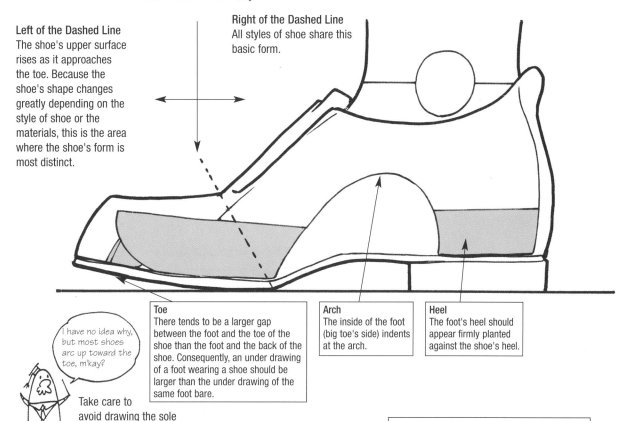

I have no idea why, but most shoes arc up toward the toe, m'kay?

Take care to avoid drawing the sole of the shoe flat against the ground.

Sole
The toe may be pointed or rounded. The sole curves inward at the arch.

Dotted Line
This line denotes where the shoe bends.

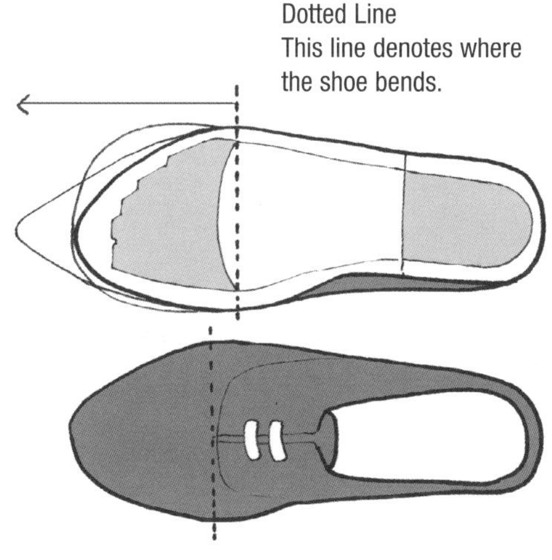

Vamp (Upper)
Note that the location of the line denoting where the shoe bends shifts depending on whether we are looking at the shoe's vamp or sole.

Parts of a Shoe
Rather than becoming lost in shoelaces and other decorations, first draw the shoe's surfaces.

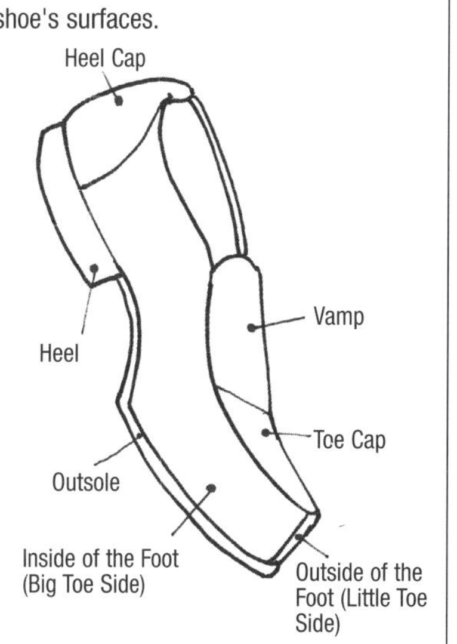

How to Draw a Shoe

These pages cover how to draw a shoe and key points in drawing a shoe looking at familiar shoe styles as reference while explaining how to evoke such elements as texture and project a sense of volume.

How to Draw Shoelaces

1 Determine how the laces will appear passing through the eyelets. Draw the shoelace passing through both of the bottommost eyelets. Next, draw the lace knotted into a bow at the uppermost eyelets. Ensure that the eyelets are positioned symmetrically.

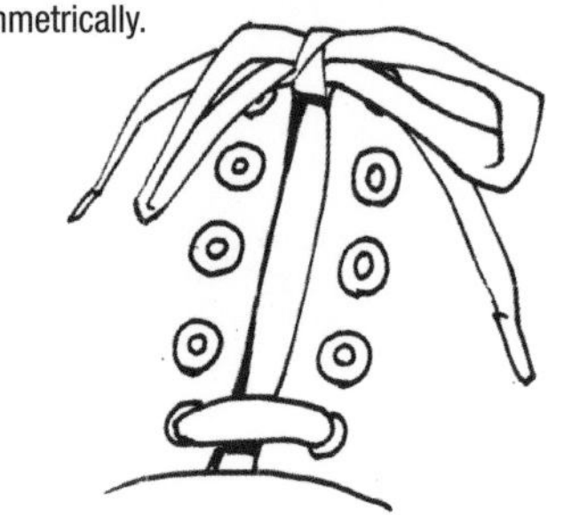

2 Draw the shoelace passing through all of the eyelets on only one side. Show the lace extending across the tongue toward the row of eyelets on the opposite side of the vamp.

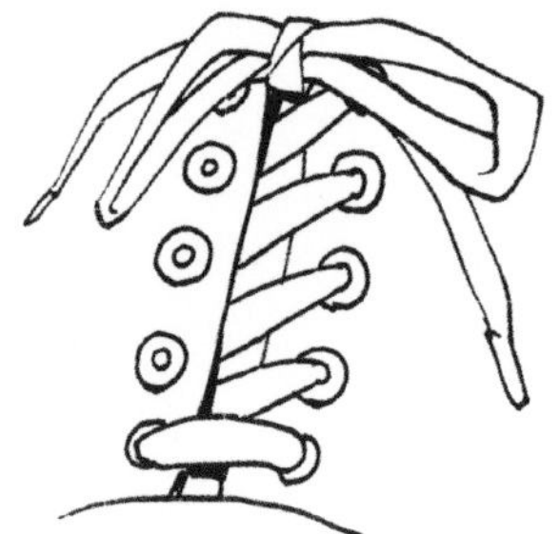

3 Draw the lacing through the second row of eyelets in the same manner as the first. Show the lace threading underneath that drawn in step 2. Voilà!

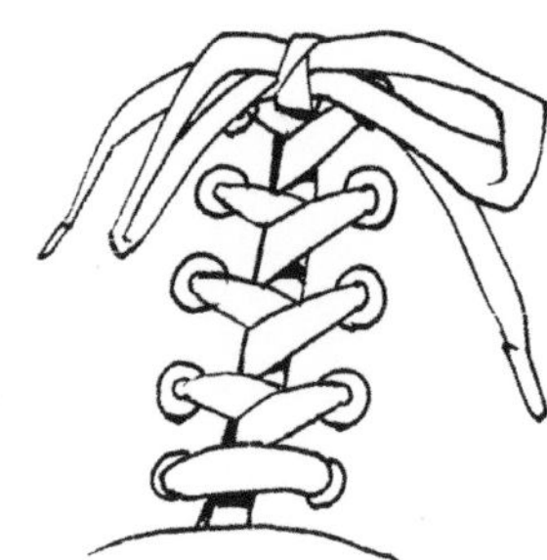

Laces on semiformal lace-up shoes are often surprisingly simple to draw. The knot is typically a limp bow that is tucked away under the vamp.

Loafers

Loafers are a popular form of leather shoe. Depicted here are penny loafers, which are (probably) the most common shoe worn by *bishonen*. Leather shoes are typically stiff, making their surfaces easy to draw. The stiff leather prevents the shoe from bending much, which in turn prevents the formation of creases. Moreover, the penny loafer has a predetermined design, making it incredibly easy to draw. Including stitched edging makes the penny loafer appear more convincing, so look around and study leather shoes in real life to learn how the stitching should be positioned. You will find little variation.

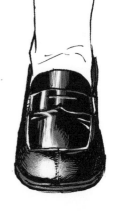

To generate the illusion of luster, leave white those areas touched by light.

To add a highlight, draw a line following the surface of the heel cap.

How to Draw a Penny Loafer

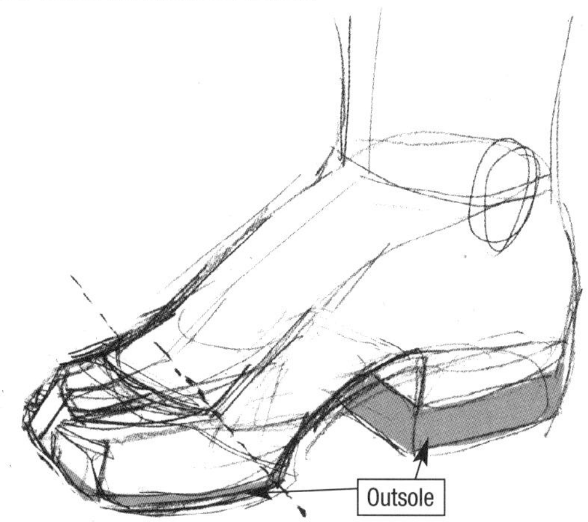

1 Draw a foot, adding extra volume for the shoe's sole. Draw a dashed line where the lowest joints of the toes meet the end of the foot (a rough, visual guess is fine). This is where the foot touches the ground. This is the only region of the shoe that bends and where creases form.

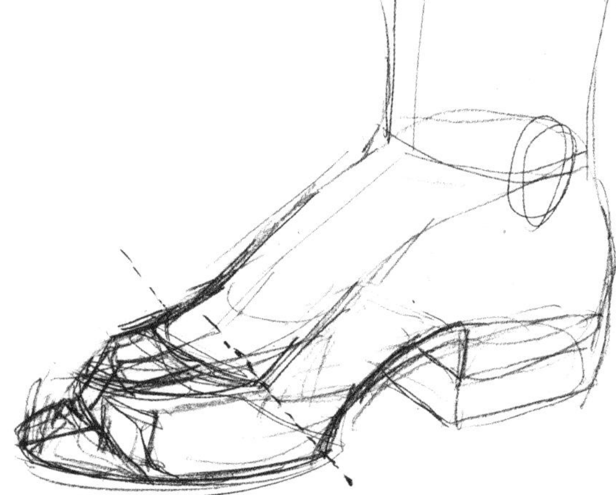

2 Determine the length of the shoe's toe. The shoe's style will affect this length. Draw the toe on the long side if the shoe is a loafer or other leather shoe. Have the toe make up approximately 2/5 of the entire vamp.

3 Delineate the shoe's surfaces.

4 Draw stitched trim and any other details.

POINT

Common Pitfall

Take careful note of where the top of the foot begins. It does not grow directly out from the ankle. Also ensure that the tip of the toe does not drop down vertically.

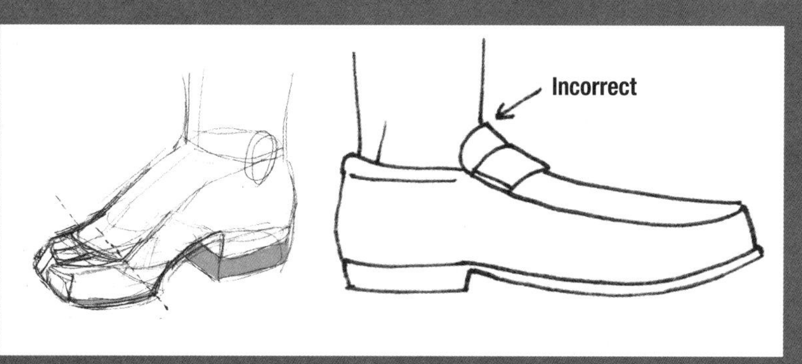

Athletic Shoes

Athletic shoes come in a wide range of shapes, materials, and designs. Athletic shoes tend to be made of soft fabrics, have roundish forms, and come with a limitless variety of components. These factors possibly make athletic shoes the most difficult of all to draw. For now, start with whatever athletic shoes you own, as they will be the most familiar to you. Before you begin to draw, pick up an actual athletic shoe or use a photograph of an athletic shoe as reference. This will help you compose the shoe without becoming confused. Repeatedly drawing shoes will enable you to create athletic shoes of your own design as needed.

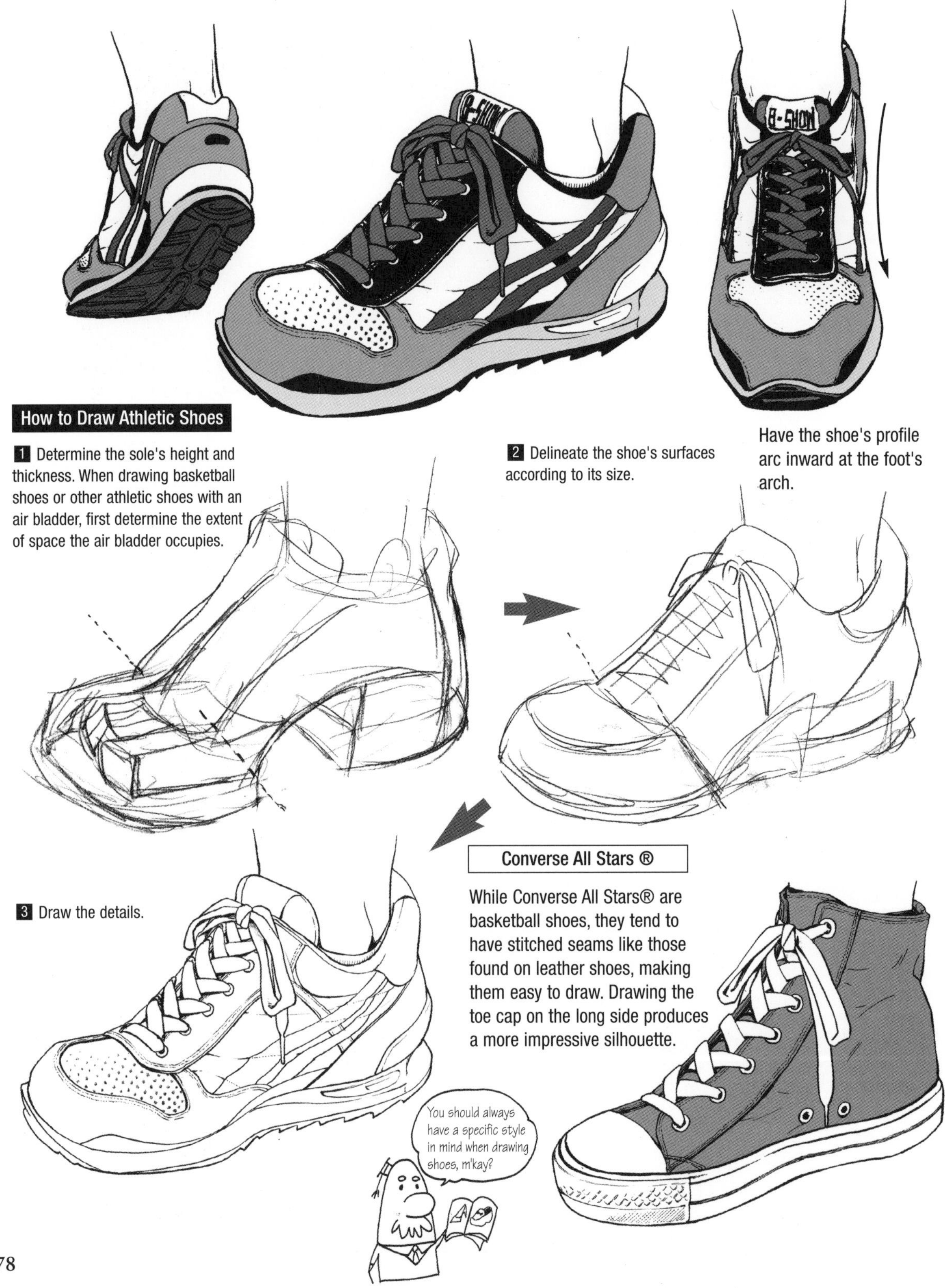

B-SHOW
B-SHOW
You should always have a specific style in mind when drawing shoes, m'kay?

How to Draw Athletic Shoes

1 Determine the sole's height and thickness. When drawing basketball shoes or other athletic shoes with an air bladder, first determine the extent of space the air bladder occupies.

2 Delineate the shoe's surfaces according to its size.

Have the shoe's profile arc inward at the foot's arch.

3 Draw the details.

Converse All Stars ®

While Converse All Stars® are basketball shoes, they tend to have stitched seams like those found on leather shoes, making them easy to draw. Drawing the toe cap on the long side produces a more impressive silhouette.

Boots

Like leather shoes, boots come in a limited range of styles, which includes cowboy boots, engineer boots, and the like. The variety of styles makes it easy to learn the tricks to their portrayal. Men's boots are typically rugged. While boots might be taller than leather shoes, there is essentially not much difference between the two when it comes to drawing.

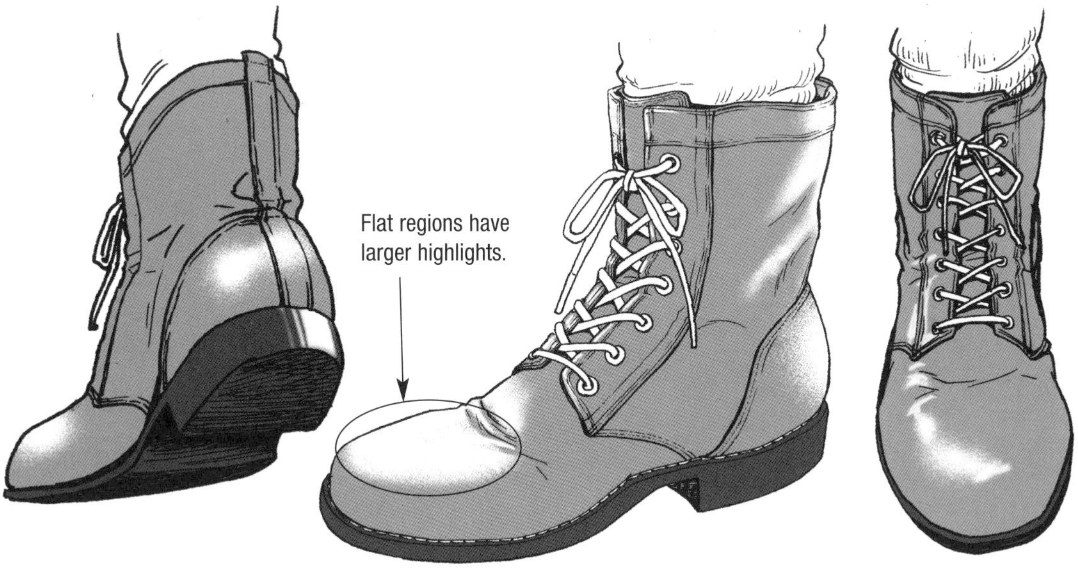

Flat regions have larger highlights.

How to Draw Boots

1 Sketch the sole and the boot's general shape.

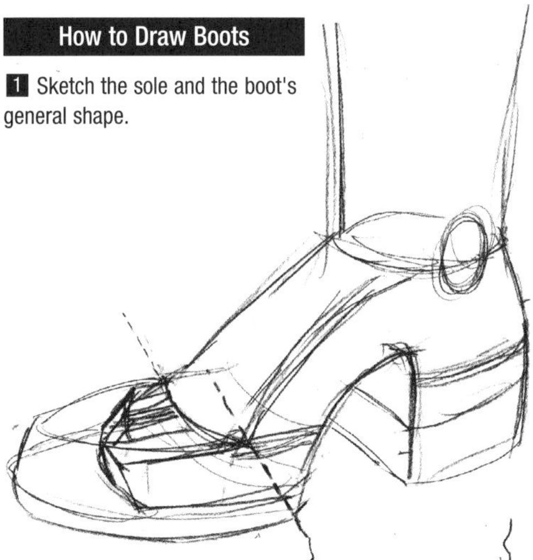

2 Delineate the shoe's surfaces according to its size.

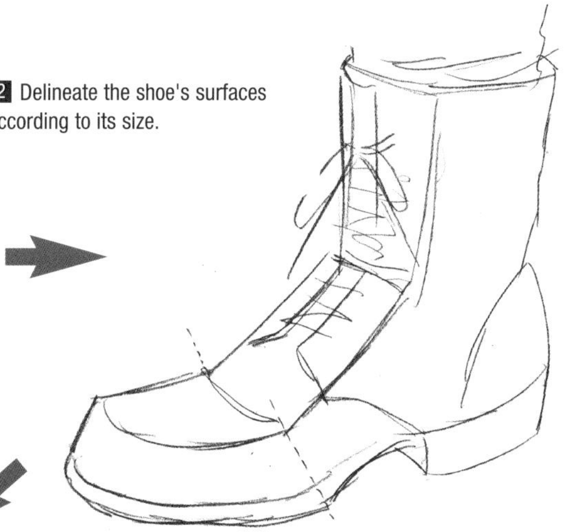

3 Draw the details.

The toe of a cowboy boot turns upward notably.

The toe of a cowboy boot tends to turn upward more dramatically than other shoe types.

Geta and Thongs

While geta and thongs might appear similar, they are actually completely different. Both are easy to compose, as most of the sketch work involves drawing a bare foot. Consequently, you should make an effort to memorize the distinguishing characteristics of these shoes.

Geta

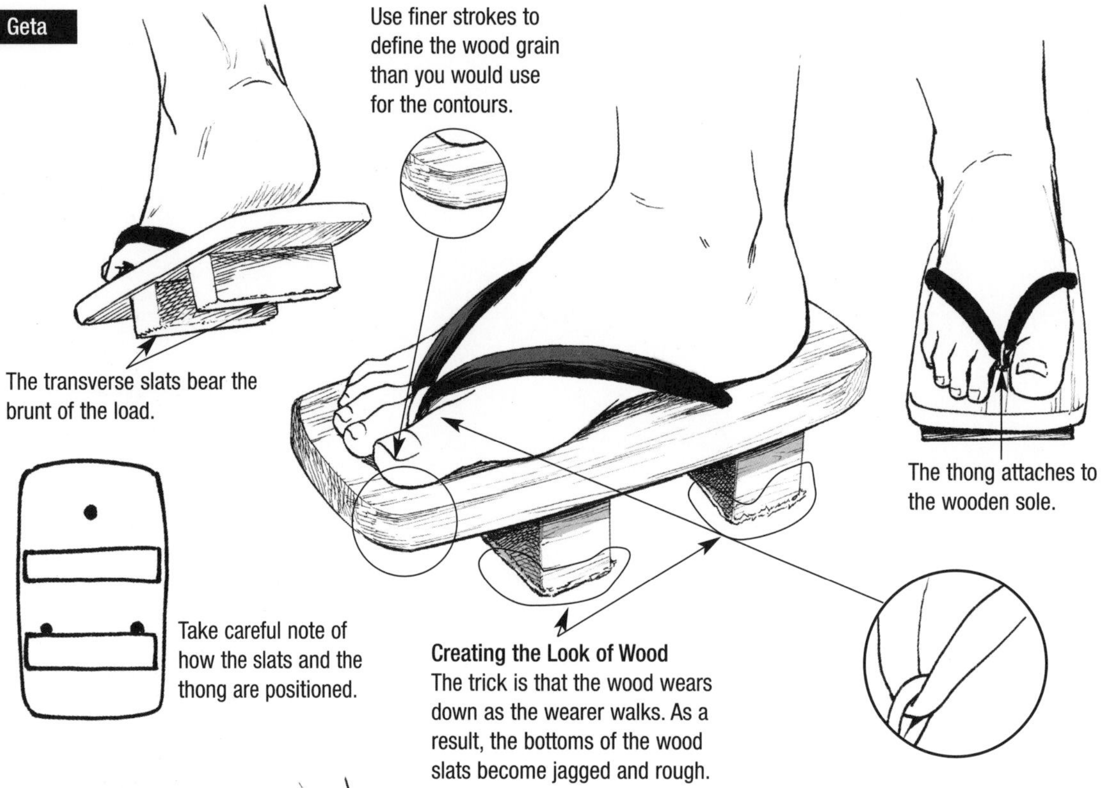

Use finer strokes to define the wood grain than you would use for the contours.

The transverse slats bear the brunt of the load.

The thong attaches to the wooden sole.

Take careful note of how the slats and the thong are positioned.

Creating the Look of Wood
The trick is that the wood wears down as the wearer walks. As a result, the bottoms of the wood slats become jagged and rough.

Thongs (Flip-Flops)

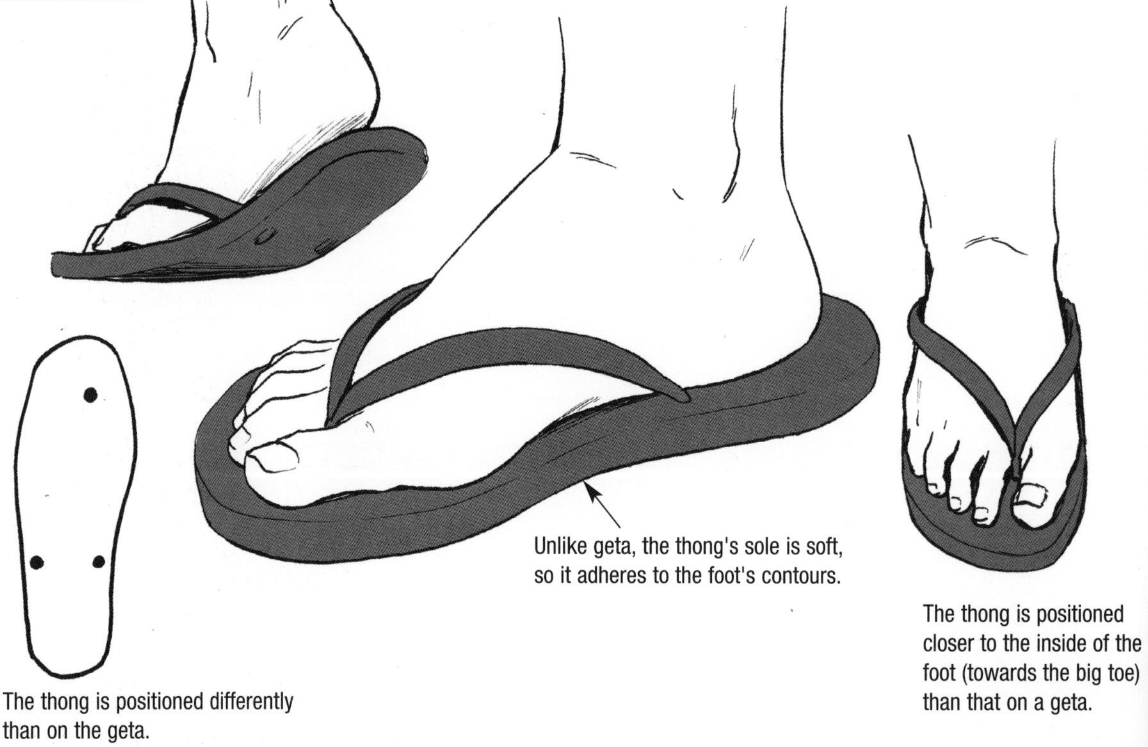

Unlike geta, the thong's sole is soft, so it adheres to the foot's contours.

The thong is positioned differently than on the geta.

The thong is positioned closer to the inside of the foot (towards the big toe) than that on a geta.

High-Heeled Shoes and Socks

When drawing shoes with high heels, pay careful attention to which point on the shoe is load-bearing and where the heel is positioned. When drawing socks, note how creases form in the fabric.

Shoes with High Heels

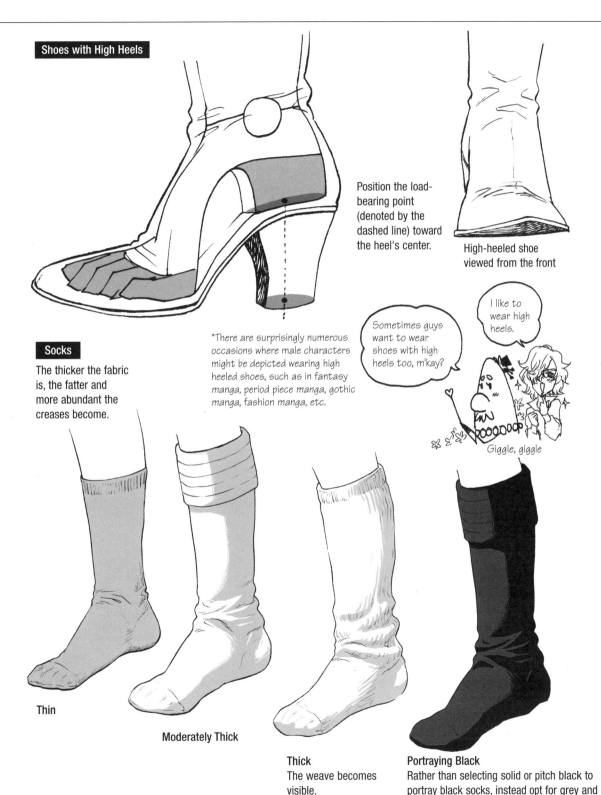

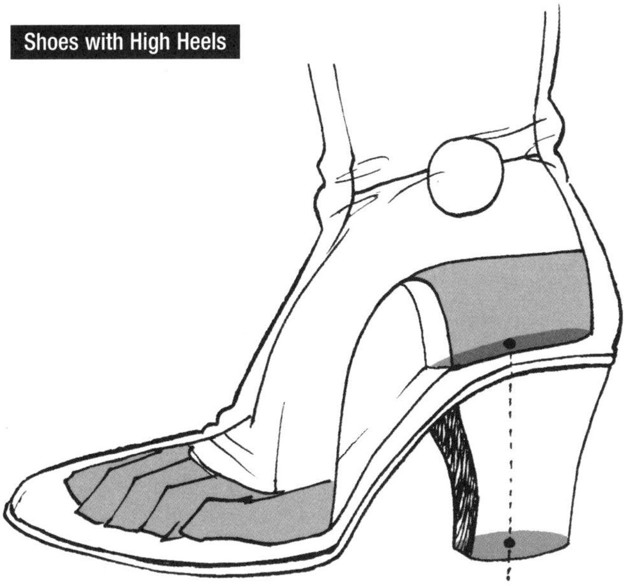

Position the load-bearing point (denoted by the dashed line) toward the heel's center.

High-heeled shoe viewed from the front

*There are surprisingly numerous occasions where male characters might be depicted wearing high heeled shoes, such as in fantasy manga, period piece manga, gothic manga, fashion manga, etc.

Sometimes guys want to wear shoes with high heels too, m'kay?

I like to wear high heels.

Giggle, giggle

Socks

The thicker the fabric is, the fatter and more abundant the creases become.

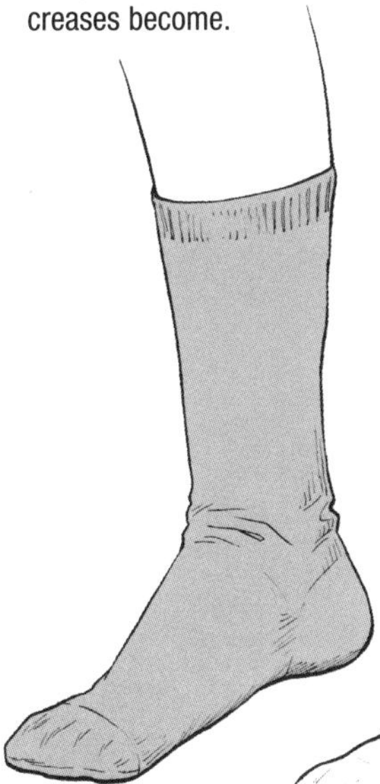

Thin

Moderately Thick

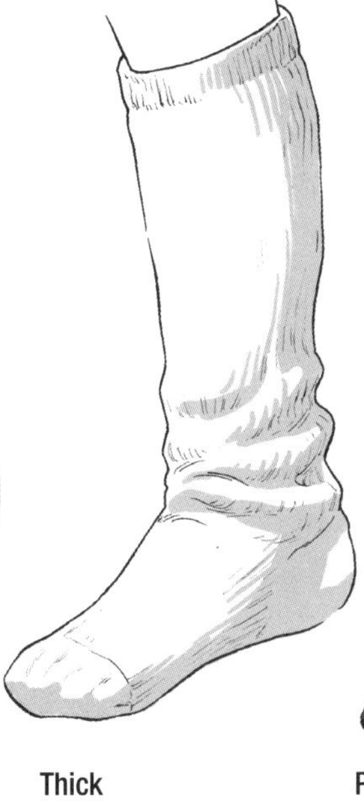

Thick
The weave becomes visible.

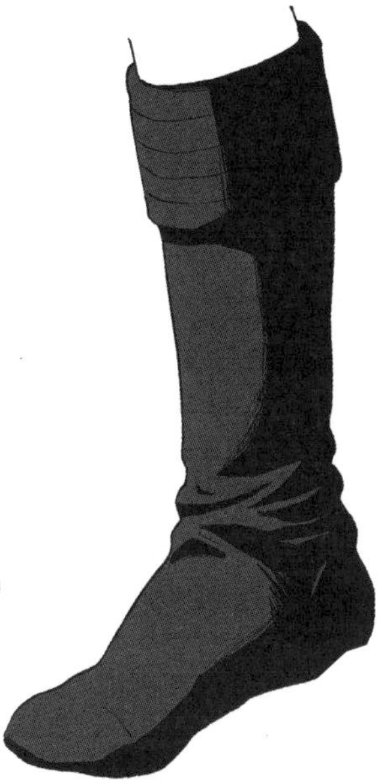

Portraying Black
Rather than selecting solid or pitch black to portray black socks, instead opt for grey and then use solid black to suggest shading. This will result in a more polished rendition.

Chapter 3
Drawing Faces

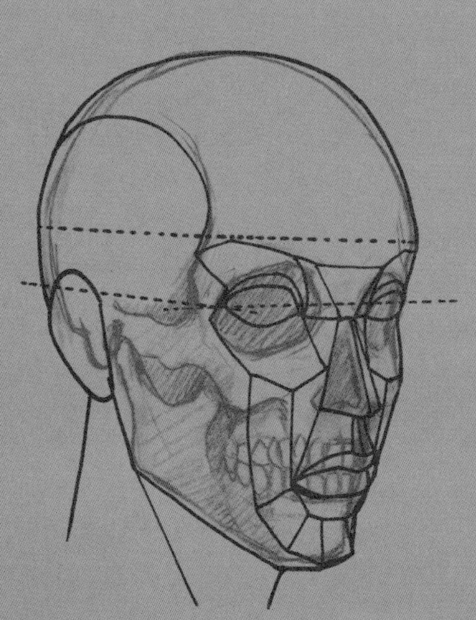

Facial Features and Proportioning

At long last, our discussion has finally turned to the most frequently drawn body part—the head. The face is the *bishonen*'s most vital feature. The head is the body part into which artists pour most of their attention and which allows artists to display their own artistic style.
This book covers only the basics, focusing on the skeletal structure, the proportioning of the facial features, and differences in portrayal according to the character's age and build.

Delineating Surfaces

In order to render the head as a solid object, the various surfaces must be carefully described. Shown below are average guides. When I draw characters' heads, I typically break the face down into its surfaces just like the samples shown below.

POINT

Bone Structure of the Head

1. Draw the head bald before adding the hair.
2. Capture the head as a solid object rather than a flat plane.
3. At the very least, never forget to draw a guideline for the eyes and a guideline for the face's center. These two guidelines form a cross.
4. Start with the nose bridge. That will make it easier to balance the face's proportioning.

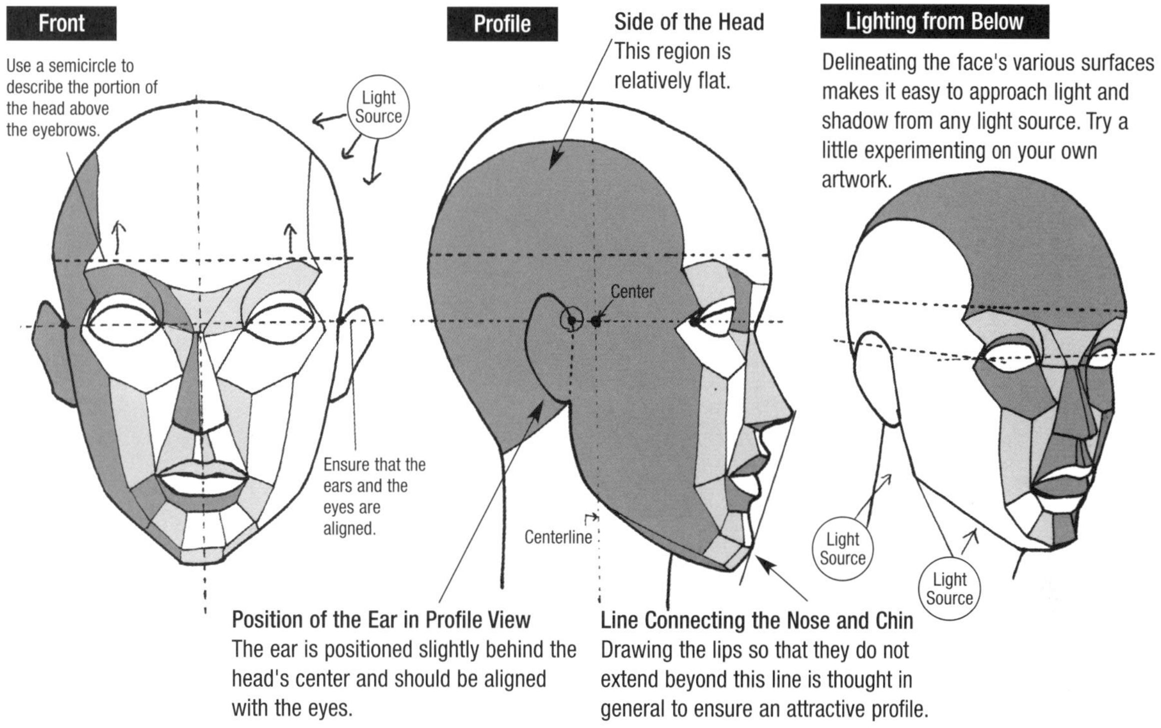

Front
Use a semicircle to describe the portion of the head above the eyebrows.
Light Source
Ensure that the ears and the eyes are aligned.
Profile
Side of the Head
This region is relatively flat.
Center
Centerline
Position of the Ear in Profile View
The ear is positioned slightly behind the head's center and should be aligned with the eyes.
Line Connecting the Nose and Chin
Drawing the lips so that they do not extend beyond this line is thought in general to ensure an attractive profile.
Lighting from Below
Delineating the face's various surfaces makes it easy to approach light and shadow from any light source. Try a little experimenting on your own artwork.
Light Source
Light Source

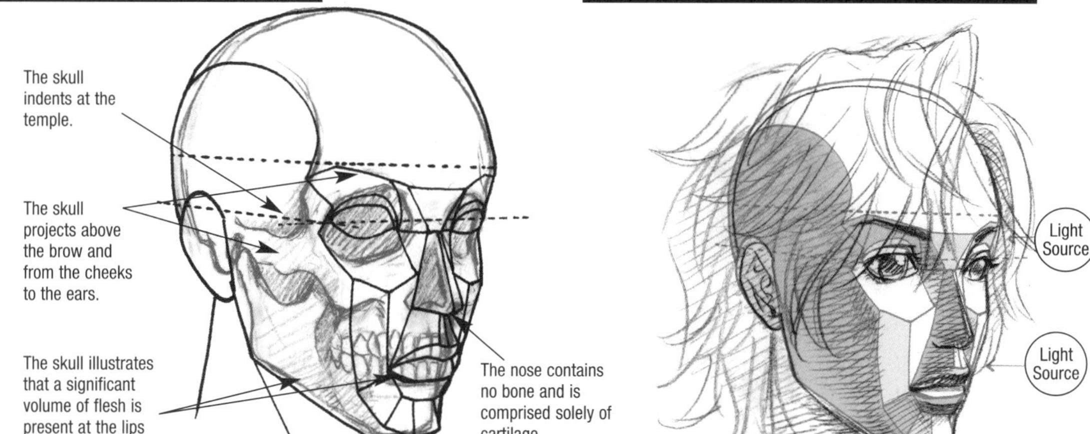

Skull Overlapping the Rough Sketch
The skull indents at the temple.
The skull projects above the brow and from the cheeks to the ears.
The skull illustrates that a significant volume of flesh is present at the lips and underneath the cheekbones
The nose contains no bone and is comprised solely of cartilage.
Rough Sketch Showing Softened Surface Edges

How to Delineate the Face's Surfaces and Portray the Bone Structure

Minor changes added to sizes and lengths in the skull yield an abundance of possible face variations. This page covers the basic guidelines in capturing the face's bone structure.

Creating Distinct Faces

Modifying the sizes or lengths of parts of the skull allows you to create a variety of faces.

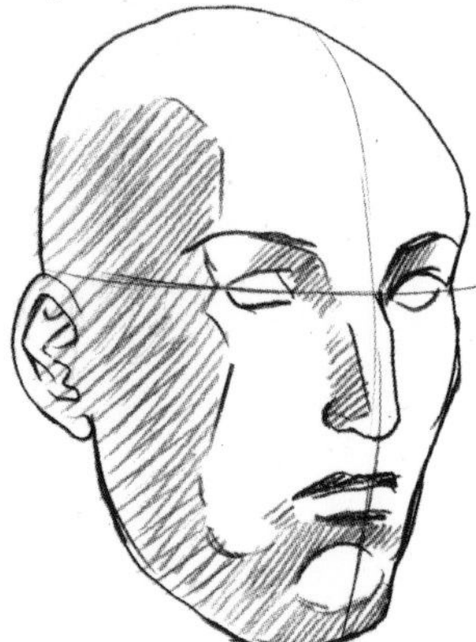

1 The above shows a long face, a rounded jaw, and a high nose bridge.

2 This face features an unusually prominent chin, cheekbones, and jaw.

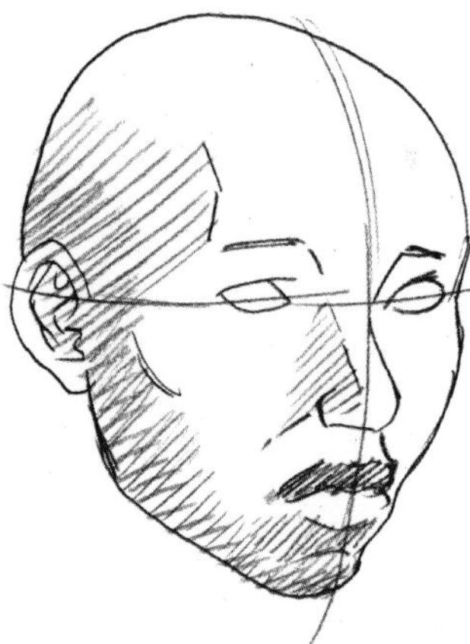

3 This face has high cheekbones but has an understated chin and jaw.

How to Capture the Bone Structure

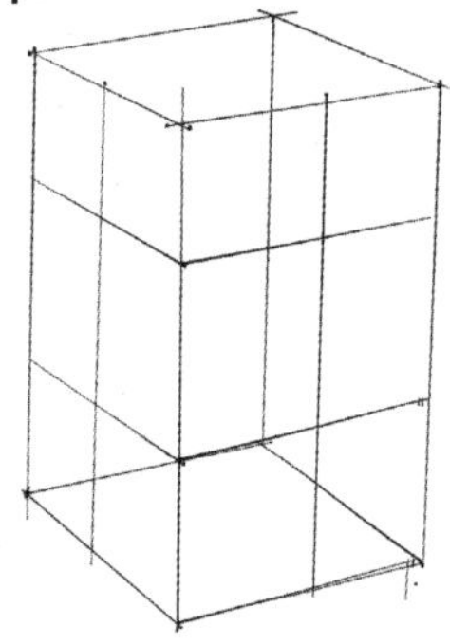

1 First, draw a box and add a few lines to serve as guides when drawing parallel contours. (The above contains two horizontal lines and one vertical line. These lines function similarly to graph paper.)

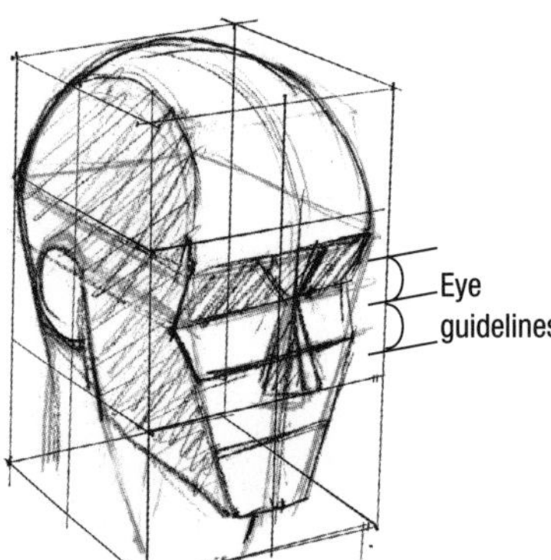

2 Using simple, straight lines, establish the positions of the eyes and the nose followed by the jaw and the ears.

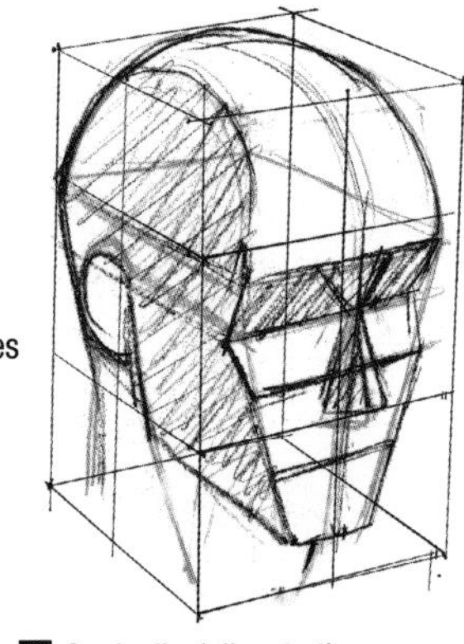

3 Gradually delineate the cheekbones and other detailed surfaces on the face..

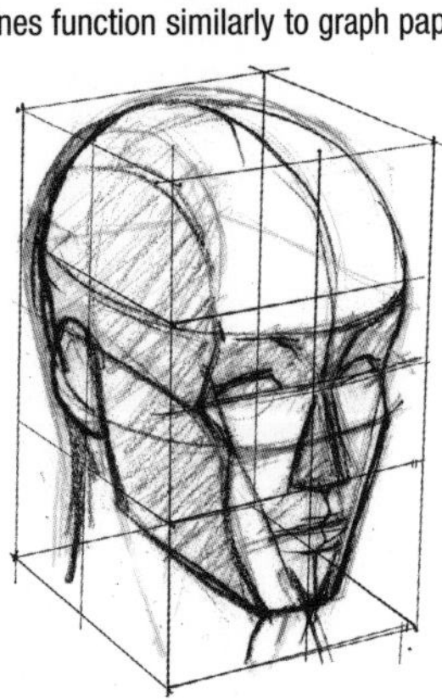

4 Draw the mouth and other finely detailed contours.

5 Finally, add in the details.

This is the face that results after it is finalized in a manga-esque style.

How to Proportion the Facial Features

Each person's facial features are proportioned differently, and each artist has his or her own personal taste. This page covers the standard proportioning used for the eyes, nose, and mouth. Use the standards as points of departure and play around until you discover a proportioning that you find satisfying.

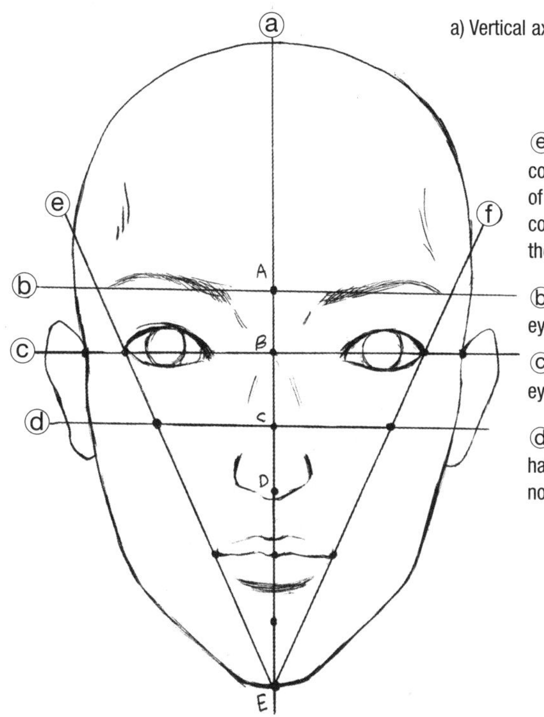

a) Vertical axial line

ⓔ and ⓕ These lines connect the far corners of the eyes and the corners of the mouth to the chin.

ⓑ This line denotes the eyebrows.

ⓒ This line denotes the eyes.

ⓓ This line marks the halfway point along the nose.

"V" Proportioning

The far corners of the eyes, the highest points of the cheekbones, the corners of the mouth, and the chin may be connected using two lines to form a "V".

- Point D denoting the tip of the nose lies along line ⓐ at the halfway point between points A and E.
- The mouth lies about 1/3 of the distance from point D to point E and does not extend beyond lines ⓔ and ⓕ.
- Point C which lies halfway between points B and D also lies along line ⓓ.

Adjusting the positions of these lines produces a variety of bone structures and faces. (For example, lengthening the distance between lines ⓒ and ⓓ results in a longer nose.) See how lines ⓐ through ⓓ would lie on one of your own drawings to learn what type of proportioning you generally prefer. Using guidelines such as these allows you to create your own proportions. This, in turn, allows you to produce more consistent artwork, and you will no longer find yourself agonizing over how to reproduce a given character's face with regularity. These guidelines also help to adjust distorted faces.

Creating Your Own Proportions

1 The above shows large eyes spaced far apart. The mouth is small. The nose is shifted slightly lower on the face. The cheekbones are located lower than is standard. Drawing the eyes on the large side and spacing them far apart results in a more juvenile appearance.

2 While this face reflects the standard almost faithfully, the mouth is still positioned slightly lower.

3 This face lacks cheekbones and instead puffs out lower along the face. Both the nose and mouth have been given extremely low positions.

Adding eyeglasses allows you to verify whether the ear and eyes are positioned properly.

As an artist, you have total liberty in positioning the eyes, nose, and mouth. If you restrict yourself, you will find it difficult to create satisfying facial expressions, m'kay? However, the positions of the eyes and ears play important roles when wearing eyeglasses. Consequently, the rules should be carefully observed in their cases, m'kay?

Remember, these are guidelines not rules!

The Effects of Age and Build on the Face's Bone Structure

Our skulls continue to grow from infancy to immediately before adolescence. Hardly any changes occur in our skulls once we reach adolescence. Only the flesh on our faces continues to reveal the story of our aging. The bald heads below trace the aging of a man from infancy to old age. Portrayal of the child's face involves drawing the facial features toward the bottom of the head. This same rule is followed when creating an ultra-stylized character.

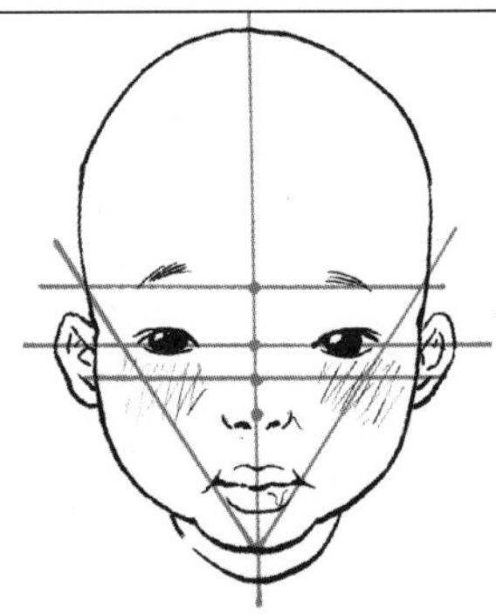

Infant to Toddler
The facial features are located low on the face. Infants have puffy, rouged cheeks, small eyes, and plump lips. (Take careful note that drawing standard human eyes will cause the character not to have a convincingly babyish look. Avoid drawing standard human eyes on characters who are too young to talk.)

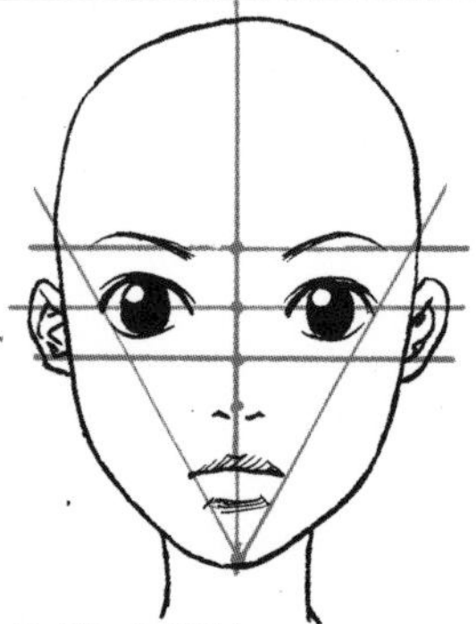

Toddler to Child
Now, the facial features are shifted somewhat higher on the head; however, they are still positioned on the low side. The skull is still growing and is still smaller than that of an adult. Portrayal of this age requires careful attention. If the facial features are not positioned low on the face, the character will appear to be an adult in miniature.d

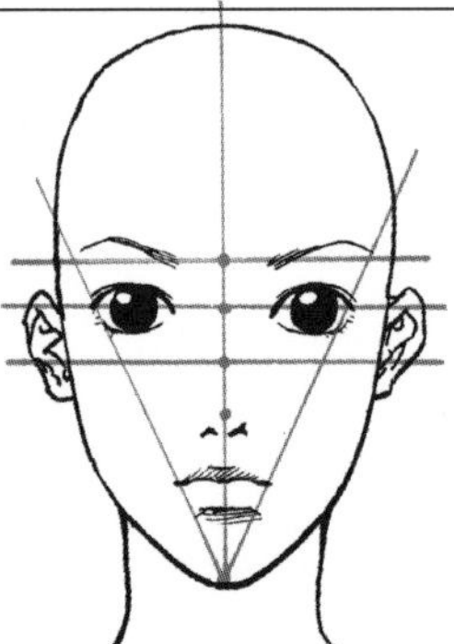

Child to Adolescent/Young Adult
Bishonen fall within this age bracket. The facial features have once again shifted slightly higher on the head. The skull is still growing. However, it is now approximately the same size as that of an adult.

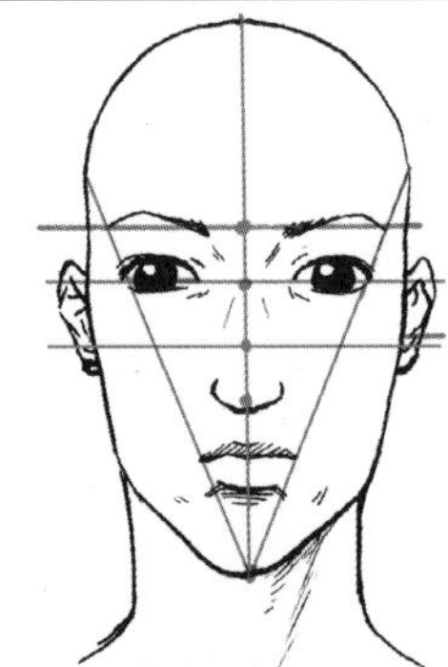

Young to Middle-aged Adult
The bone structure has completely matured and aging, which we often dread, has started to set in. The neck is sturdy and muscular. From this age until his death, the eyes, nose, ears, and chin will remain in the same position. (The mouth will lower.) This image reflects a man in his prime, who has amassed experiences in life.

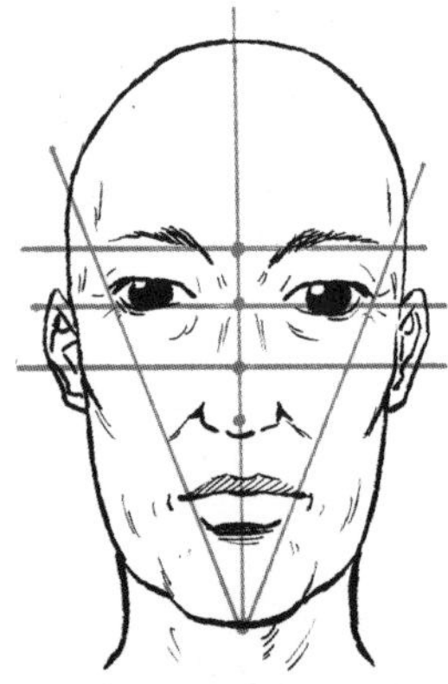

Middle-aged to Retired Adult
The head above primarily reflects a middle-aged man. He has a sturdy brow. Tiny wrinkles appear around his eyes. The flesh on his cheeks is beginning to sag.

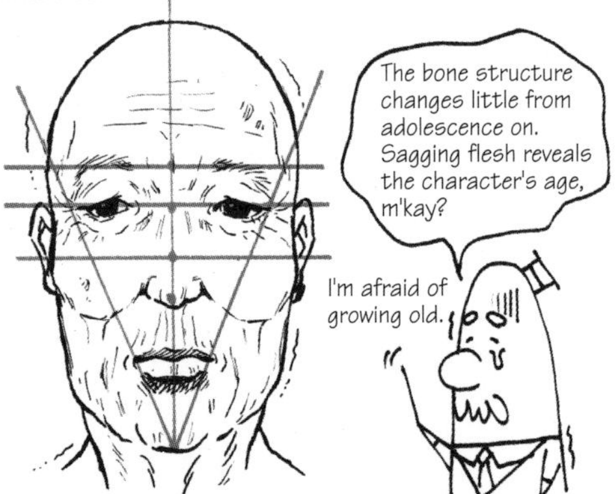

The bone structure changes little from adolescence on. Sagging flesh reveals the character's age, m'kay?
I'm afraid of growing old.

Retired to Elderly Adult
While the bone structure remains unchanged from that of the middle-aged face, gravity has pulled at his flesh, causing it to sag. The flesh underneath his chin also sags, blurring the juncture where the neck and jaw meet. The mouth contains no bones, so it has dropped as well. He has lived a life full of vicissitudes.

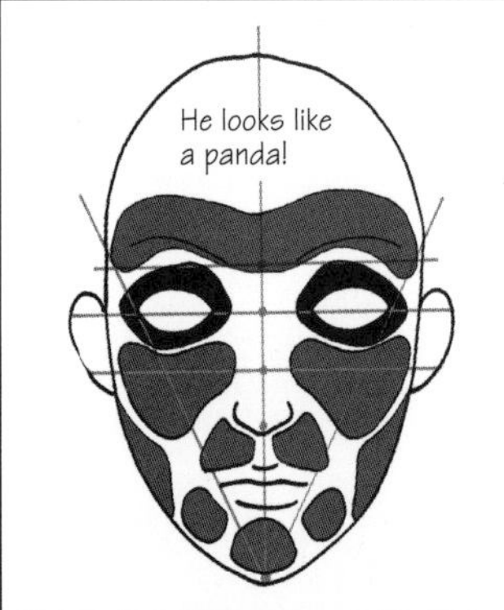

He looks like a panda!

Distribution of Flesh across the Face
Have the flesh sag, bulge and swell, or become drawn and haggard to portray aging or the character's build.

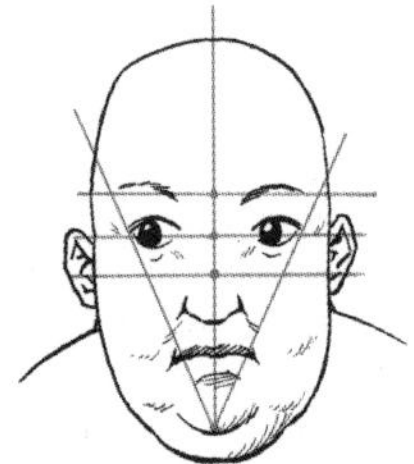

Obese I
Note the extreme volume of flesh underneath the chin. The head appears larger owing to the thick flesh.

Obese II
Note the presence of fatty flesh behind the neck.

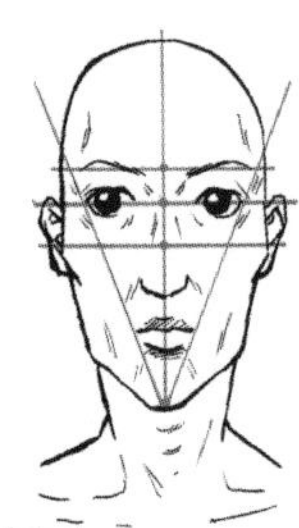

Emaciated
The bones of the neck are distressingly visible. Here, the man has scarcely any flesh. His bones jut out. He is covered in wrinkles, despite not being old.

Assorted Characters

This lesson module discusses the proportioning of the clueless boys starring in the *manga* at the end of this book. Take careful note of the grey guidelines and how the "V" rule used to draw these six characters handles differences in how lines are distributed across the face and the affects of varying distances between facial features.

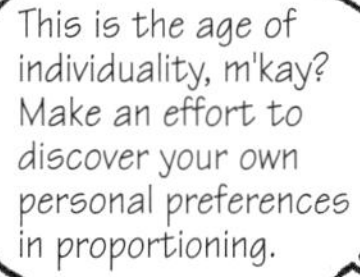

This is the age of individuality, m'kay? Make an effort to discover your own personal preferences in proportioning.
My features are all higgledy-piggledy.

Bontaro Hei
Bontaro Hei's head is neither long nor short nor wide nor narrow. His eyebrows, eyes, and cheeks lie at equal distances. Refer to Bondaro's face as the standard sample when studying the remaining five characters.

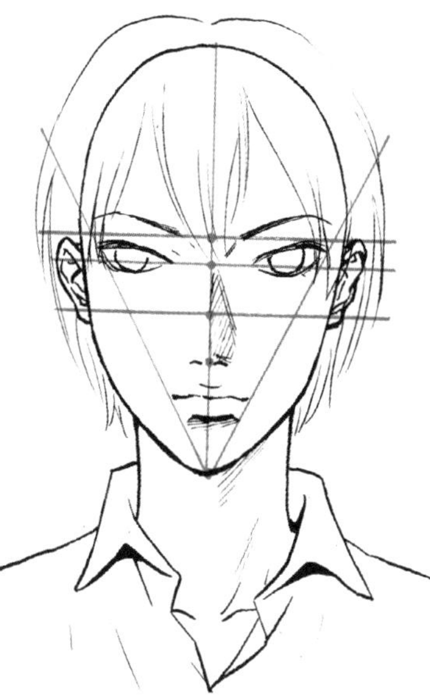

Sugita Hinekure
Sugita's head is long. His eyes lie close to his eyebrows, and he has a long nose bridge. His eyes are spaced slightly far apart. He has a mature face.

Kosaku Inochigake
Inochigake's facial features are positioned low on his head, giving him a childlike appearance. His features from his eyebrows to the tip of his nose are all evenly spaced. He lacks a nose bridge. His mouth is clearly shifted off center, reflecting a bit of that *manga* charm.

Otsuteru Yumebakari
Otsuteru Yumebakari has the largest eyes and the sharpest chin of the six characters. Shortening the distance between his eyebrows and eyes would give him a more manly face. Giving him a more prominent nose bridge would evoke the air of a Westerner. (Remember this technique. It comes in handy!) The corners of his mouth fall well within the "V" guide. His facial features are positioned low on his head, giving him a childlike appearance.

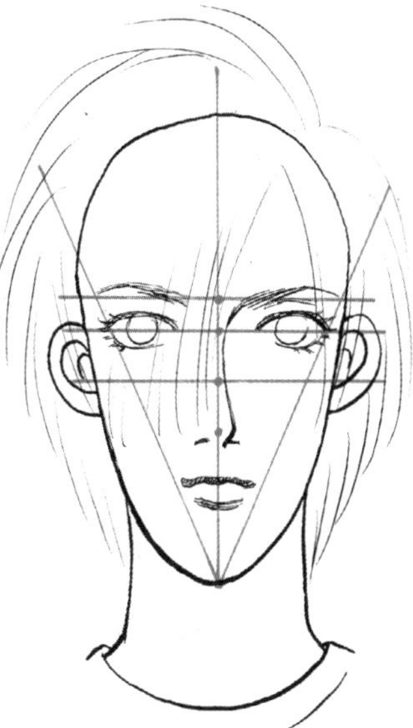

Jotaro Sho
Jotaro Sho has a round chin and a thick neck. He has the most prominent nose of the six characters, and his eyes slope downward, giving him the look of a Westerner. His face is longish overall.

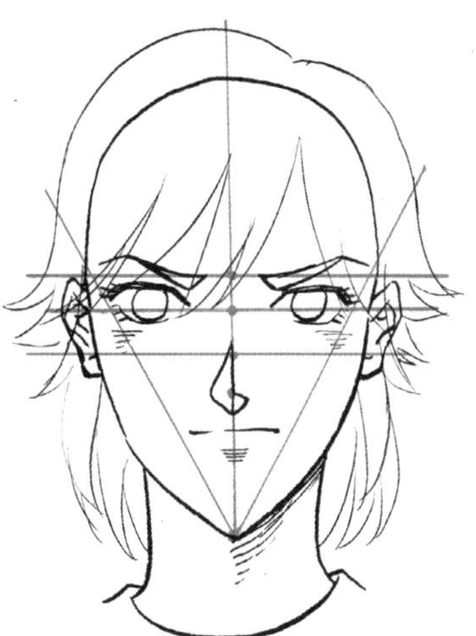

Nentaro Sho
Nentaro Sho's head is proportioned more similarly to Bontaro Hei's than are those of the remaining four boys. His nose bridge is relatively flat, and his eyes and eyebrows lie close to one another, giving him a more manly and Asian appearance. Keeping a short distance between the nose and upper lip, as seen here, is a great trick to making a character appear manly.

Structure of the Eye

Bishonen faces come in a countless variety of forms, and each artist has his or her own preferences. Consequently, there is no set way to draw an eye. However, being aware of the eye's structure and basic sketching techniques may be applied to any *bishonen* character and any emotional portrayal of the eye. This lesson module covers the basics.

Structure of the Eye

Front

The eyeball rests within a bony socket.

Profile **Closed Eyes**

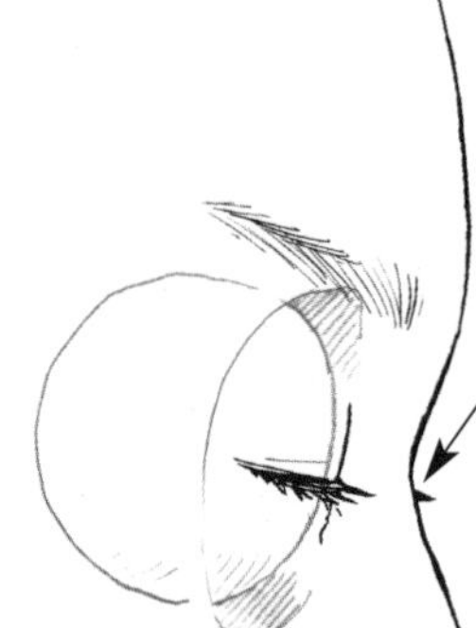

Note how the eyelashes of the far eye are positioned when the eyes are closed.

The eyelids conform to the shape of the eyeball, taking on a spherical form.

Realistic Eye and Manga-esque Eye

Realistic Eye

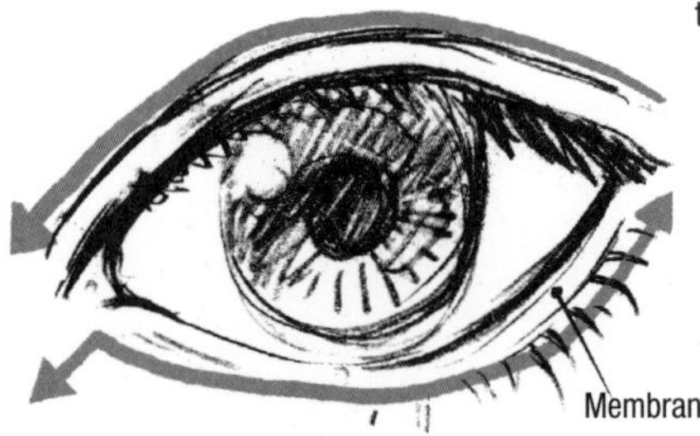

The upper eyelashes are thicker than the lower eyelashes, making the arc described by the upper eyelashes darker than that of the lower eyelashes.

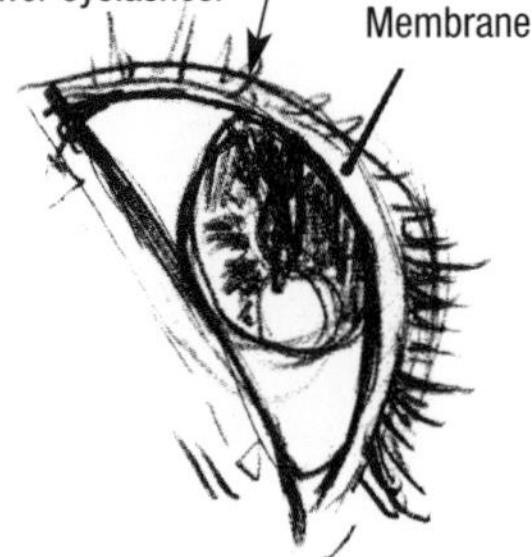

Giving the eyelids rounded forms and including the membrane in your drawing imbues the eye with a sense of three-dimensionality, m'kay?

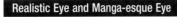

Draw these.

POINT

Take careful note that symmetrical, almond-shaped eyes eliminate any sense of emotion on the face.

Manga-esque Eye

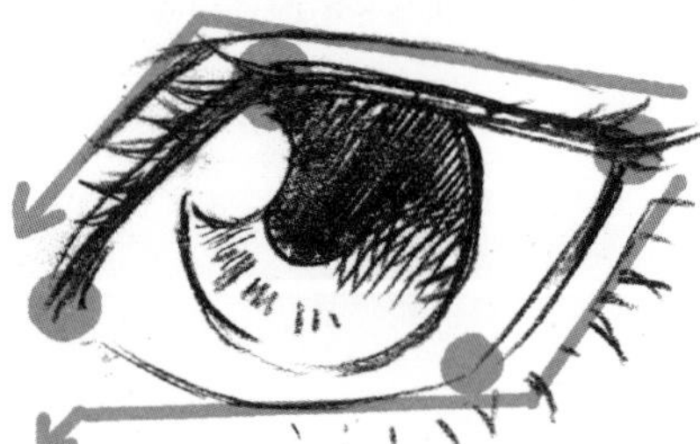

As indicated by the grey arrows and dots, the addition of angles adds textual diversity that results in a more distinctly *manga* style. Where to position the angles and how much volume to give the eyelashes are up to the artist.

The eyelashes are not drawn thickly across the eyelid but rather are drawn in strategic locations.

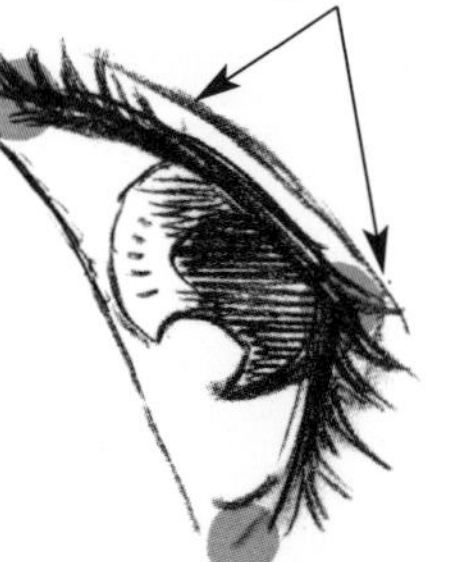

Using straight lines for the eyes instead of curved contours projects a sense of three-dimensionality.

Incorrect

Correct

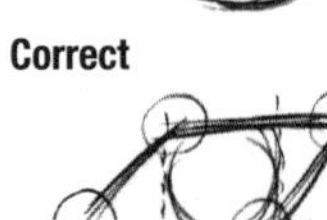

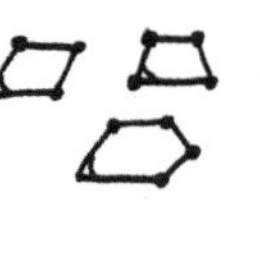

Sample Manga-Style Eyes When stylizing the eye to an extreme degree, employ highlights and carefully render eyelashes to indicate that the symbol drawn on paper is in fact an "eye."

Defiant Eyes with White Almost Completely Surrounding the Iris

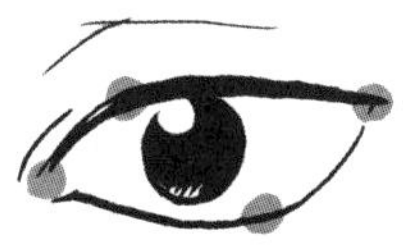

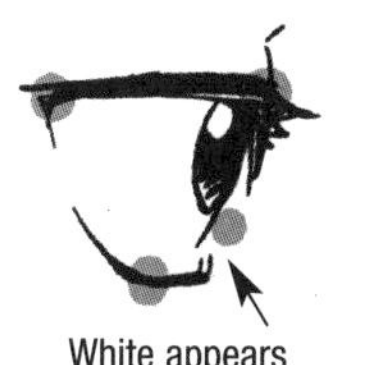

White appears underneath the iris.

Irises with Straight Contours

The upper eyelid contour drops at a dramatic angle.

Stereotypical *Bishonen* Eyes

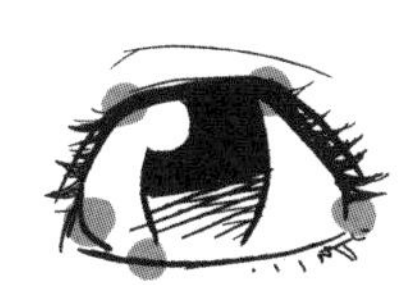

The lengths of the upper and lower eyelids are the same.

Left ←

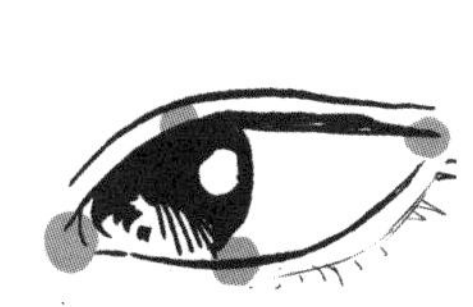

→ **Right**

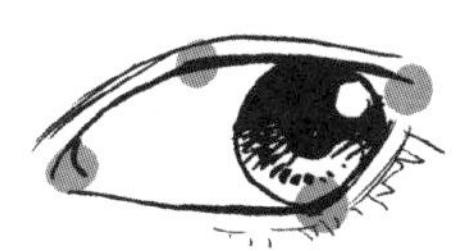

Note how angles in the eye's contours shift as the eye looks from left to right.

Sample Manga-Style Eyes Rather than conceiving of the face as spherical, instead think of it as a flat surface with lumps.

Incorrect
Composing the head like a balloon makes the character look like his head is a ball with eyes and a nose stuck on it. The resulting face has no three-dimensionality. One of the eyes looks cut off too.

Correct
This example shows the face's surface rendered as a flat plane.

The Eye's Appearance in Four Stages Unless the face is composed from an extreme side angle, the eyes should appear in their entirety on the face and not be cut off. Note that the distance between the eyes decreases as the face turns to the side.

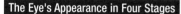

1 Here, the face is turned almost toward the picture plane. As the stages progress, the face turns gradually toward a profile view.

2 The gap between the right eye (the viewer's right) and the face's exterior contour is closing.

3 Now the eyelashes touch the face's exterior contour.

4 Here, the face has turned to the extent that the eyeball's contour has become part of the face's silhouette.

Portrayal of Emotion in the Eyes and Other Features

Naturally, the eyes are able to portray a host of emotions. However, the eyelashes, eyebrows, and other peripheral features also play important roles in conveying a character's emotional state. This lesson module examines key points in their portrayal.

Assorted Eye Emotions

The eyes express as much as the mouth. Make an effort to master a variety of emotions conveyed through the eyes so that these emotions may be communicated without words.

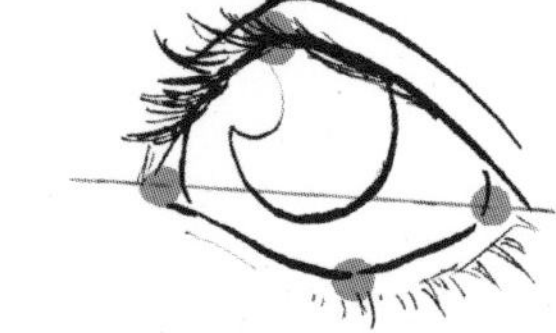

1 Gazing Up
The eye is open wide with much of the lower half exposed.

2 Narrowed Eyes
The eye forms a crescent. The upper half is drawn proportionally larger.

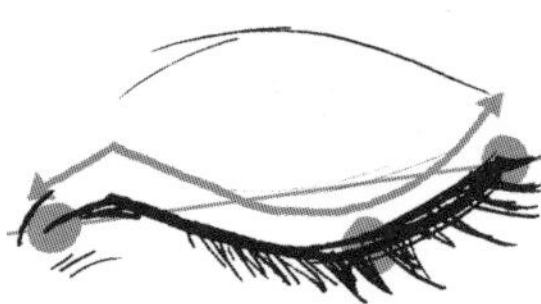

3 Closed
Note the directions traced by the arrows. The sharp drop of the inside corner of the eye constitutes a key compositional point.

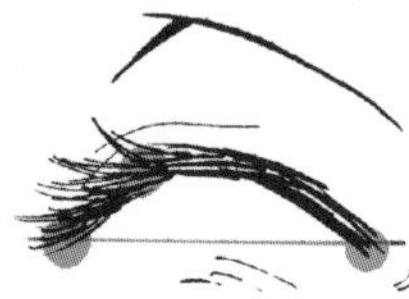

4 Tightly Shut Eyes
Adding a few diagonal strokes underneath the eye projects the sense of a tightly shut eye.

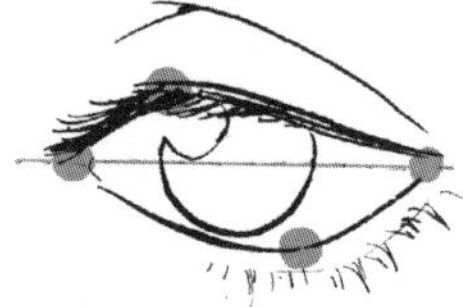

5 Unfocussed Eye
The upper eyelid is half shut, and the lower half occupies a large portion of the composition. Carefully rendering the eyelid contour using two lines creates the impression of a heavy-lidded, half-shut eye.

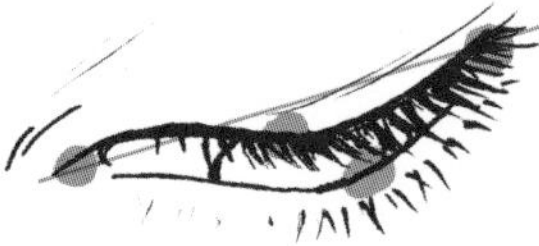

6 Downcast Eye
The eyelid always lowers when the eye is cast downward. As with 3, having the inside corner drop sharply gives the eye an alluring air. Without the lowered eyelid, the character would merely appear to be looking down at a specific object.

POINT

Low and High Angle Eyes

- The distance between the eyebrow and eye narrows.
- The "V" at the brow between the eyes becomes an increasingly obtuse angle.

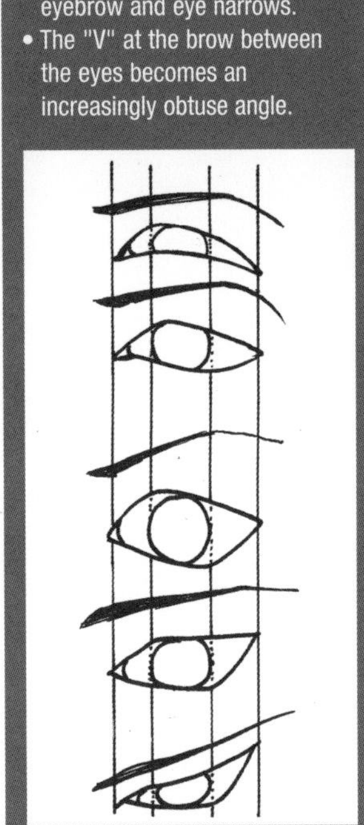

Eyebrows

Directions of Eyebrow Growth

The eyebrows grow in two directions.

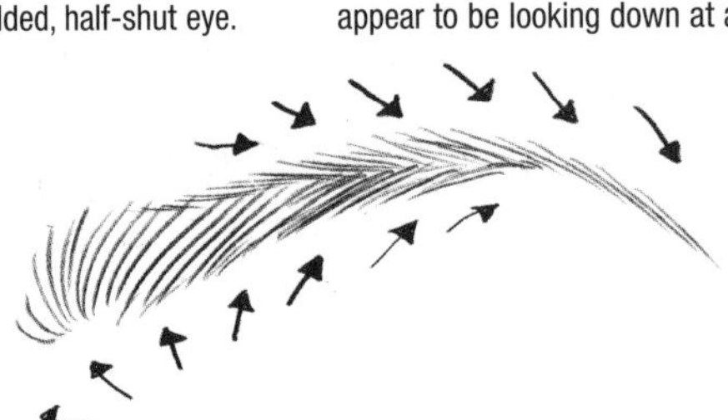

Eyebrow Movements

The eyebrows are capable of portraying a myriad of emotions owing to the muscles located at the brow between the eyes and the movements of the eyebrows' corners. Pairing these eyebrows with happy eyes, angry eyes, or sad eyes makes the emotions you are able to portray limitless. Any subtle emotion is now within your ability.

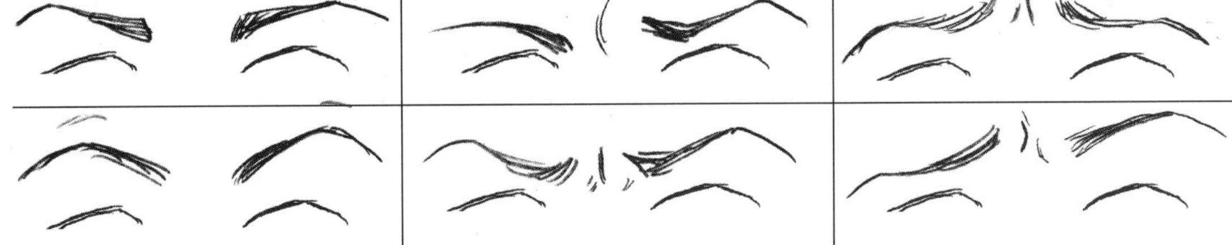

Eyelashes

The trick to drawing attractive eyelashes is to have a portion of the lashes be longer than the others. Typically, the eyelashes are drawn the longest toward the outside corners.

Lower Eyelashes

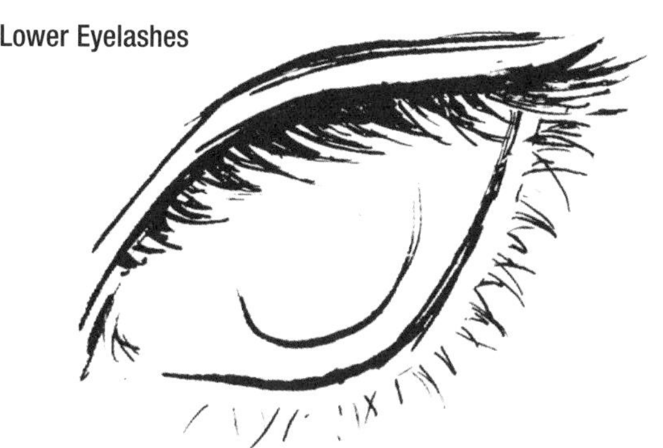

The lower eyelashes are fewer than and not as lush as the upper eyelashes. Avoid drawing a thick contour for the lower eyelid's rim. Using the eyelashes to define the lower eyelid's rim will produce a more natural look.

Upper Eyelashes

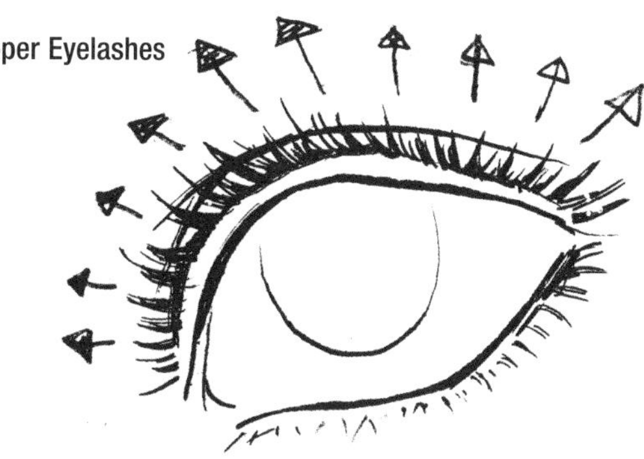

Key Points in Giving Eyelashes a Cosmetic-Free Look

1. Draw the eyelashes in random bunches and lengths.
2. Show the upper eyelashes dipping downward.

Key Points in Creating Feminine Eyelashes (Made-up Eyelashes)

1. Draw the eyelashes in regular bunches and lengths.
2. Show the upper eyelashes curling upwards.

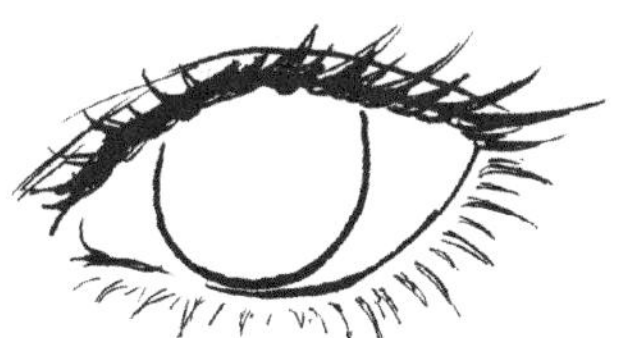

POINT

Note how the lashes appear to grow when viewing the eye in profile. Avoid drawing the eyelashes in the same manner that you would from a front view.

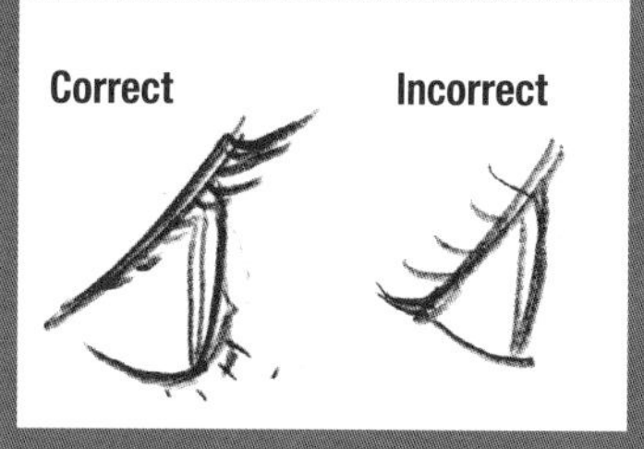

Assorted Eyelashes

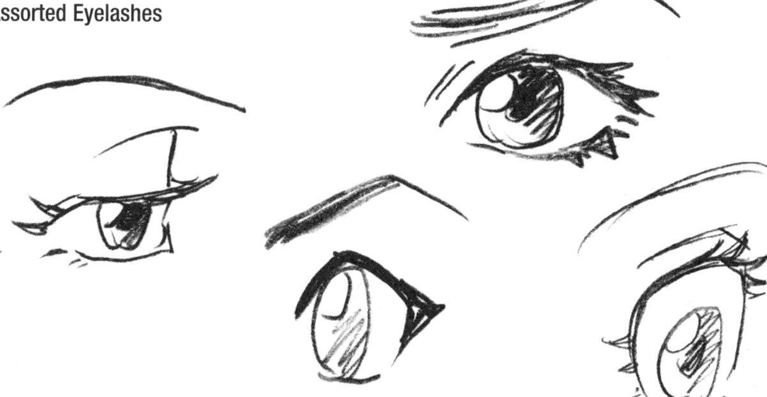

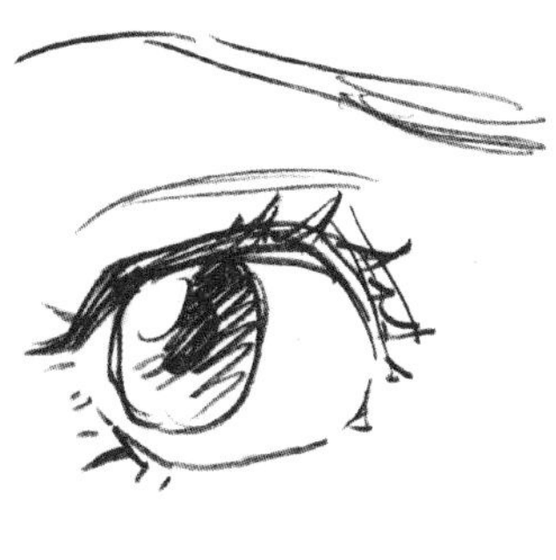

Portraying Irises and Pupils

Often artists express frustration in drawing the eye's interior. And yet, the eye's interior is really up to the individual artist's discretion. However, since real irises and pupils are being used as reference models, the pupils should be given some form.

Realistic Eye

The black circle at the eye's center is called the "pupil." Radiating black lines around the pupil define the "iris."

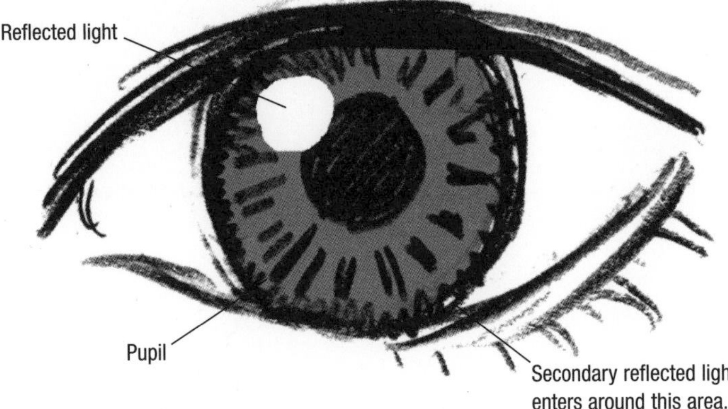

Reflected light
Pupil
Secondary reflected light enters around this area.

How to Portray Reflected Light

Often the word, "highlight" is used. In all cases, drawing reflected light on an eye is akin to drawing light reflected off a sphere.

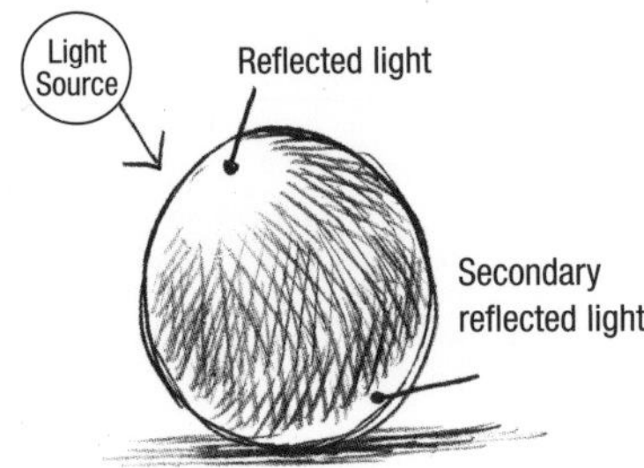

Stylized Irises and Pupils

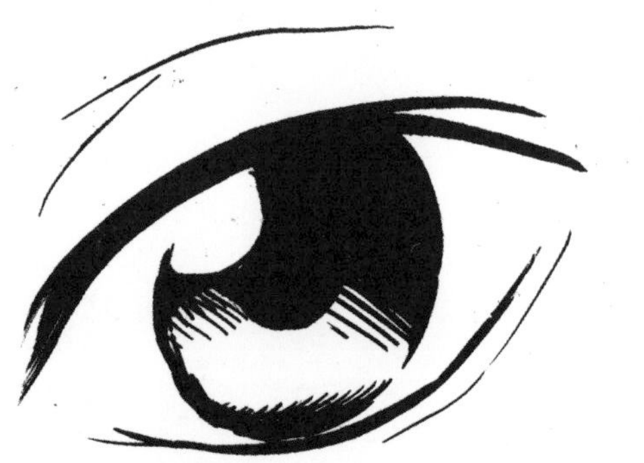

This is the most popular style of rendering the eyes today (according to Dr. *Bishonen*'s research).

The large, black oval merges the iris with the pupil.

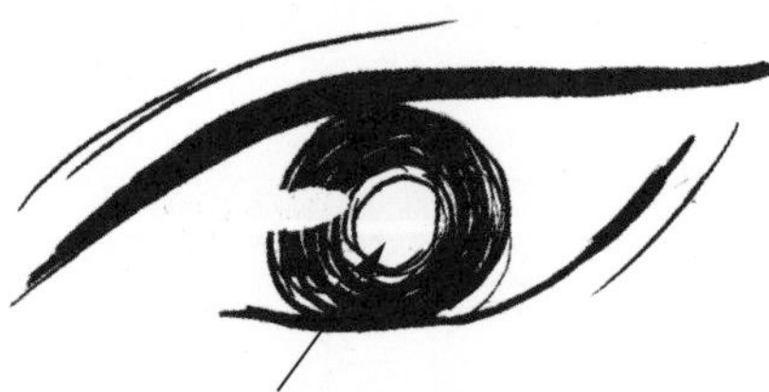

There is an unusually large amount of white used in the pupil here. Oddly enough, this style of rendition appears perfectly natural. Avoid using this technique with exceptionally large eyes.

Crosshatching was used in the pupil above.

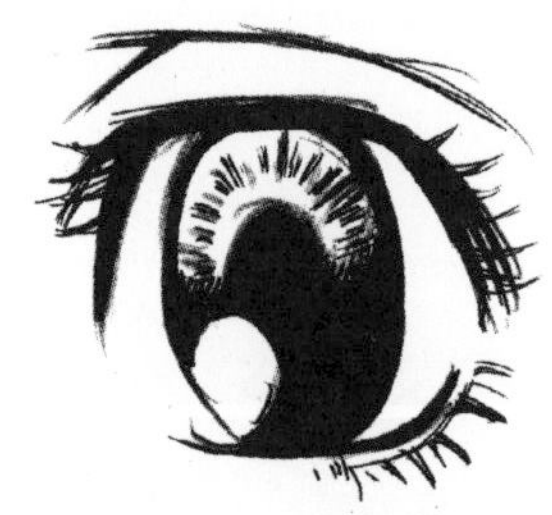

When the light source is located beneath the eye, reverse how you normally would draw the iris and pupil, adding a highlight below and showing a portion of the iris above.

Eyes of Various Characters

This lesson module further explores how to draw eyes using the six boys appearing in the back of this volume as reference. The same steps should be followed when drawing the eyes of any character. Key points requiring attention vary as discussed below.

Kosaku Inochigake (1960s Style)

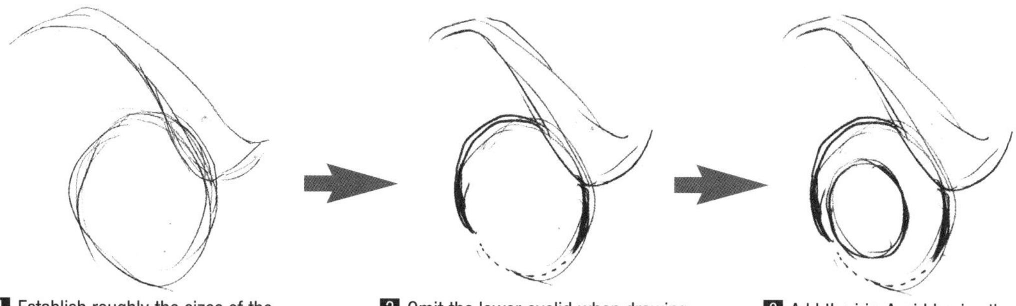

1 Establish roughly the sizes of the eyebrow and eye. The key point here is that the eyebrow overlaps the eye, creating a perpetually frowning appearance.

2 Omit the lower eyelid when drawing Kosaku's eyes. Draw a circle to represent the upper eyelid alone.

3 Add the iris. Avoid having the iris touch the top, bottom, right, or left side of the eye.

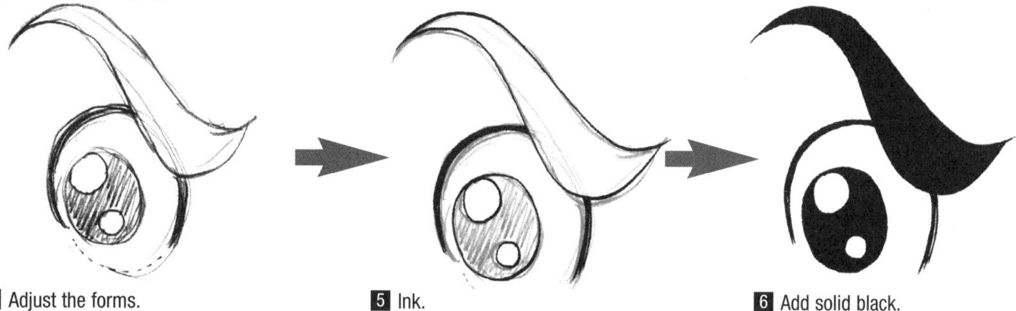

4 Adjust the forms.

5 Ink.

6 Add solid black.

Otsuteru Yumebakari (1970s Style)

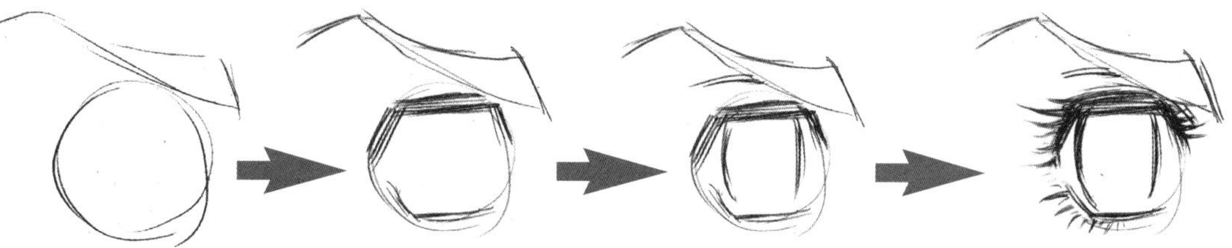

1 Establish roughly the sizes of the eyebrow and eye. Have the eyebrow touch the eye. Note that the shapes of the corners of Otsuteru's eyebrows are different from those of the other characters.

2 Add angled contours to the eye, and give the upper eyelid a thick rim.

3 Draw the iris. Use a squarish form and leave a gap between the iris and the lower eyelid rim. Draw a line to define the upper eyelid fold approximately in the center of the upper eyelid.

4 Draw the eyelashes while adjusting the forms. Draw the eyelashes so that they extend to the right and left instead of up and down. Make the eyelashes in the inside and outside corners of the upper eyelid and in the outside corner of the lower eyelid the longest. Do not draw the eyelashes touching the rim of the lower eyelid.

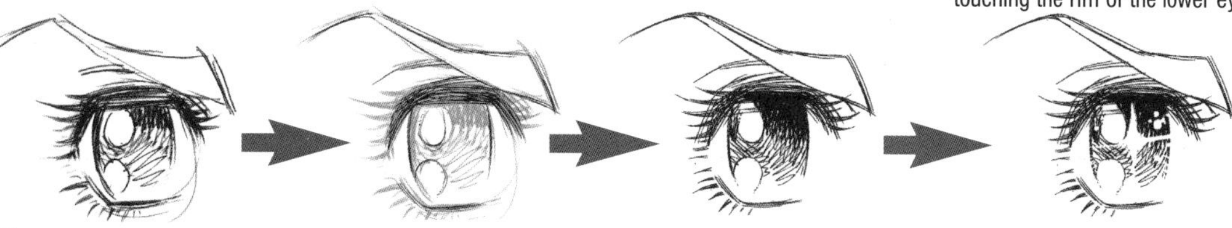

5 Draw the iris's interior. Use a zigzagged stroke to create hatching, making the iris increasingly shaded toward the top. The more random the stroke placement, the more the eye will appear moist, so shift the stroke direction frequently.

6 Use fine strokes for all of Otsuteru's eyes. The care you take is vital to this character.

7 Lastly, spatter white correction fluid across the eye to create highlights. In the case of this character, go ahead and add as many highlights as you like.

otaro Sho [In the Style of 1980s *Shojo* Manga*]

**Manga* targeted at girls

1 Capture the eye's general shape, using an oblong form.

2 Sketch the upper and lower eyelid rims, ensuring that they are parallel to one another.

3 Draw the iris so that it just barely touches the rim of the upper eyelid. Draw a contour denoting the fold of the upper eyelid approximately 1/3 of the distance between the iris and the eyebrow.

4 Draw the eyelashes while adjusting forms overall. Key points of Jotáro's eyes are the relatively sparse upper eyelashes and the long and abundant lower eyelashes.

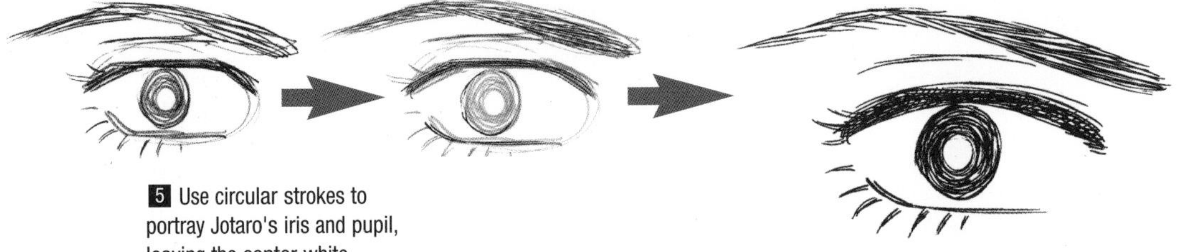

5 Use circular strokes to portray Jotaro's iris and pupil, leaving the center white.

6 Use a pen with a fine nib to ink Jotaro's entire eye.

Nentaro Sho ([In the Style of 1980s *Shonen* Manga*]

**Manga* targeted at boys

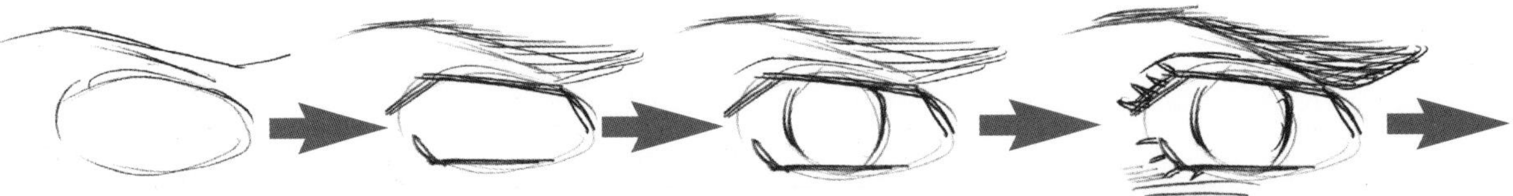

1 As with Nentaro Sho's younger brother Jotaro, use an oblong form. Unlike Nentaro, always draw Jotaro with prominent eyebrows.

2 Draw the upper and lower eyelid rims so that the eye appears to have a moderate downward slant. Include well-defined angles in the contours.d

3 Draw the iris so that it just barely touches the rim of the upper eyelid. Draw a contour denoting the fold of the upper eyelid approximately 1/3 of the distance between the iris and the eyebrow.

4 Draw the eyelashes while adjusting forms overall. In the outside corner of the eye, draw four tufts of eyelashes on both the upper and lower eyelid rims. Space the eyelash tufts evenly and at short distances from one another. The eyelash tufts should be even in length and thickness. Add horizontal hatching underneath the eye. While this hatching has no specific meaning, for some reason it gives the character an unruly, feral air.

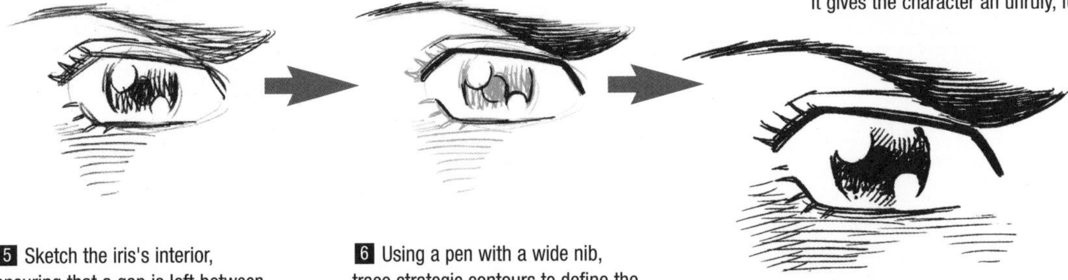

5 Sketch the iris's interior, ensuring that a gap is left between the iris and the upper and lower eyelids.d

6 Using a pen with a wide nib, trace strategic contours to define the eye's form in general.

7 Add in the details using fine strokes.

Bontaro Hei (In the Style of the 1990s to the Present)

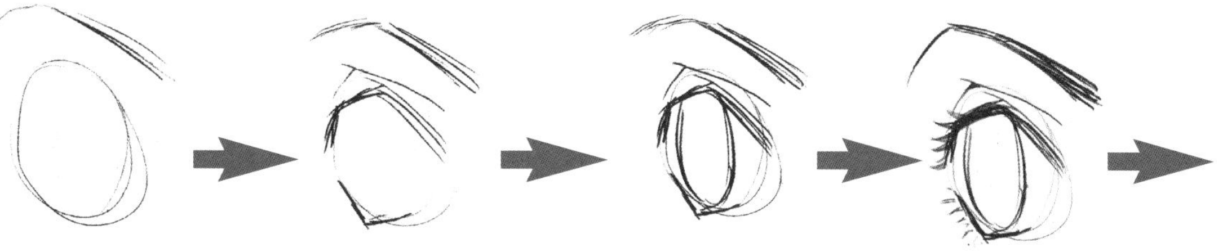

1 Establish roughly the sizes of the eyebrows and eye.

2 Using straight strokes, sketch the rims of the upper and lower eyelids, incorporating angles.

3 Sketch the iris.

4 Draw the eyelashes while smoothing out the contours defining the upper and lower eyelid rims.

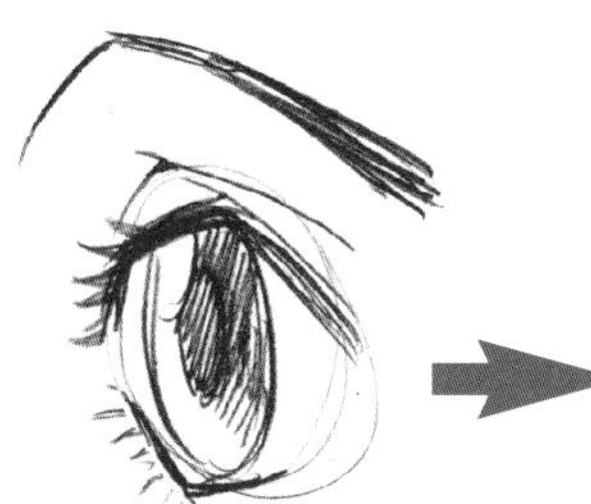

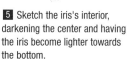

5 Sketch the iris's interior, darkening the center and having the iris become lighter towards the bottom.

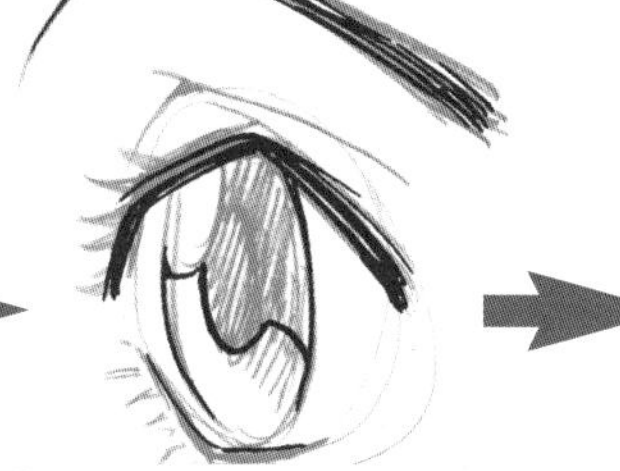

6 Using a pen with a wide nib, trace strategic contours to define the eye's form in general.

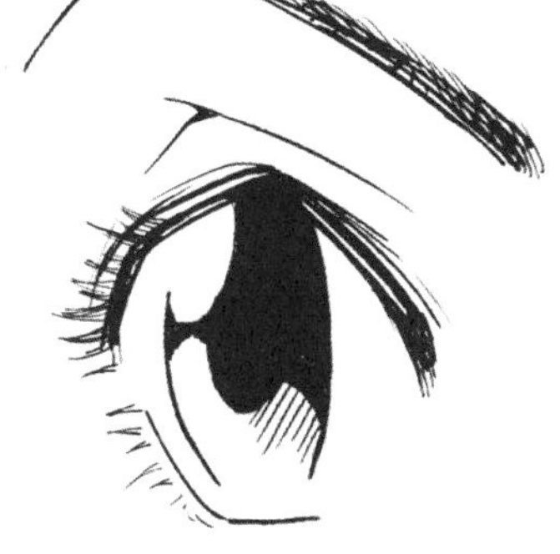

7 Add in the details using fine strokes.

Sugita Hinekure (In the Style of the 1990s to the Present)

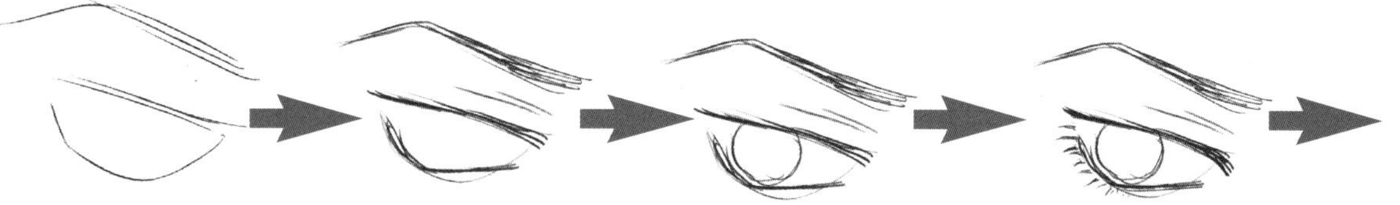

1 Draw a semicircle with the flat edge directed upward. Leave a generous gap between the eye and the eyebrow.

2 Use a single line to define the upper eyelid's rim, arcing it slightly upward. Use a gentle "V" for the lower eyelid rim.

3 Sketch the iris. Avoid letting the iris touch the lower eyelid rim.

4 Draw the eyelashes while adjusting the forms. Sugita has only lower eyelashes. Take care to leave a gap between the eyelashes and the lower eyelid rim.

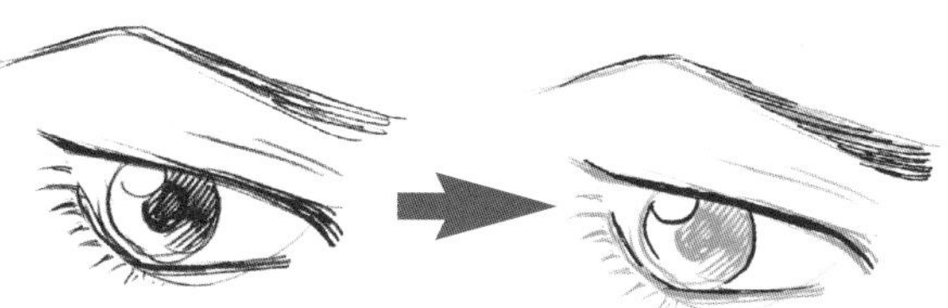

5 Sketch the iris's interior in the same manner used for Bontaro Hei.

6 Using a pen with a wide nib, trace strategic contours to define the eye's form in general.

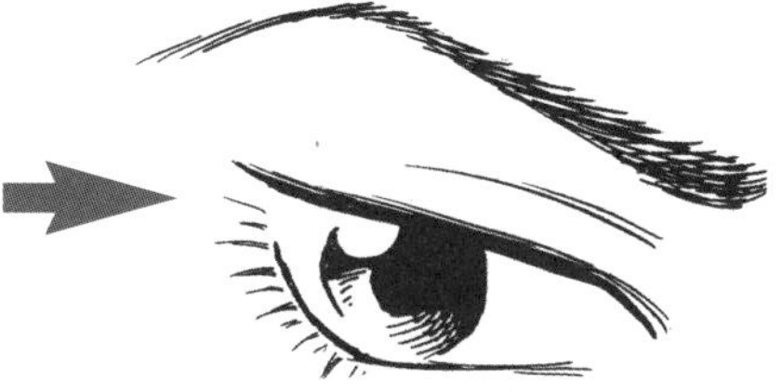

7 Add in the details using fine strokes.

How to Draw Three-Dimensional Noses and Mouths

This lesson module examines the basic structure of the nose and mouth. Maintaining awareness of the play of light and dark when drawing the nose and of the swell of the lips when drawing the mouth results in three-dimensional looking face.

Structure of the Nose and Mouth

The mandible and the zygomatic bone divide at the base of the ear. The black circle marks the pivot point from which the mandible's movements originate. To us, the mouth appears to be opening and closing independently. However, as an artist, you should never forget that the chin also moves every time the mouth does. The nose contains no bone but, rather, is formed of cartilage.

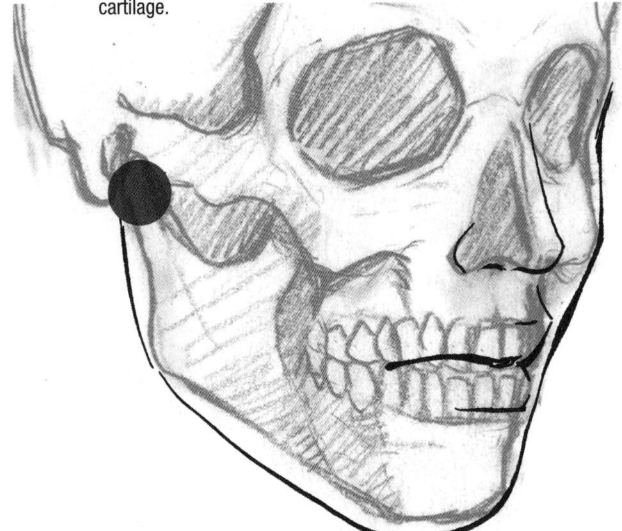

Bone Structure of the Nose

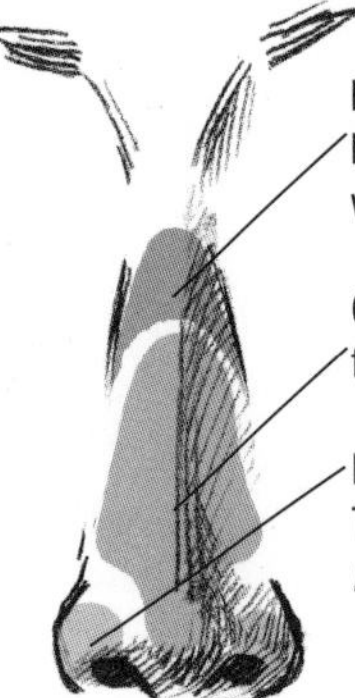

Nasal Bone: This contains genuine, hard bone and is what breaks when we are punched in the nose.

Cartilage: This gives the nose its form.

Nostrils: These twitch and flare. The nostrils are often omitted in *manga* and *anime*.

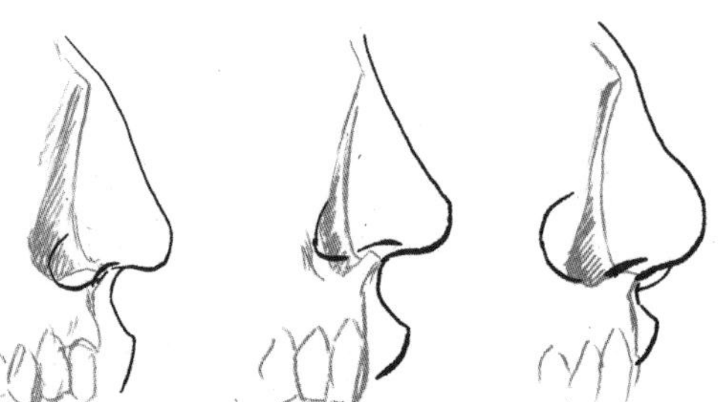

Modifying the forms of the cartilage and nostrils produces numerous different noses.

Motion of the Jaw

When the mouth opens, the lower jaw does not drop visually but rather shifts backward. In other words, when the mouth opens, the angle of the jaw changes rather than extends. Artists particularly fall into pitfalls when drawing the mouth from a front composition, so take extra care.

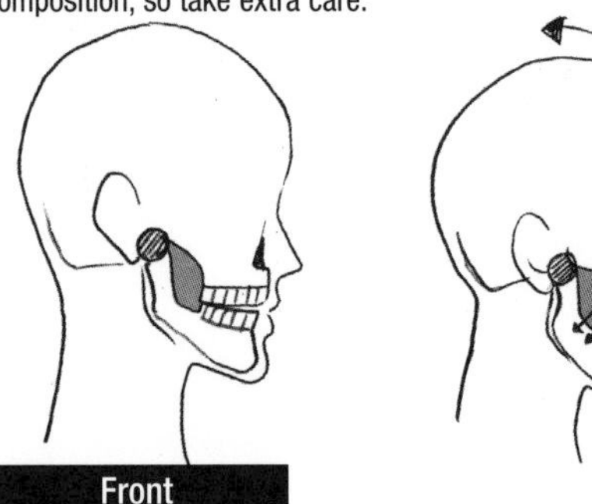

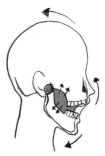

Front

Compare each face with the tiny skull drawn next to it. Also note that when the mouth opens, the flesh of the cheeks becomes pulled.

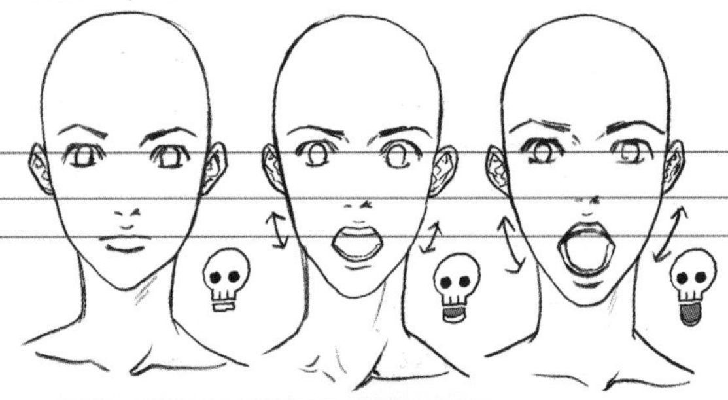

Portraying a Nose from a Front View

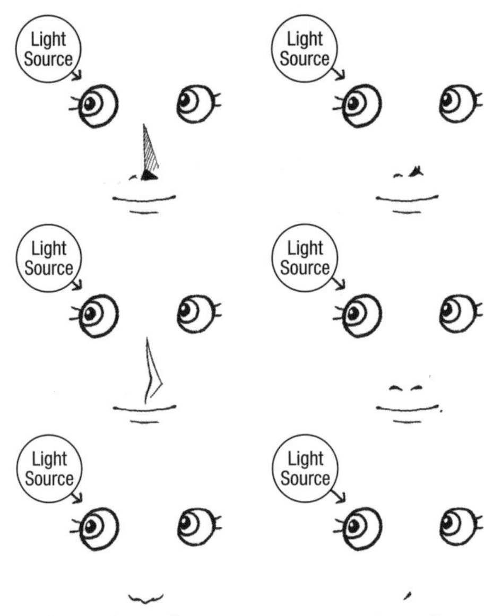

The Lips

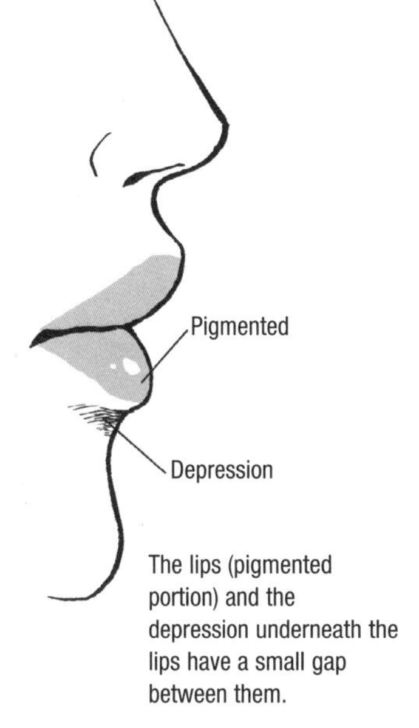

The lips (pigmented portion) and the depression underneath the lips have a small gap between them.

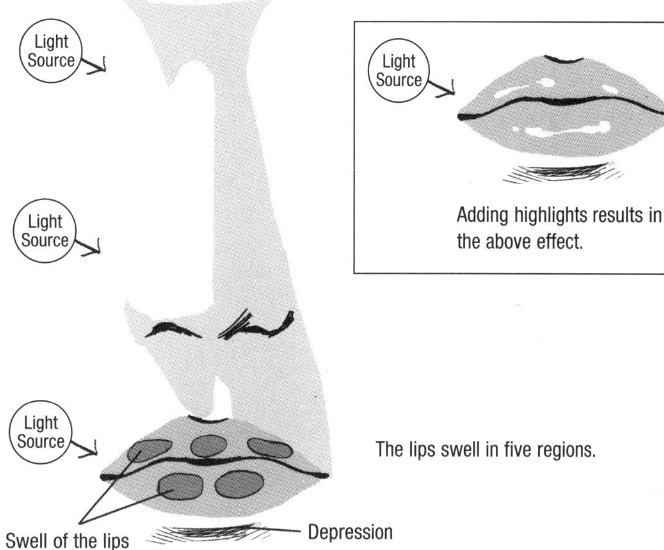

The lips swell in five regions.

Adding highlights results in the above effect.

Low and High Angles

When composing the face from a low or high angle, first establish the angle of the nose bridge.

POINT

Low Angle: Show the upper lip and the inside of the nostrils. Use an inverted "V" for the lips.
High Angle: Include a little of the nose bridge. Draw the upper lip on the narrow side. The corner of the mouth should turn slightly upward.

Lip Forms and Highlights

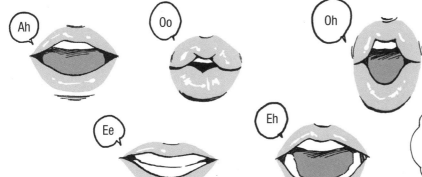

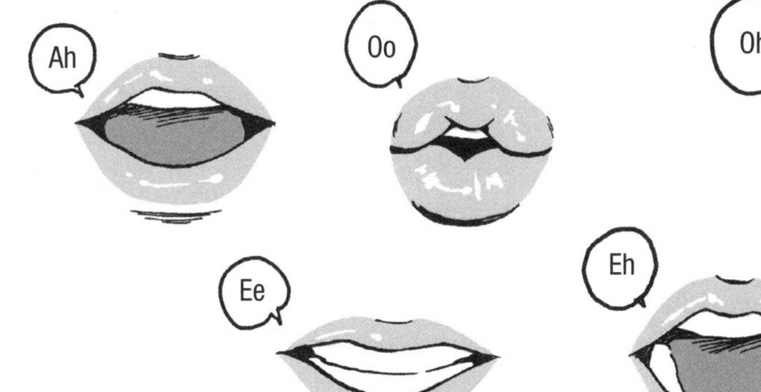

Ah
Oo
Oh
Ee
Eh

Since the nose is located in the center of the face, drawing it first will make it easier to proportion the rest of the face correctly, m'kay?

Displaying the Teeth

There is no need to produce a realistic rendition of the teeth. However, learning techniques of stylizing the teeth will allow you to create an abundant array of facial expressions featuring an open mouth.

Realistic Teeth

Including this much detail on a *manga* character would most likely produce repulsive results.

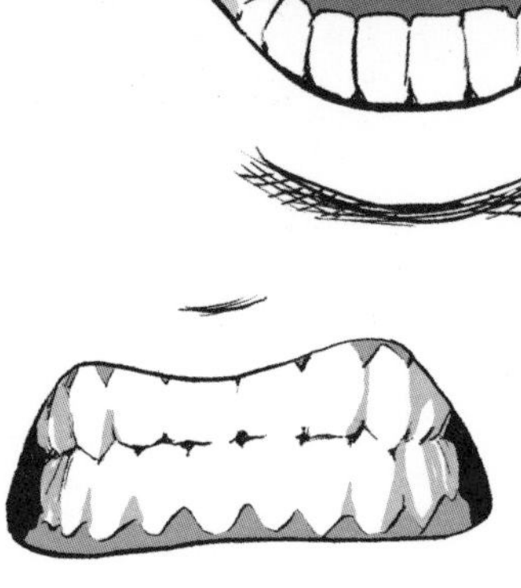

Stylization 1

The contours of the teeth are rendered in silhouette rather than having each tooth clearly delineated. Crosshatching has been used for the back teeth.

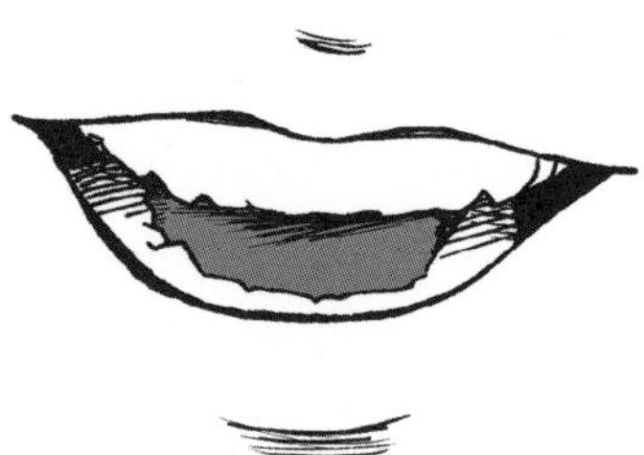

Laughing
Avoid drawing vertical lines to delineate each tooth. Instead, only include the jagged silhouette contours.

Clenching the Teeth
Avoid clearly delineating the contours where the upper teeth and lower teeth meet. Instead, use negative space formed between the gaps as the teeth meet.

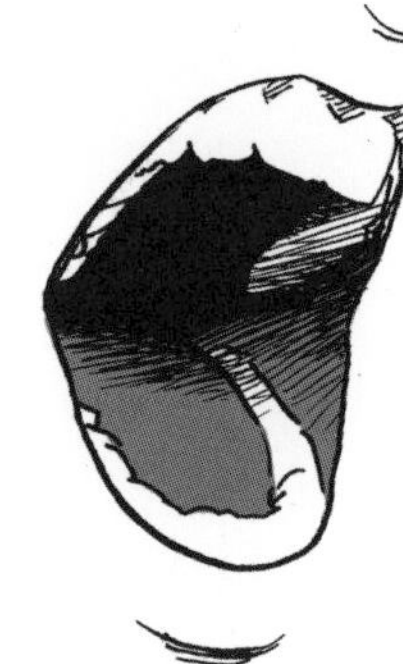

Open Wide
Crosshatching is used to shade the back teeth and the throat.

Stylization 2

None of the irregular jaggedness of the teeth is portrayed. Instead, the teeth are rendered using modulated contours.

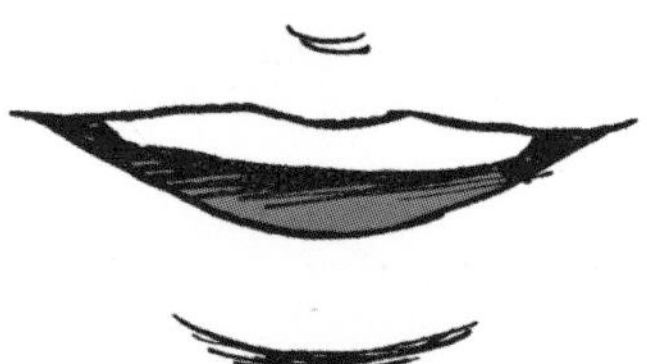

Laughing
Omit the lower row of teeth and use crosshatching to blur the mouth's interior.

Clenching the Teeth
Use a straight contour to delineate where the two rows of teeth meet. If the character has a snaggletooth, then delineate only that tooth as a focal point. When intending to include the gums, use tone alone.

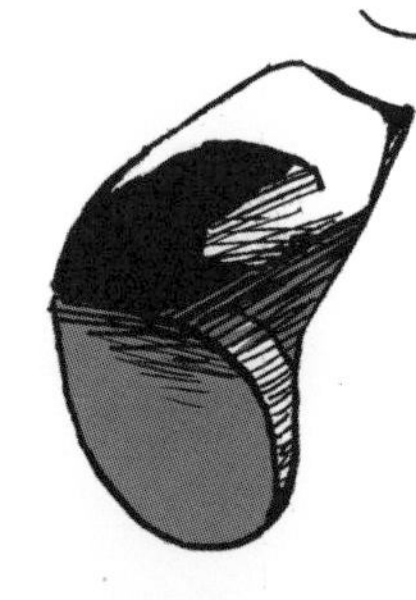

Open Wide
Eliminate clear reference to the teeth's jagged edges. Use crosshatching to render the inside of the mouth.

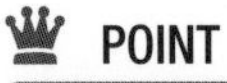

POINT

Open Wide: An Even Easier Technique

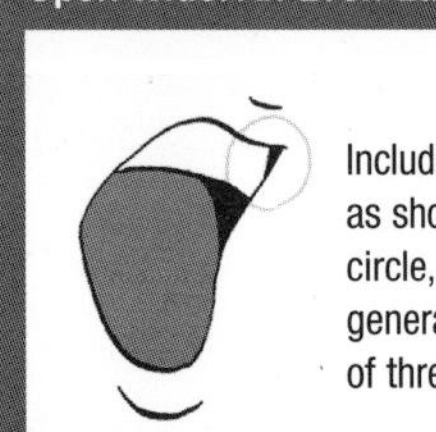

Including a sharp angle, as shown inside the circle, allows you to generate a clear sense of three-dimensionality.

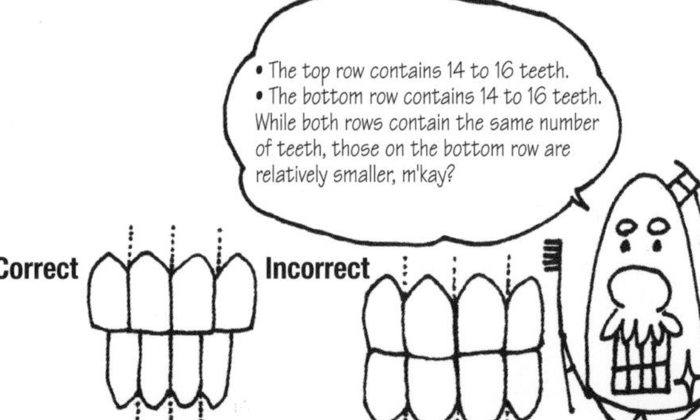

• The top row contains 14 to 16 teeth.
• The bottom row contains 14 to 16 teeth.
While both rows contain the same number of teeth, those on the bottom row are relatively smaller, m'kay?
Correct
Incorrect

The Tongue and Mouths with Something in Them

This lesson module covers how to draw a mouth with something in it to achieve the proper look. Carefully observing the facial expressions people wear when they eat and the mouth's movements will allow you to convey your characters' personalities in a natural manner.

The Tongue

This may seem obvious, but the tongue is attached to the lower jaw. Draw the tongue extending not from the back of the throat but from low in the mouth. Note that a relaxed tongue and an extended tongue (tensed tongue) have different shapes.

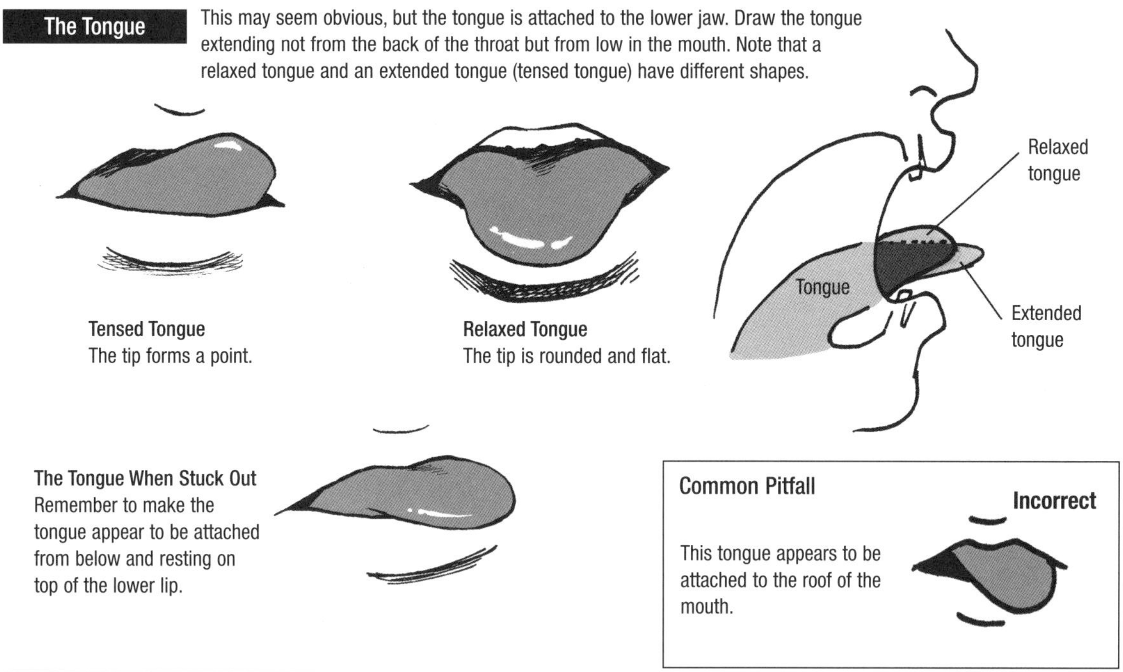

Tensed Tongue
The tip forms a point.

Relaxed Tongue
The tip is rounded and flat.

The Tongue When Stuck Out
Remember to make the tongue appear to be attached from below and resting on top of the lower lip.

Common Pitfall
This tongue appears to be attached to the roof of the mouth.

Mouths with Something in Them

A Full Mouth
Adding a little hatching to the cheek (just underneath the eye) evokes the air of a full mouth.

Biting a Hard Object
Draw the mouth using straight strokes and evoke the atmosphere of clamping down on something hard. Showing one eye squinting is a dramatic effect that projects the feel of the boy straining with the tough object.

Sucking
The mouth should form an "oo". Show the mouth pursed and pointed outward. Including the underside of the nose projects the atmosphere of puckering.

Holding Something in the Mouth
Tension in the lips causes the corners of the mouth to rise. Drawing the lips on the narrow side evokes the feeling of tightly clamped lips.

Licking
We do not lick with our mouths closed. Always show the mouth open! I won't even mention how erotic licking looks.

Assorted Noses and Mouths

This lesson module examines the noses and mouths worn by the boys starring in the *manga* at the end of this book.

Bontaro Hei (Standard)

From a front view, Bondaro's nose and mouth comprise simply the tip of the nose and the inside of the nostrils. The distinguishing characteristics of Bondaro's nose and mouth are that they have no distinguishing characteristics.

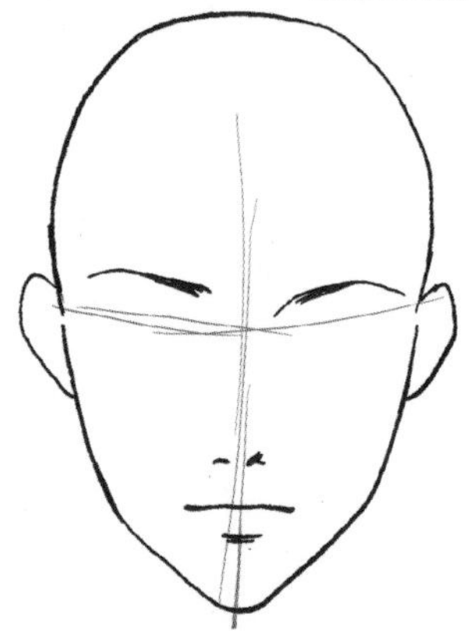

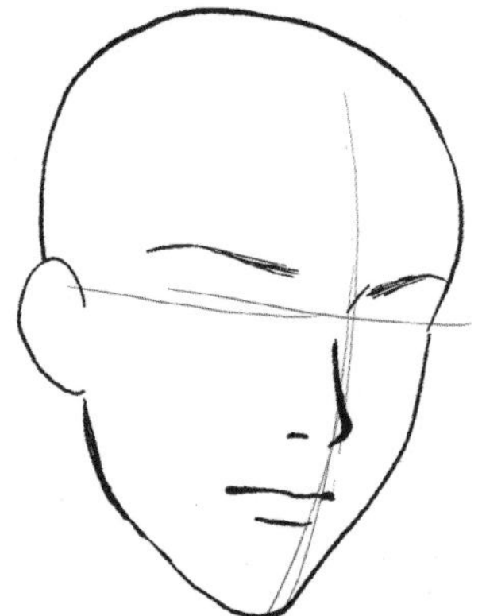

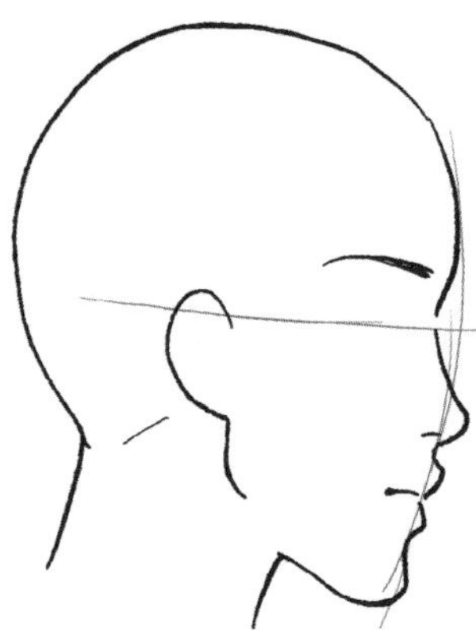

Kosaku Inochigake (1960s Style)

Kosaku Inochigake's nose is an adorable ball attached to his balloon of a head. His mouth is shifted conspicuously to the left. This causes Kosaku almost to project a simultaneously humorous and out-of-control atmosphere and gives the character a stylishly drawn look. The distinguishing characteristic of Kosaku's nose is that it always appears the same, regardless of the angle of perspective.Å

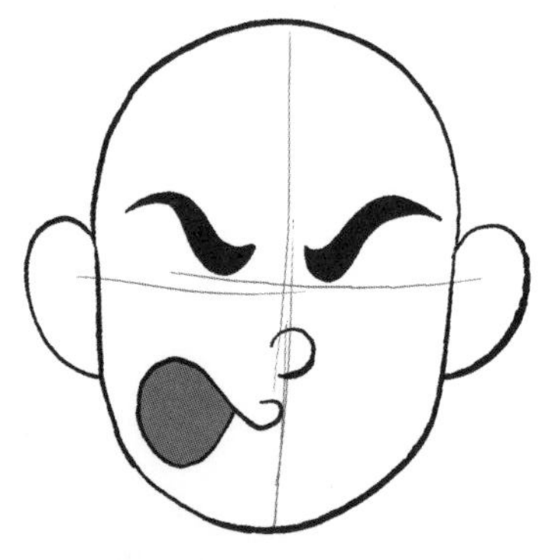

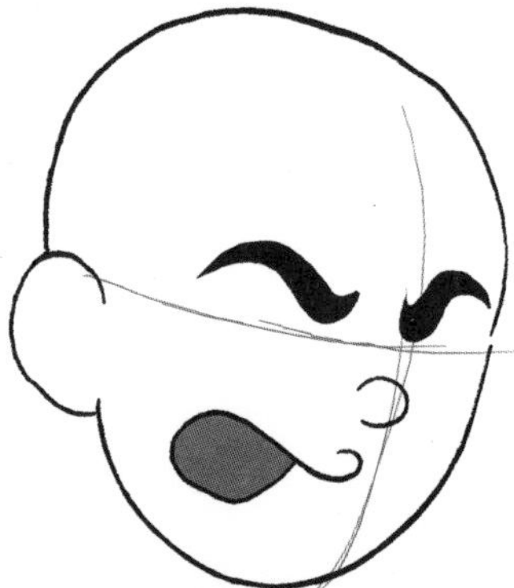

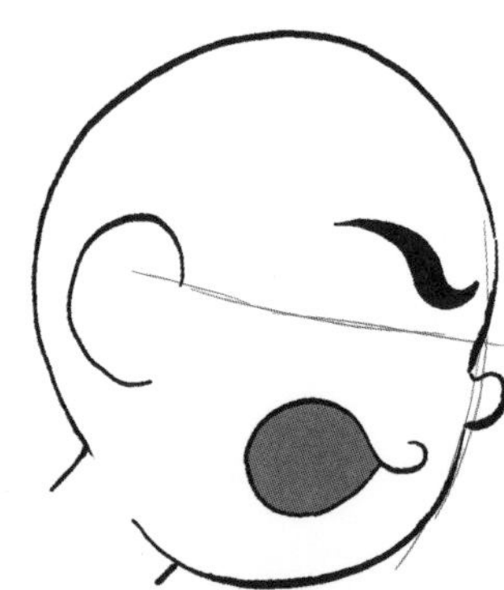

Otsuteru Yumebakari (1970s Style)

Otsuteru has a straight nose and small, bowtie mouth. His nose bridge maintains its elevation as it continues up between the eyes. Incidentally, the small line that you see at the side of his nose does not represent the inside of a nostril but rather the exterior contour of a nostril. The two corners and center of his mouth are darkened and clearly defined. The rest of his mouth is either not defined or is filled in using fine strokes. Lastly, "rouge" in the form of a circle is added to the lips.

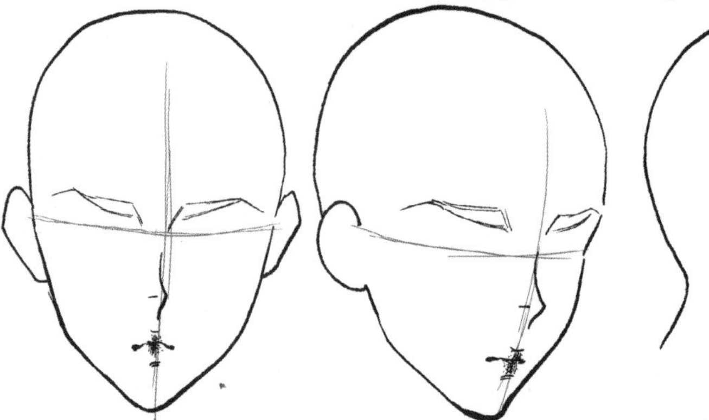

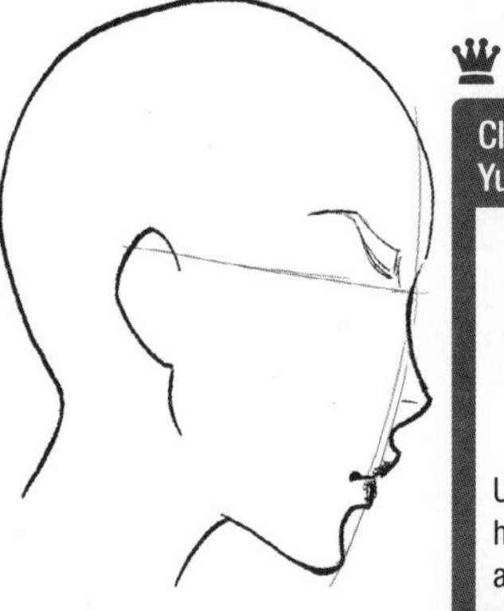

POINT

Close-up of Otsuteru Yumebakari's lips

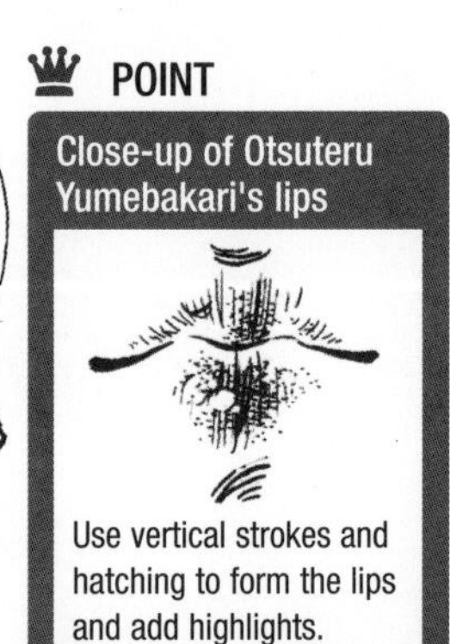

Use vertical strokes and hatching to form the lips and add highlights.

Jotaro Sho [In the Style of 1980s *Shojo* Manga]

Jotaro Sho's nose and mouth are rendered using an unusual technique. The exterior contours are drawn with a fine nib and the rest is shaded using crosshatching, ensuring that the strokes used are delicate and fine. While his nose bridge is long, his chin is long as well, maintaining the face's overall proportional balance.

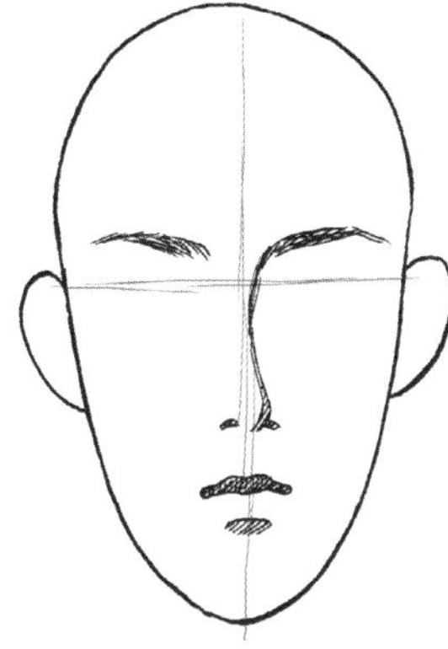

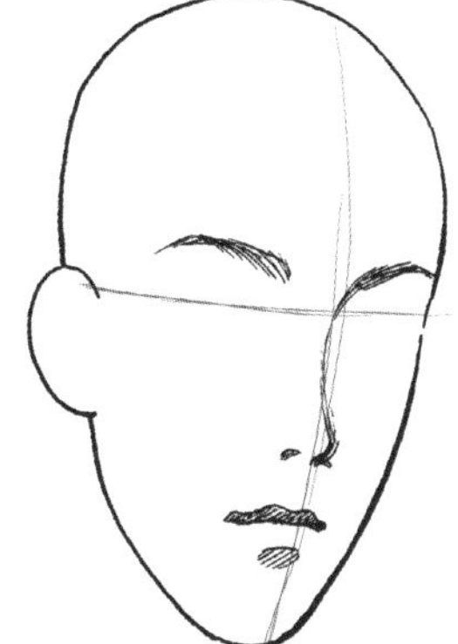

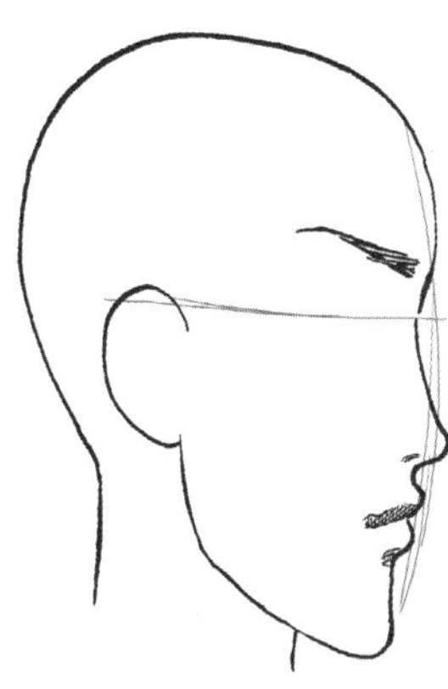

Nentaro Sho [In the Style of 1980s *Shonen* Manga]

Nentaro Sho's mouth is essentially a straight line. It is not necessary to connect the mouth's two corners with a continuous line, provided that the corners are clearly drawn. A few strokes underneath the lip also provide adequate definition. The shadow on his nose is emphasized by drawing the shadow's surrounding borders as contours. While the techniques used to draw Nentaro may seem a little obsolete, adjusting the silhouette contours to suit your own preferences yields surprisingly fresh results.

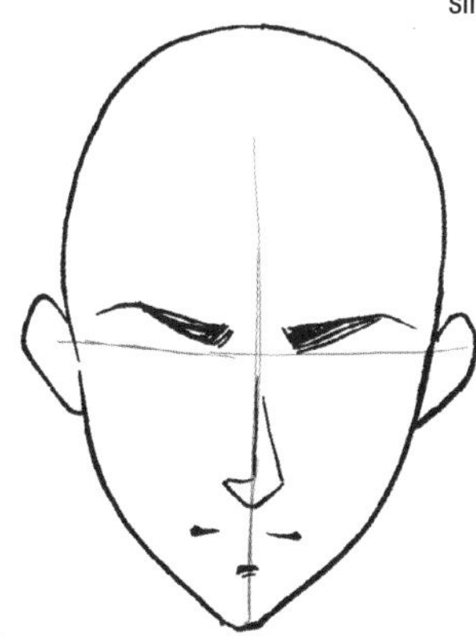

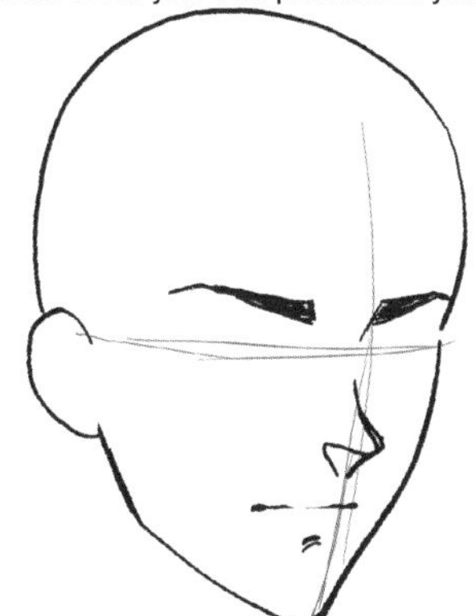

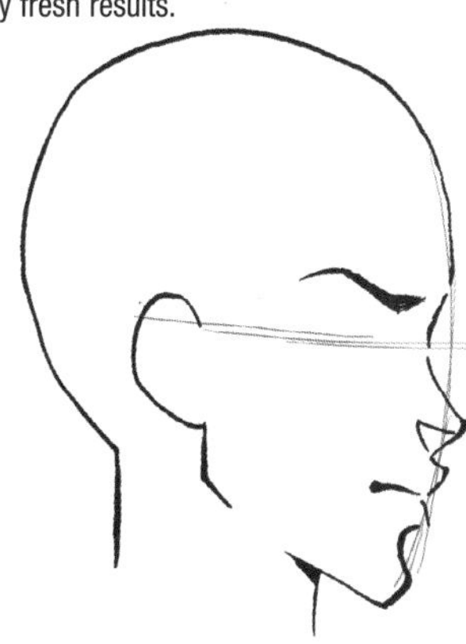

Sugita Hinekure (1990s Style)

When drawing Sugita's face from the front, the nose is divided using an axial line. Solid black is applied to the side of the nose opposite the light source, while hatching is applied to the nose bridge. The hatched strokes gradually become lighter and spaced farther apart toward the tip of the nose, which results in a natural look. The mouth's corners are clearly defined, and the lips are described using an inverted "V".

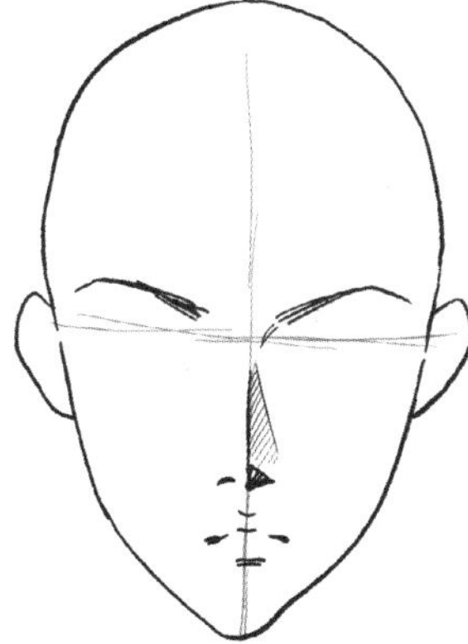

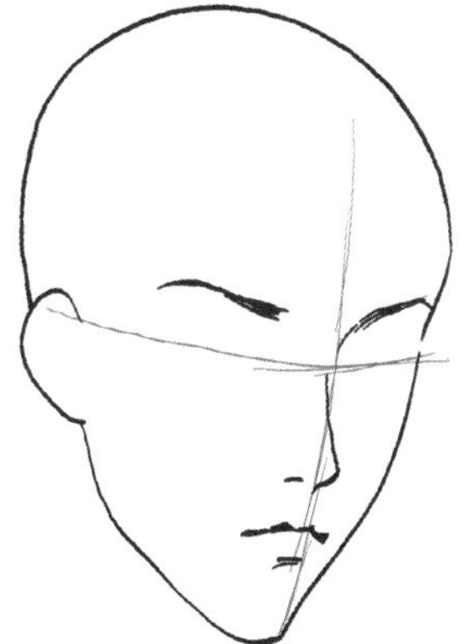

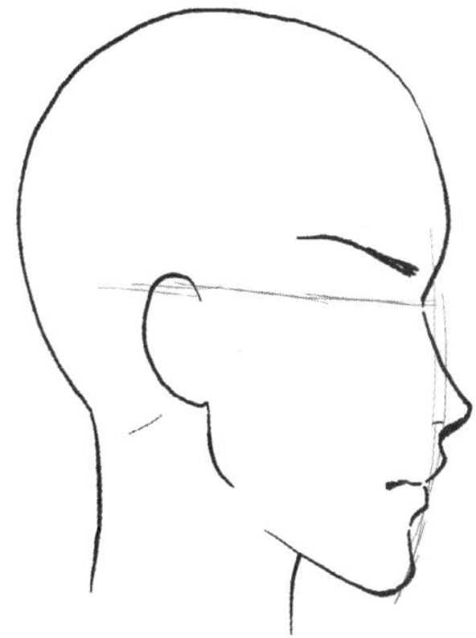

Composing the Ear

While in *manga* each character's eyes, nose, and mouth are different, not much individuality is given to the ears. Mastering the form shown below is ample for now. While the ear below might seem complicated at first glance, if you memorize the steps to composing it, you will find the ear infinitely easier than the eyes, nose, and mouth.

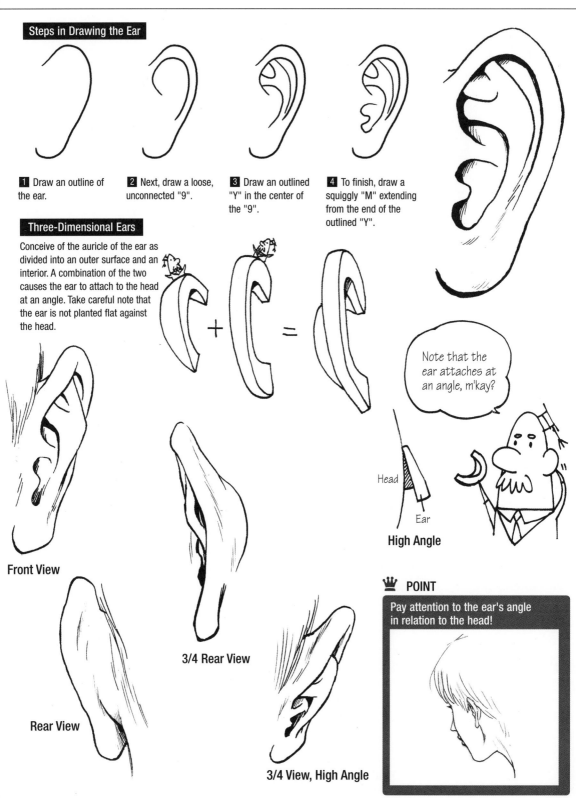

Steps in Drawing the Ear

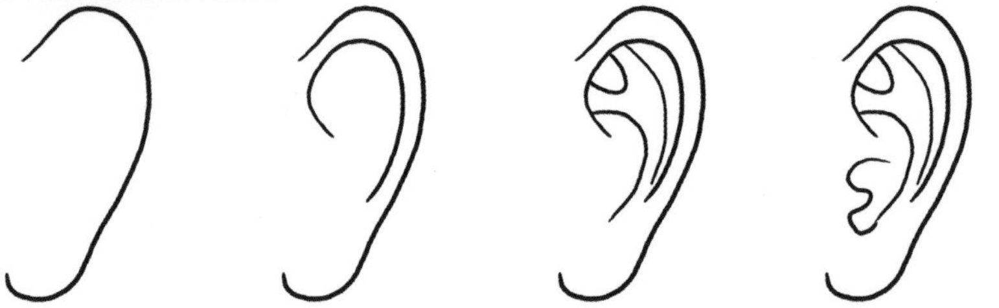

1 Draw an outline of the ear.

2 Next, draw a loose, unconnected "9".

3 Draw an outlined "Y" in the center of the "9".

4 To finish, draw a squiggly "M" extending from the end of the outlined "Y".

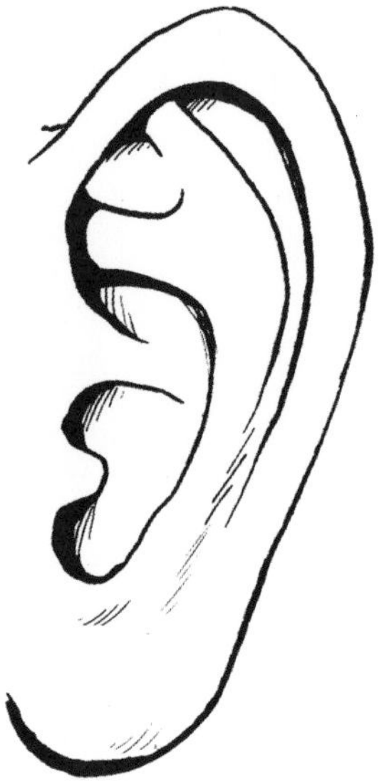

Three-Dimensional Ears

Conceive of the auricle of the ear as divided into an outer surface and an interior. A combination of the two causes the ear to attach to the head at an angle. Take careful note that the ear is not planted flat against the head.

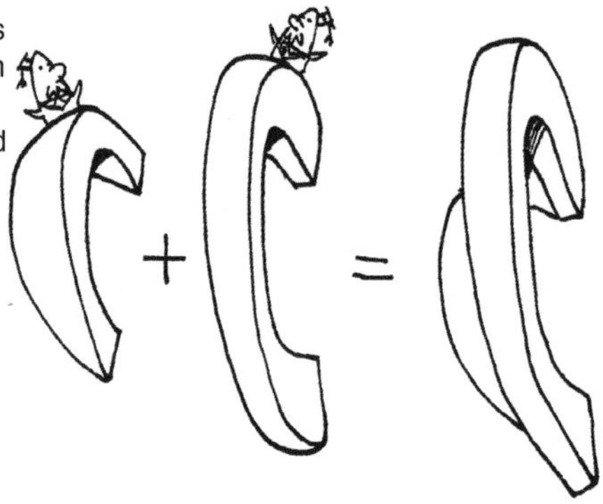

+
=
Note that the ear attaches at an angle, m'kay?
Head
Ear

High Angle

Front View

3/4 Rear View

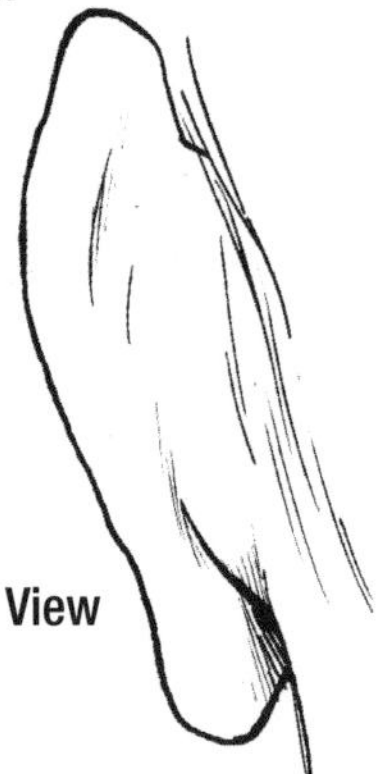

Rear View

3/4 View, High Angle

POINT

Pay attention to the ear's angle in relation to the head!

Low and High Angle Sample Collection

The three heads appearing in the central box are not composed from a low or high angle. Use these as guides when drawing a head from a skewed perspective.

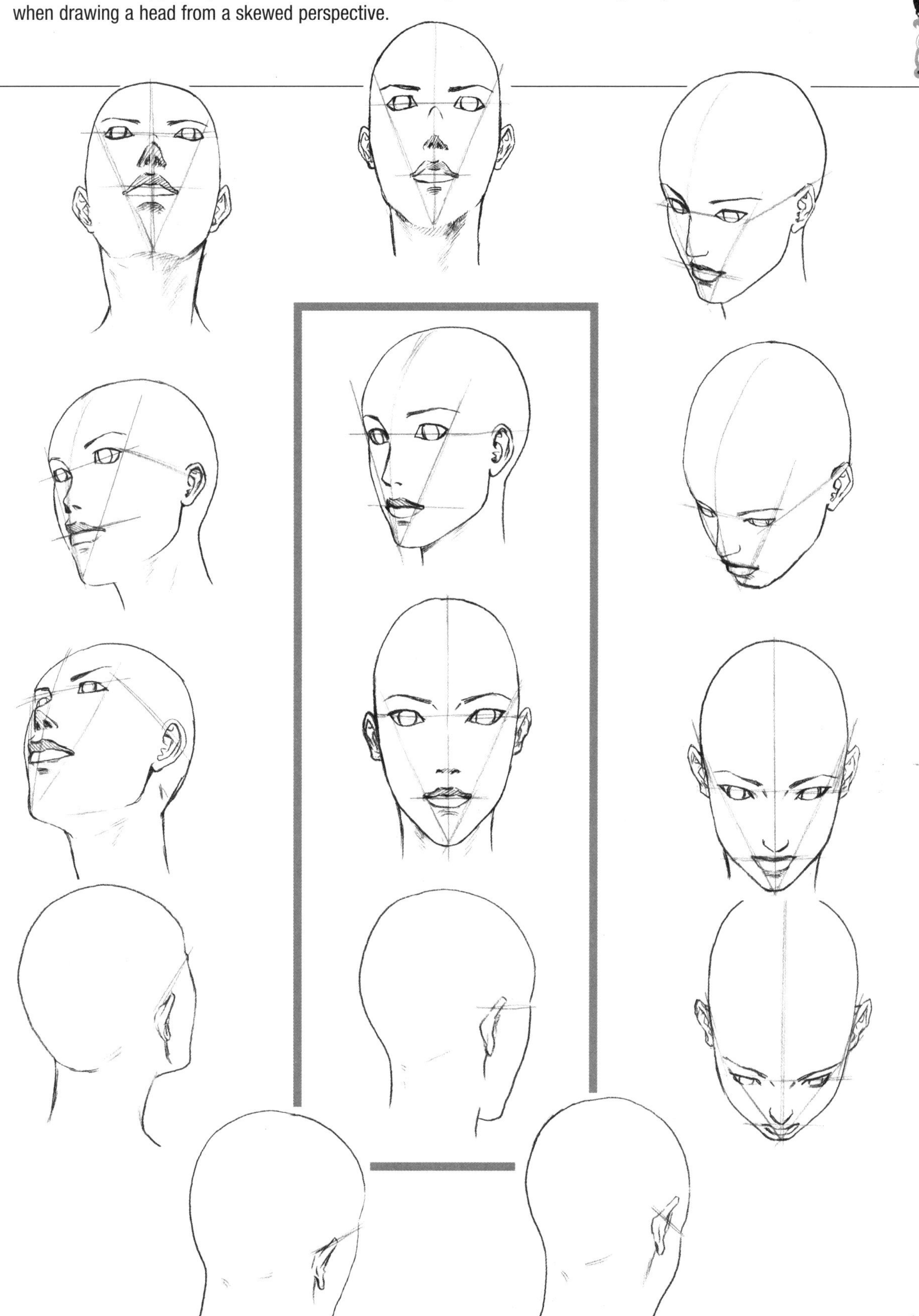

Bontaro Hei's Collection of Facial Expressions

A typical *bishonen*, Bondaro tends to be slightly narcissistic. Bondaro recently transferred to *Bishonen* Academy to engage in *bishonen* studies under the tutelage of Dr. *Bishonen* and the more senior *Bishonen* Academy students. Bondaro tends to become deeply emotionally involved and is easily influenced by others. His hope for the future is to become a "worthy *bishonen*." Bondaro is not very bright.

Kosaku Inochigake's Collection of Facial Expressions

Kosaku is a senior (third year student) at *Bishonen* Academy. He is always risking his life for a mysterious organization that employs him. Despite all that, he is still a genuine retro-style ca. 1960s *bishonen*. Kosaku's only fault is that he dedicates too much of his effort to espionage adventures and becomes unable to see the forest for the trees. But he is a good-hearted older student. Incidentally, since Kosaku only appears as a hyper-stylized character, I decided to include a more realistic rendition of him below.

Otsuteru Yumebakari's Collection of Facial Expressions

Otsuteru Yumebakari is a senior at *Bishonen* Academy. Otsuteru tends to daydream. He suffered countless traumas in his past and consequently is susceptible to feel jealous and unloved about three times as much as keenly as the average person. Otsuteru is drawn in a retro-*bishonen* style, ca. the 1970s. He seduces others at random and leads them to their downfall. While Otsuteru is not a degenerate by any means, in a certain sense he is lacking in character. He is excessively given to fantasies and, if given the slightest opportunity, tends to lose himself in his fantasy world.

Jotaro Sho's Collection of Facial Expressions

Jotaro is a junior (second year student) at *Bishonen* Academy. He has a twin brother and is the younger of the two. He has somewhat of a muscular build, which is virtually unheard of at *Bishonen* Academy. Jotaro is a vocalist in a band and gets plenty of attention from the girls; however, he complains that girls annoy him. Jotaro is drawn in the retro-style of a *shojo manga* character from the 1980s. Jotaro loses his temper easily and is constantly fighting with his older brother, Nentaro.

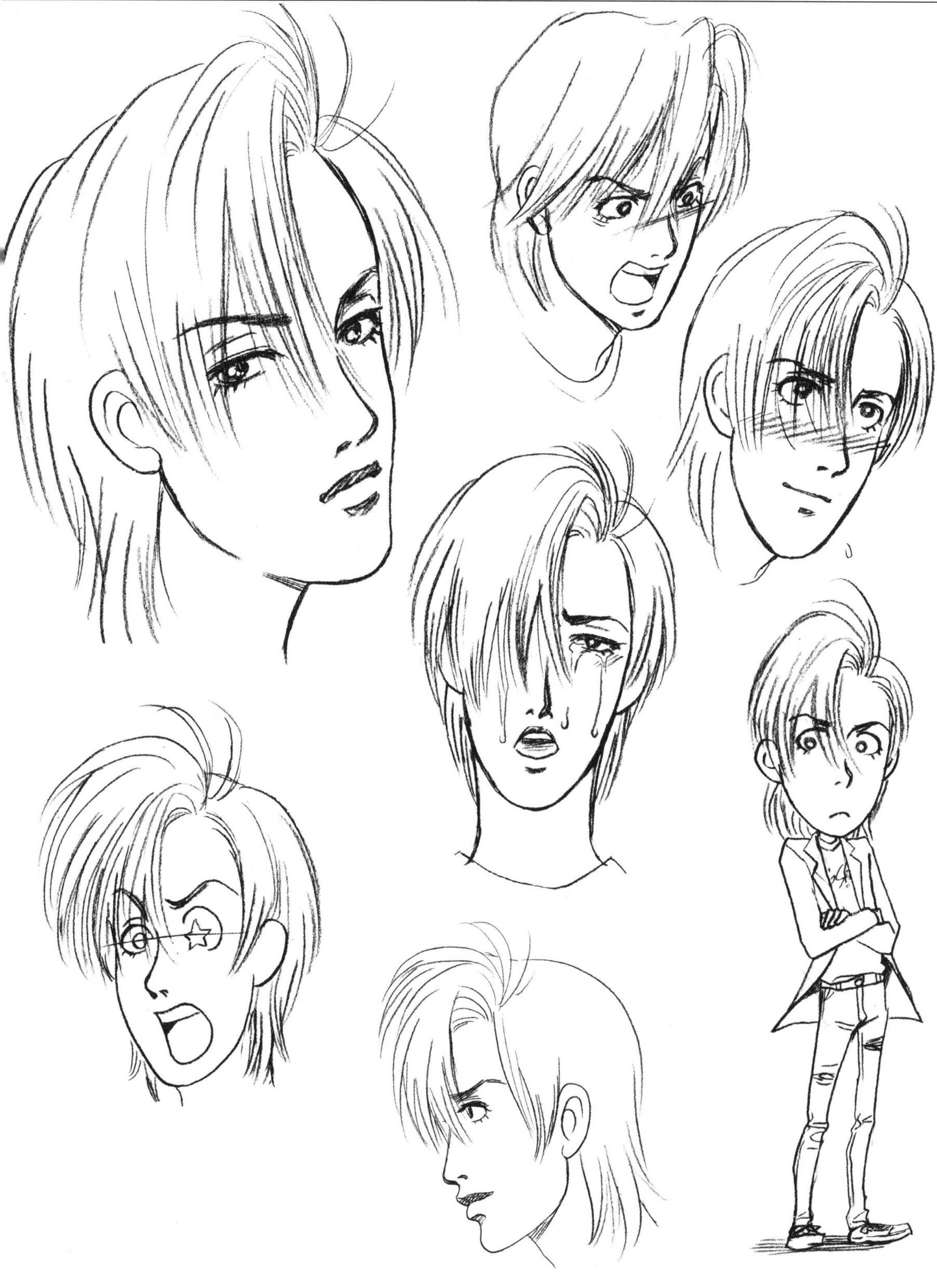

Nentaro Sho's Collection of Facial Expressions

Nentaro Sho is a junior at *Bishonen* Academy and is the older Sho twin. He has a strong sense of right and wrong, is a passionate young man, and can become a little too fiery at times. He is straightforward in everything he says and does and there is nothing scheming, disguised, or complicated about him. He is drawn in the retro-style of a *shonen manga bishonen* from the 1980s. Nentaro's little brother, Jotaro, is always in a snit and is constantly giving him trouble. Netaro and Jotaro come from a poor family.

Sugita Hinekure's Collection of Facial Expressions

A problematic student, Sugita Hinekure is a freshman at *Bishonen* Academy. While in elementary school, Sugita became addicted to the Internet and still continues along this twisted path. If Sugita does not get along with someone, he engages in a social affront that is borderline criminal. Even Dr. *Bishonen* finds him difficult to handle. When confronted with a just argument, Hinekure will come back with a shockingly sophistic response.

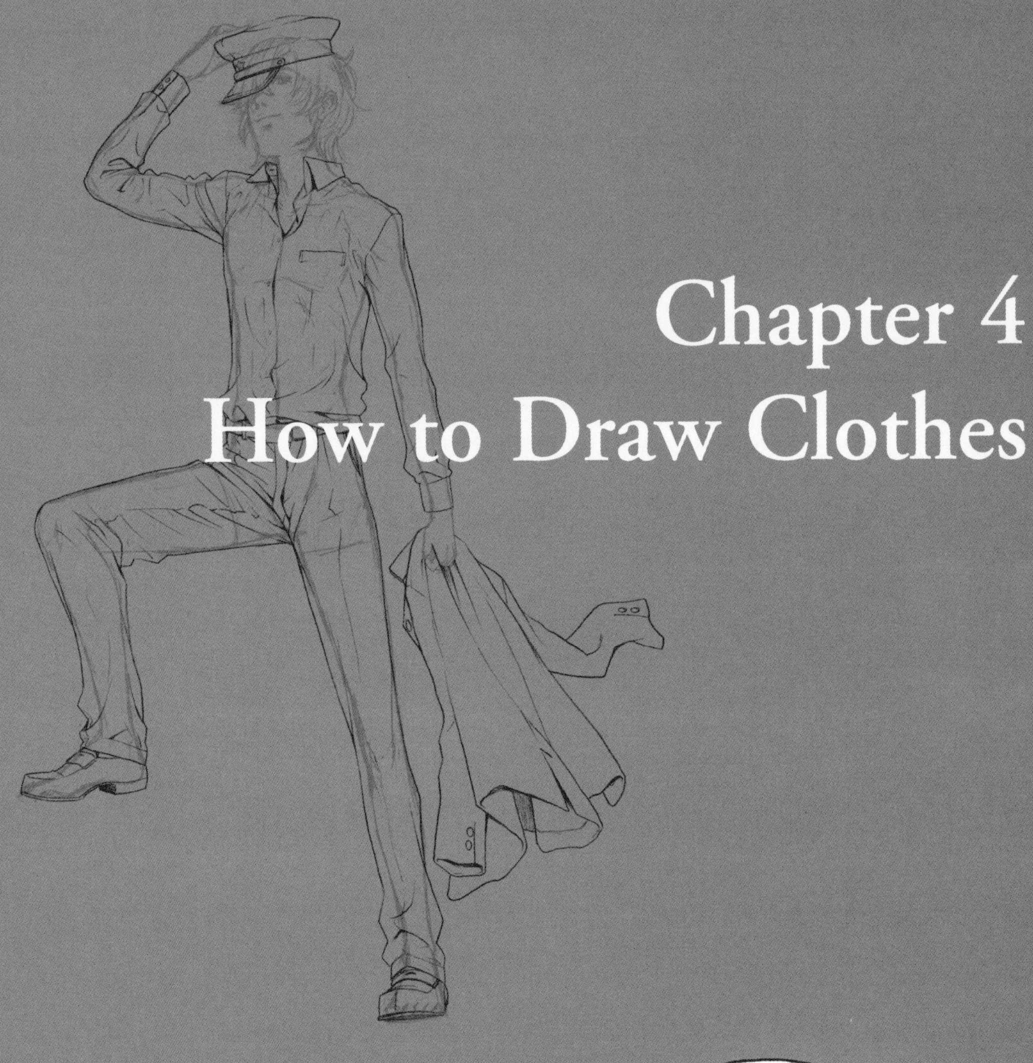

Chapter 4
How to Draw Clothes

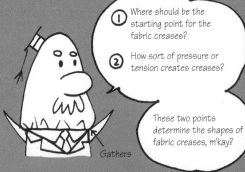

① Where should be the starting point for the fabric creases?

② How sort of pressure or tension creates creases?

These two points determine the shapes of fabric creases, m'kay?

Gathers

Mastering Fabric Wrinkle and Crease Patterns

Wrinkles and creases might seem haphazard and complex at first glance; however, they may be roughly divided into two types: gravity-made creasing and manmade creasing. These two types of creases merely change their appearance, depending on the shape of the fabric and how tension is applied. Because gravity-made creases can become transformed into manmade creases, the reader should look around and observe how various types of creases form in fabrics.

Gravity-made Creasing

As the heading indicates, creasing types 1-3 result from gravity. Unlike manmade creases, the trick to drawing gravity-made creases is to use straight strokes. Gravity-made creases do not form loops.

1. Hanging Ripples

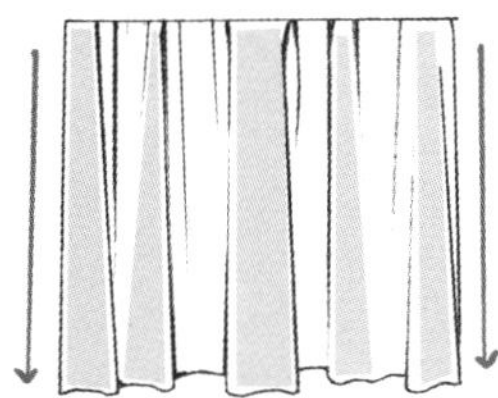

Characteristics: These straight ripples fall like those on a curtain. Few of the ripples are small.

How: Draw the ripples as if long, inverted trapezoidal boards where propped vertically. Show the forward and back undulation of the ripples.

Where: Skirts, capes, and the sleeves of long-sleeved shirts

2. Bunches

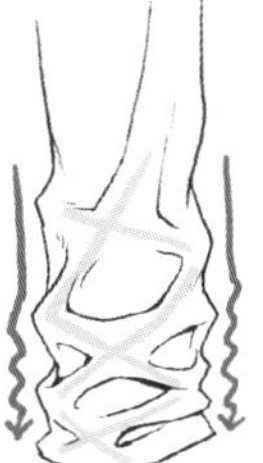

Characteristics: These creases form when a tubular-shaped fabric bunches on the ground.

How: Draw as if small strips of wood were nailed to a pipe in an "X" like pattern. As the eye travels downward, the strips of wood become increasingly horizontal.

Where: Pant leg cuffs, sleeve cuffs, towards the hem of tucked-in shirts, and at the joints when clothes are closely tailored to the body.

3. Bowed Ripples

Characteristics: These are creases forming an inverted "V" when parts of a fabric are supported while the rest is allowed to hang.

How: Start by drawing an arc, giving the stroke a sketchy, tapering ending. Show the creases becoming smaller as the eye travels down.

Where: The tops of capes, the chest regions of shirts, the shoulders of sleeves

Manmade Creasing

These are looped creases that form when tension other than gravity is exerted on fabric. Manmade creases adhere to the shapes of the body underneath the clothing, and when parts of the body bend or twist or pull the fabric.

4. Draped Ripples

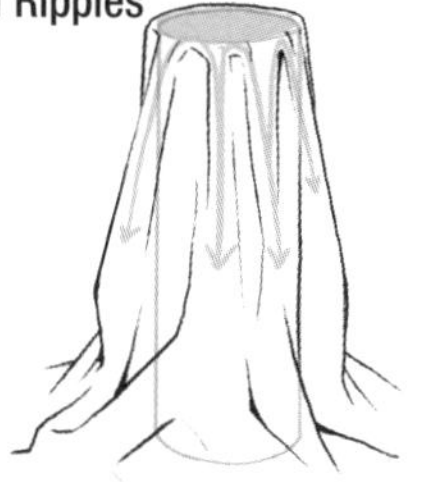

Characteristics: These subtly arcing creases form when a hard object lies beneath the fabric. The creases adhere to the shape of the object underneath.

How: Avoid drawing creases where the object and the fabric are in direct contact.

Where: The peaks of bent elbows and knees and chests

5. Bent Creases

Characteristics: These looped creases form when a tubular-shaped piece of cloth bends.

How: Compose as if drawing the mouth of a bag.

Where: The inside of bent elbows and knees and underarms

6. Round, Pulled Creases

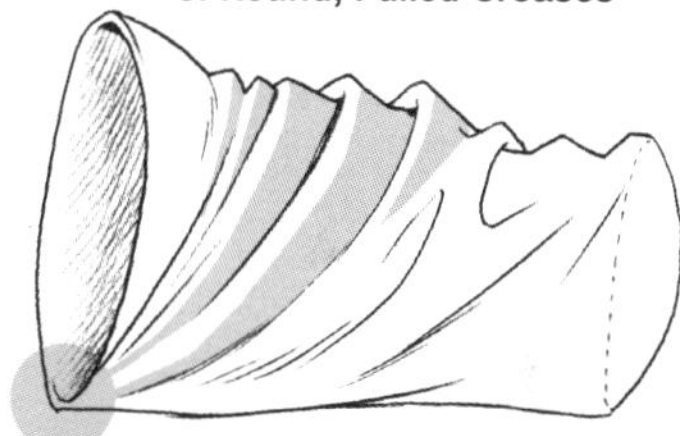

Characteristics: These tiered, overlapping creases form when a tubular-shaped piece of fabric is pulled.

How: Imagine you are drawing the segmented shell of a pill bug. Draw the creases moving in a singular direction and overlapping.

Where: Shoulders when the arm is raised and the tops of thighs

7. Gathers

Characteristics: When the fabric is bunched, an extravagant display of looped creases results.

How: The trick is to draw creases evenly and abundantly both above and below where the fabric is gathered.

Where: Waist and the cuff of puff sleeves

8. Pulled Creasing

Characteristics: These are straight creases that result when the fabric is pulled or other strong pressure is exerted on the fabric.

How: Use rigidly straight strokes that taper off.

Where: Tight clothes

9. Twisted Creasing

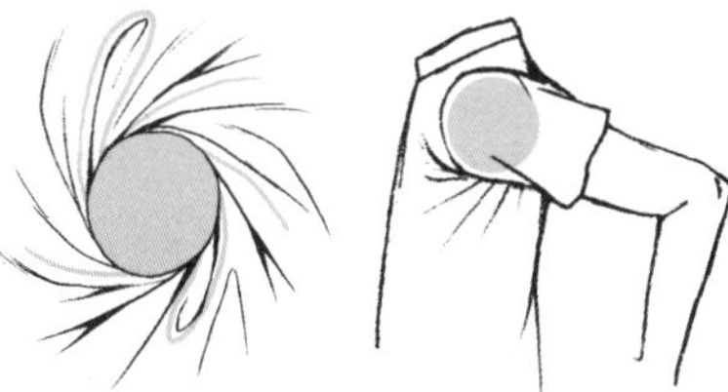

Characteristics: These are creases that form a radiating pattern when a portion of fabric becomes twisted.

How: Draw the creases in a whorl, following the direction of torsion.

Where: When the arms and legs move forward and back

Following a Pattern

After the detailed description of creases in the preceding lesson module, do you feel capable of distinguishing when to draw a straight crease and when to draw a circular crease? As a practice exercise, this next lesson module examines where and how creases form on clothing. The example used below is a *bishonen* wearing a school uniform, the likes of which the world has never seen.

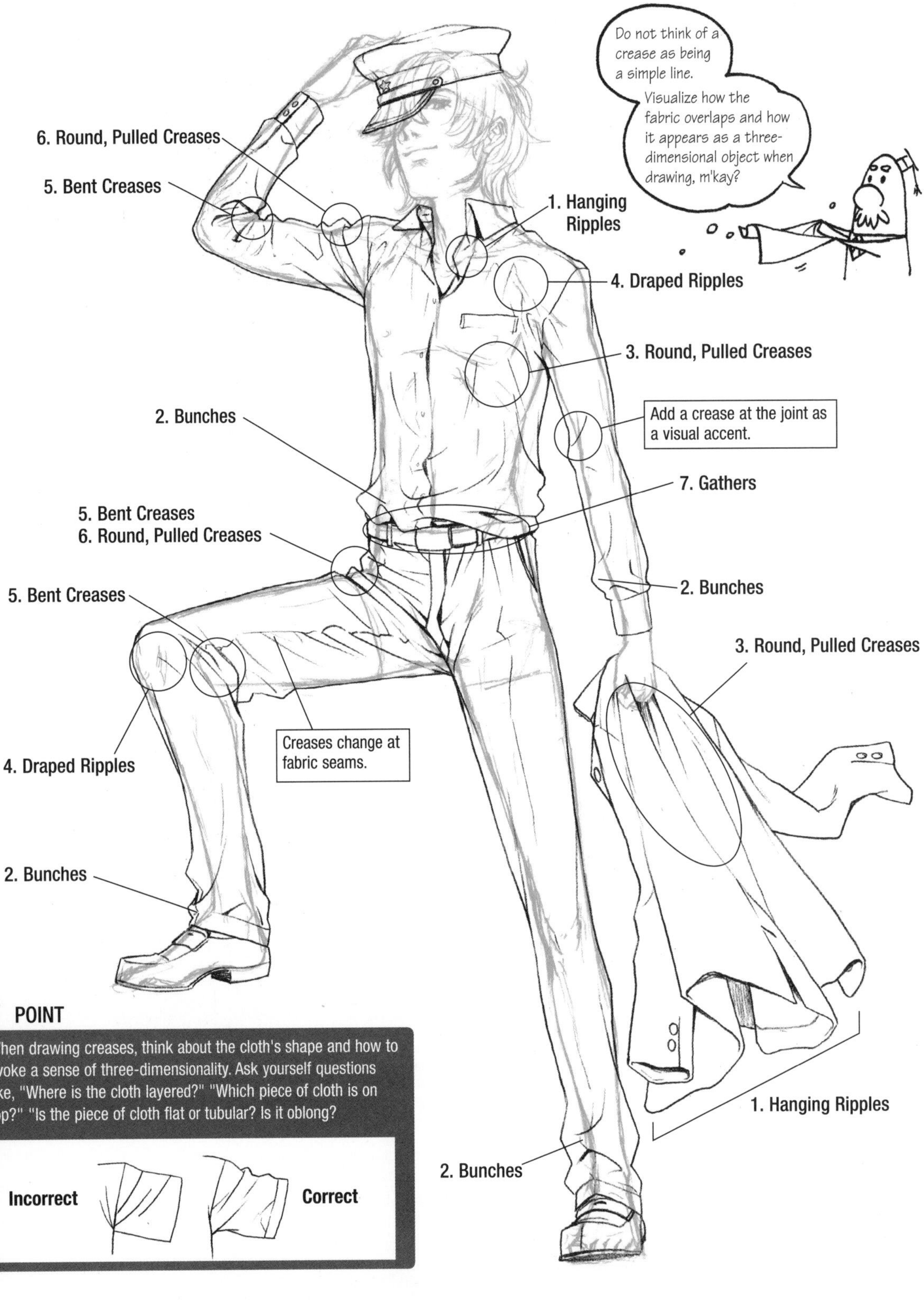

Do not think of a crease as being a simple line.
Visualize how the fabric overlaps and how it appears as a three-dimensional object when drawing, m'kay?

6. Round, Pulled Creases
5. Bent Creases
1. Hanging Ripples
4. Draped Ripples
3. Round, Pulled Creases
Add a crease at the joint as a visual accent.
2. Bunches
7. Gathers
5. Bent Creases
6. Round, Pulled Creases
5. Bent Creases
2. Bunches
3. Round, Pulled Creases
4. Draped Ripples
Creases change at fabric seams.
2. Bunches
1. Hanging Ripples
2. Bunches

POINT

When drawing creases, think about the cloth's shape and how to evoke a sense of three-dimensionality. Ask yourself questions like, "Where is the cloth layered?" "Which piece of cloth is on top?" "Is the piece of cloth flat or tubular? Is it oblong?

Incorrect

Correct

The Steps in Drawing Wrinkles and Creases

First, draw the general silhouette. Next, establish where the predominant creases should go. Last, draw small, detailed creases that accompany the larger ones.

1 Draw the Body, the Foundation.
The body acts as a guide in determining where creases form. Never forget to draw the body first.

2 Draw the Clothing's Silhouette.
Using straight strokes, produce a rough sketch of the silhouette contours, maintaining awareness of how thick the fabric is.

3 Add the Seams
Clothing seams also determine where creases will form. Always draw the seams before embarking on the creases.

4 Draw the Largest Creases
Draw the deepest-cut creases already indicated in the silhouette contours sketched earlier.

5 Draw the Smallest Creases
Add the shallow, detailed creases.

6 Clean up the Lines
If the fabric is supple, then adopt rounded contours. If the fabric is stiff, then use straight contours. Develop the fabric's texture while adjusting the lines.

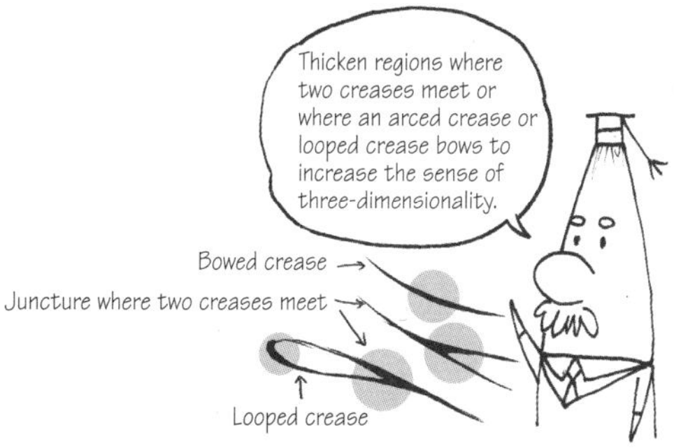

Thicken regions where two creases meet or where an arced crease or looped crease bows to increase the sense of three-dimensionality.

Bowed crease

Juncture where two creases meet

Looped crease

Ideal Clothing = Stiffness + Thickness + Size

To portray a garment's texture, first establish how stiff and how thick the fabric should be. What about the garment's size. Should it have a snug or loose fit? Combining these factors is the trick to creating ideal clothing.

Stiffness

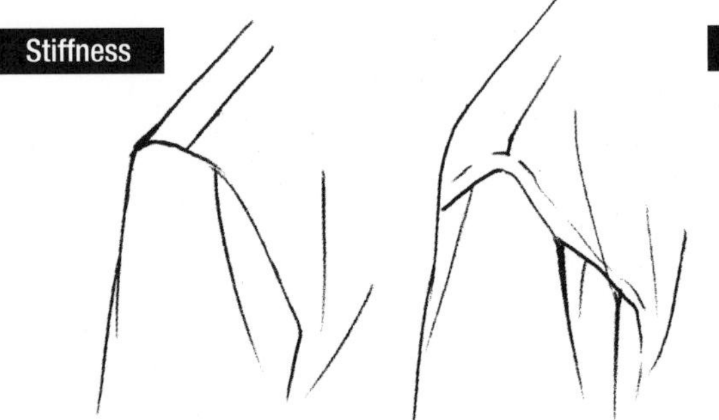

Stiff Fabric
Use straight lines to define seams and creases. This will give the garment a crisp, starched look. Make the contour of the sleeve's shoulder angular rather than showing it hug against the body.

Soft Fabric
Use gentle, smooth contours to define seams and creases. Supple fabrics easily show the effects of gravity. The sleeve's shoulder adheres to the body, while the fabric hangs.

Thickness

Thin Fabric
Smallish creases form in response to slight undulations in the body underneath. The creases tend to be narrow and abundant.

Thick Fabric
Only large creases (primarily toward the body's lower region) form on thick fabric. Avoid drawing small, detailed creases. The creases tend to be wide and few in number.

Size

Loose Clothing (Left)
Gravity pulls at the fabric, causes large, bunches to form at the cuffs and hem. Maintain awareness of gravity, and show the fabric hanging in draped ripples.

Snug Clothing (Right)
The fabric hugs to the body, revealing its silhouette. Minor hills and valleys on the body cause creases to form. Bunching appears primarily at the joints. There is little variation in crease size.

Nylon Jacket = Stiff + Thin + Loose

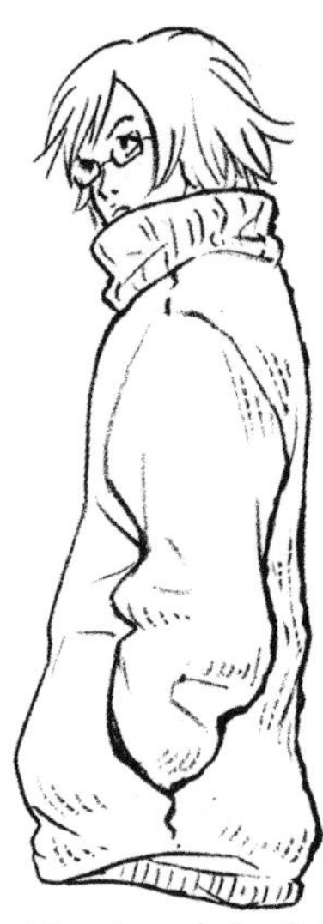

Cable Knit, Wool Sweater = Soft + Thick + Loose

Thin Turtleneck Sweater = Soft + Thin + Snug

School Uniforms and Suits

Projecting a crisply starched look is crucial when drawing school uniforms, suits, and other dress clothes. Pay attention not to use amorphous, wavy lines. The trick is to figure out the extent to which you are able to evoke a sense of three-dimensionality using just a few lines. Take careful note in that there are areas on these garments where creases will not form, even if the wearer moves his body. Be sure that you establish key points such as garment lengths, how the buttons should look, and the collar design and position.

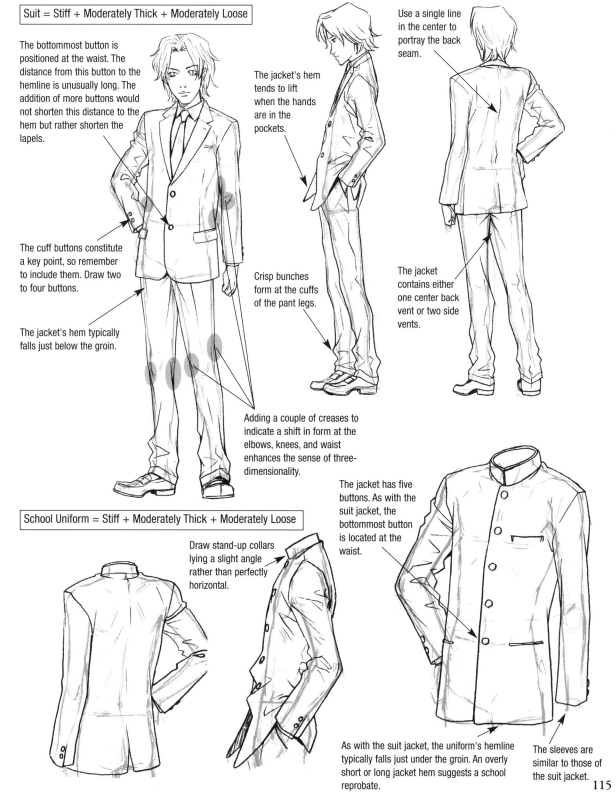

Suit = Stiff + Moderately Thick + Moderately Loose

The bottommost button is positioned at the waist. The distance from this button to the hemline is unusually long. The addition of more buttons would not shorten this distance to the hem but rather shorten the lapels.

The cuff buttons constitute a key point, so remember to include them. Draw two to four buttons.

The jacket's hem typically falls just below the groin.

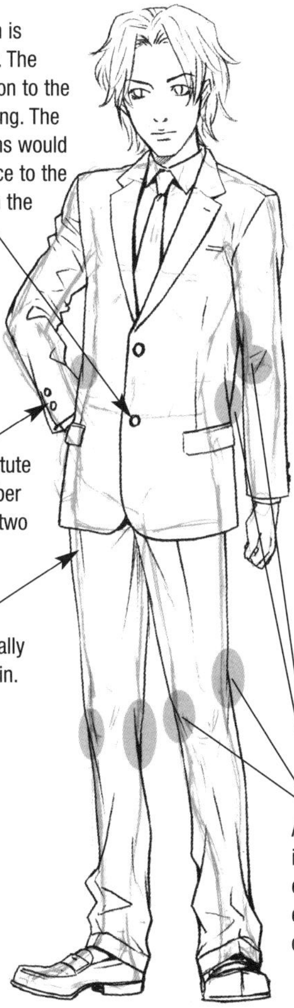

The jacket's hem tends to lift when the hands are in the pockets.

Crisp bunches form at the cuffs of the pant legs.

Use a single line in the center to portray the back seam.

The jacket contains either one center back vent or two side vents.

Adding a couple of creases to indicate a shift in form at the elbows, knees, and waist enhances the sense of three-dimensionality.

School Uniform = Stiff + Moderately Thick + Moderately Loose

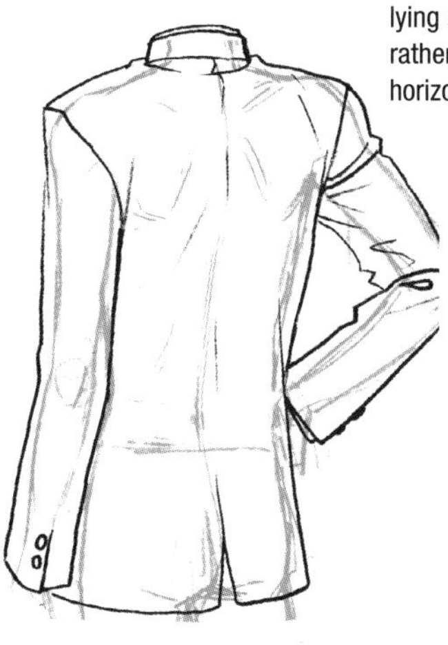

Draw stand-up collars lying a slight angle rather than perfectly horizontal.

The jacket has five buttons. As with the suit jacket, the bottommost button is located at the waist.

As with the suit jacket, the uniform's hemline typically falls just under the groin. An overly short or long jacket hem suggests a school reprobate.

The sleeves are similar to those of the suit jacket.

Special Characteristics of a Jacket

Master the key points in making a jacket look convincing.

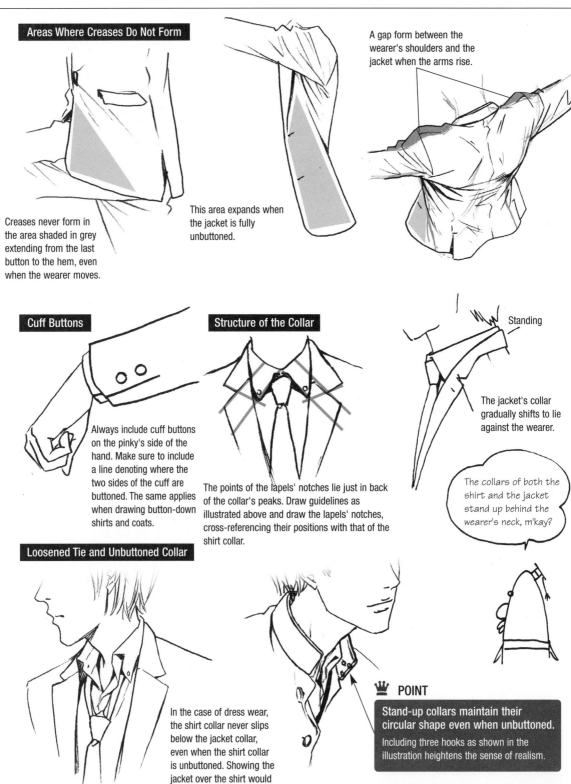

Areas Where Creases Do Not Form

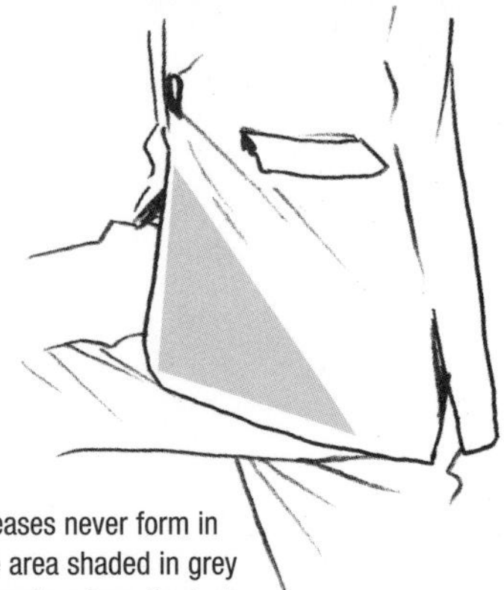

Creases never form in the area shaded in grey extending from the last button to the hem, even when the wearer moves.

This area expands when the jacket is fully unbuttoned.

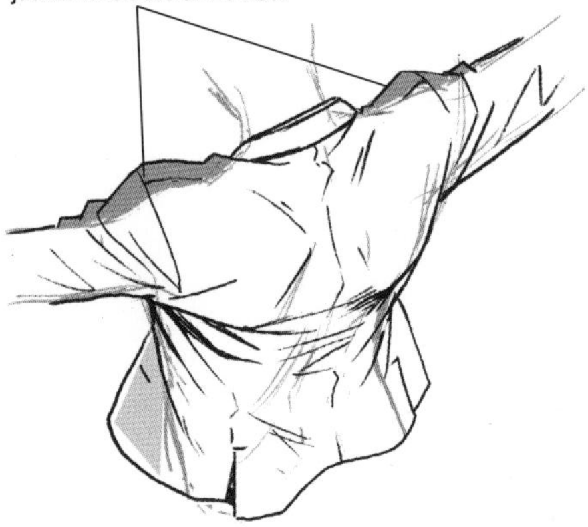

A gap form between the wearer's shoulders and the jacket when the arms rise.

Cuff Buttons

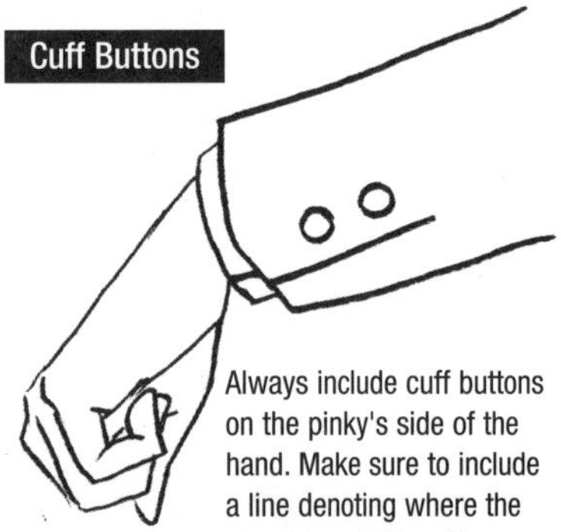

Always include cuff buttons on the pinky's side of the hand. Make sure to include a line denoting where the two sides of the cuff are buttoned. The same applies when drawing button-down shirts and coats.

Structure of the Collar

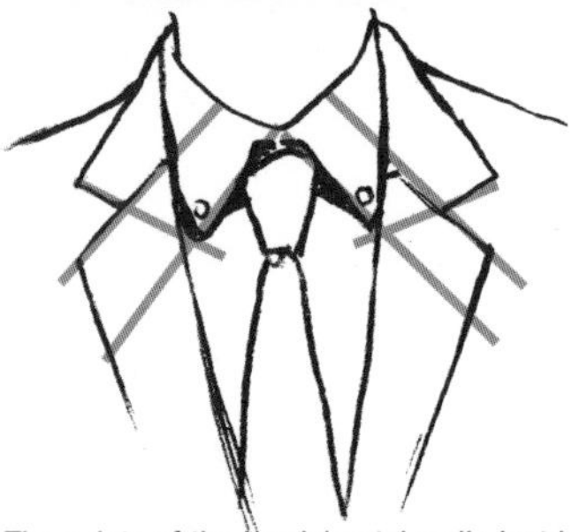

The points of the lapels' notches lie just in back of the collar's peaks. Draw guidelines as illustrated above and draw the lapels' notches, cross-referencing their positions with that of the shirt collar.

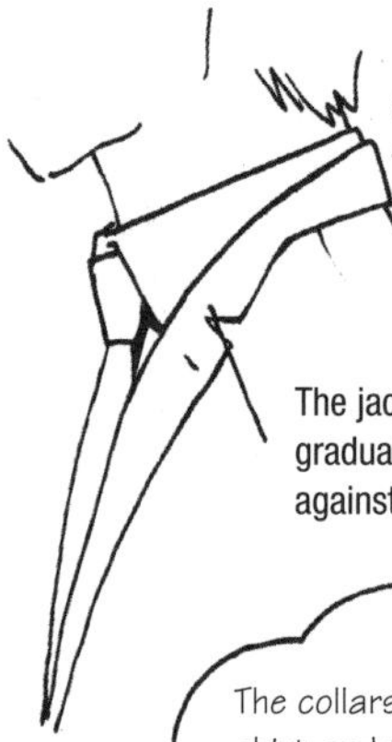

Standing

The jacket's collar gradually shifts to lie against the wearer.

The collars of both the shirt and the jacket stand up behind the wearer's neck, m'kay?

Loosened Tie and Unbuttoned Collar

In the case of dress wear, the shirt collar never slips below the jacket collar, even when the shirt collar is unbuttoned. Showing the jacket over the shirt would create more a look of casual wear.

POINT

Stand-up collars maintain their circular shape even when unbuttoned.

Including three hooks as shown in the illustration heightens the sense of realism.

Shirts

Naturally, students wear button-down shirts underneath their school uniforms. A multitude of different crease types from large to small easily form on button-down shirts. Different creases project different impressions regarding the fabric composing the shirt. Distinguish the strokes you use to portray creases, using straight lines to portray a crisply starched shirt and curved strokes to portray soft, silky fabrics like satin.

Long-sleeved Button-down Shirt = Thin + Moderately Stiff + Loose

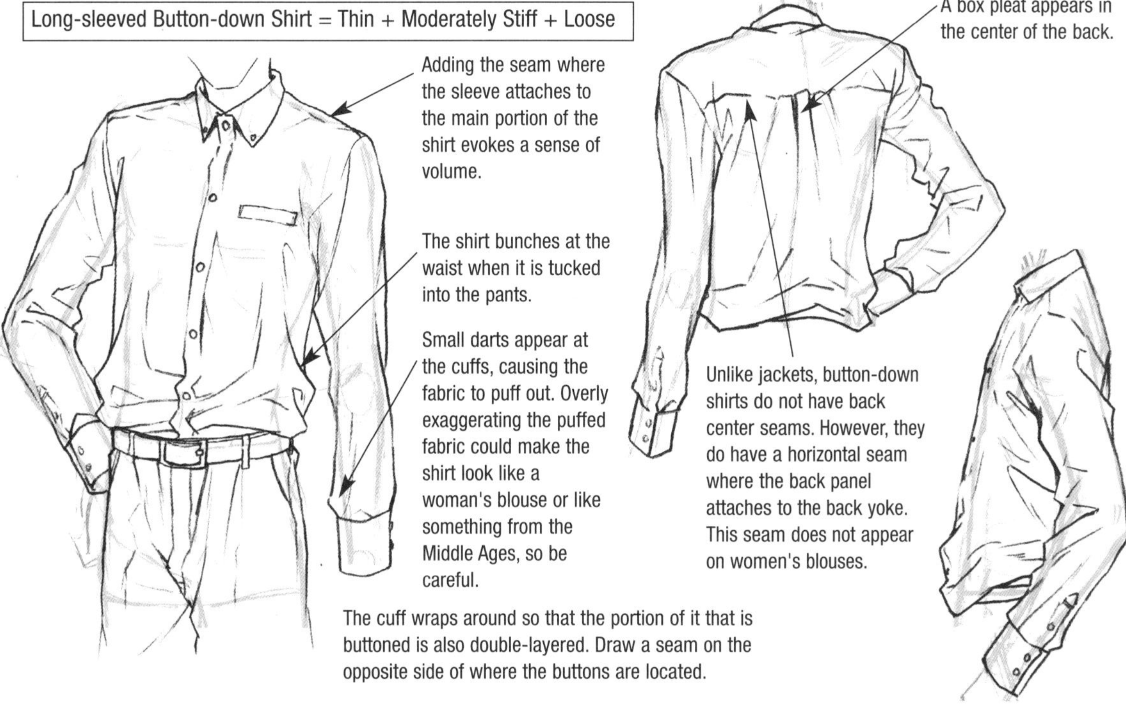

Adding the seam where the sleeve attaches to the main portion of the shirt evokes a sense of volume.
The shirt bunches at the waist when it is tucked into the pants.
Small darts appear at the cuffs, causing the fabric to puff out. Overly exaggerating the puffed fabric could make the shirt look like a woman's blouse or like something from the Middle Ages, so be careful.
A box pleat appears in the center of the back.
Unlike jackets, button-down shirts do not have back center seams. However, they do have a horizontal seam where the back panel attaches to the back yoke. This seam does not appear on women's blouses.
The cuff wraps around so that the portion of it that is buttoned is also double-layered. Draw a seam on the opposite side of where the buttons are located.

Short-sleeved Button-down Shirt = Thin + Moderately Stiff + Loose

Button-down shirts typically have six buttons.

Collar Structure

Flat Collar

Flat collars often appear on the shirts of summer school uniforms, Hawaiian shirts, and other shirts intended to keep the wearer cool in warm weather. The collar comprises the same soft fabric as the sleeves and other parts of the shirt.

Turn-down Collar

This is a dressier collar worn underneath school uniforms and suit jackets. Draw the collar as if wrapped around the neck. Give the collar the appearance of standing up stiffly around the neck.

Polo Shirts, Cuffs, and Assorted Creases

Polo shirts are made of a different fabric from that of button-down dress shirts, so take care when drawing.

Polo Shirt = Moderately Thin + Soft + Moderately Loose

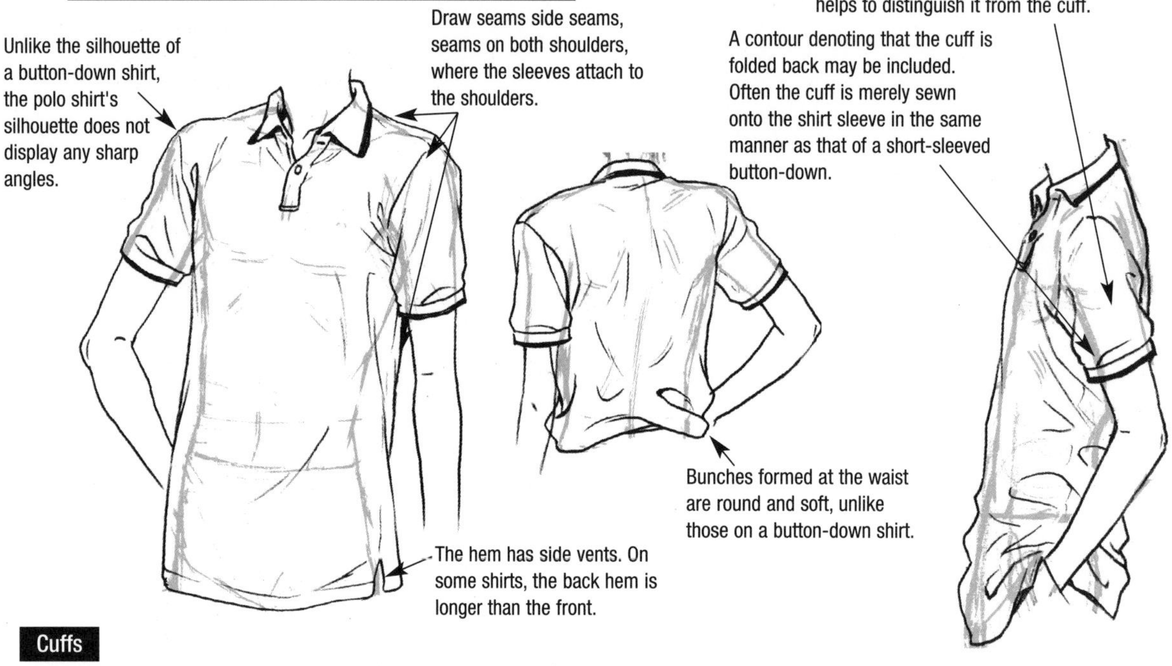

Unlike the silhouette of a button-down shirt, the polo shirt's silhouette does not display any sharp angles.

Draw seams side seams, seams on both shoulders, where the sleeves attach to the shoulders.

The hem has side vents. On some shirts, the back hem is longer than the front.

Bunches formed at the waist are round and soft, unlike those on a button-down shirt.

Giving the sleeve a soft, puffed appearance helps to distinguish it from the cuff.

A contour denoting that the cuff is folded back may be included. Often the cuff is merely sewn onto the shirt sleeve in the same manner as that of a short-sleeved button-down.

Cuffs

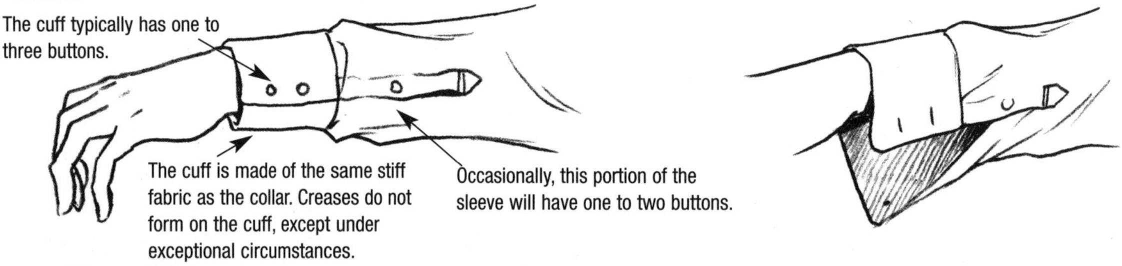

The cuff typically has one to three buttons.

The cuff is made of the same stiff fabric as the collar. Creases do not form on the cuff, except under exceptional circumstances.

Occasionally, this portion of the sleeve will have one to two buttons.

Assorted Creases

When drawing creases, consider what kinds of creases form as a result of the wearer's movements and where the garment lifts off the wearer's body, forming a gap between fabric and skin. Establish a distinct difference between prominent and small creases.

The buttons are pulling the fabric.

The fabric is lifted off the skin.

The shirt is pulled upward.

Gravity

Rounded, pulled creases

The buttons are pulling the fabric.

Pulled creases

Hanging ripples

Rounded, pulled creases

Clothing Catalogue

This lesson module includes an array of garments frequently worn by *bishonen*. Pay attention to the shapes of creases (straight, rounded, etc.), the width of creases, and where seams are located. While the below is written rather definitively, remember that these are nothing more than a sample of common garments. From catalogs to fashion magazines, there is an abundance of reference materials available, so do a little investigation on your own.

Coats

Duffle Coat

The toggle button is distinctive, and the seam attaching the reinforcement panel of wool to the shoulders creates a stylish look. No seams appear at the back.

Trench Coat

The trench coat is thin and belts at the waist, cuffs, and neck.

Peacoat

The peacoat's collar and buttons are like those of the trench coat. However, the peacoat is made of thick fabric and does not have a tailored waist. The sleeves have a buttoned belt.

Down Jacket

Showing light creases form at the seams forming the jacket's padding enhances the sense of realism.

Assorted Bottoms

Bottoms come in a variety of forms. Give consideration to differences in the fit and fabrics when drawing.

Slacks

Note the pressed crease running down each leg's center. Use straight strokes when rendering fabric wrinkles.

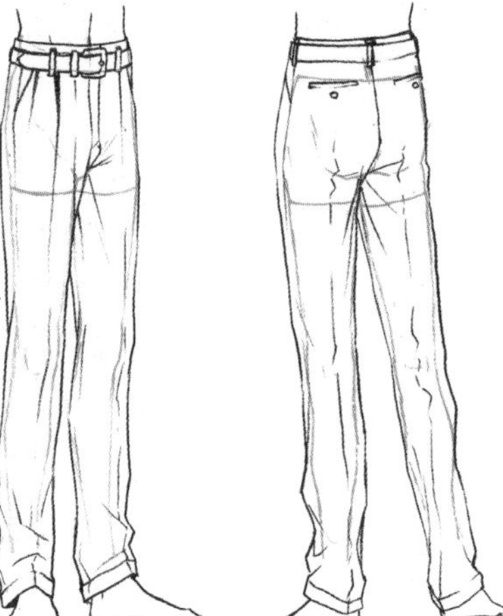

Low-Rise, Slim-Leg Jean

Crease form in concentration at the knees and ankles.

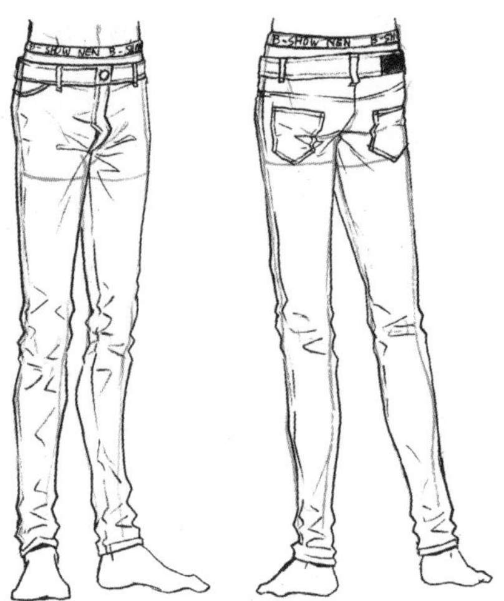

Straight-Leg Jeans

Denim is a stiff fabric. The legs of jeans tend to bunch around the ankles.

Boot-cut Jeans

The legs flare at the hem.

Cargo Pants

Cargo pants are constructed of thin fabrics, have a baggy fit, and are covered in pockets.

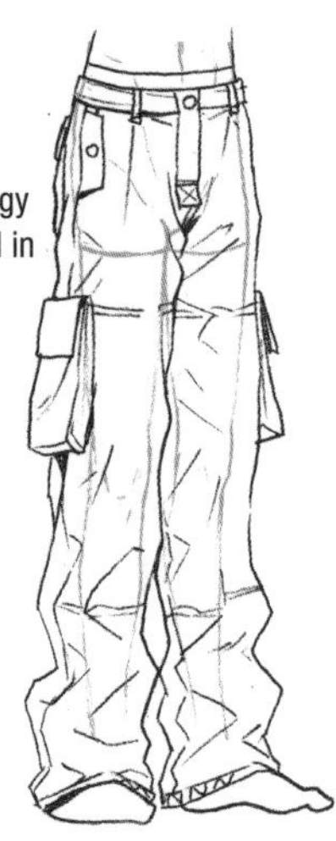

Shorts and Swim Trunks

Have firm grasp of how to convey the fabric's texture and include key elements, such as the drawstring hem. Shorts come in a host of lengths.

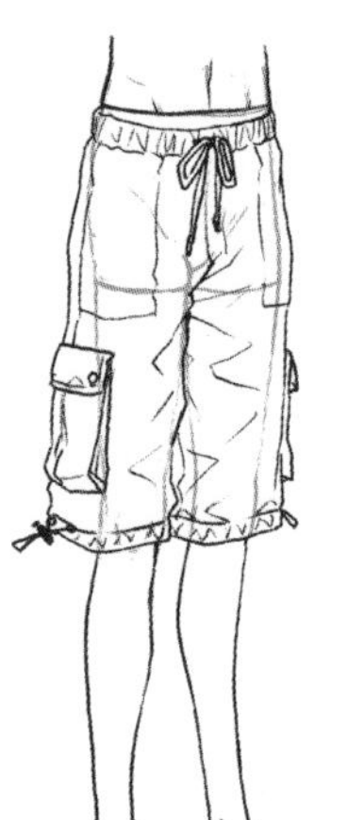

Sports and Martial Arts Uniforms

Sports uniforms symbolize youth. They become smelly and stained with sweat. Martial arts uniforms tend to share the same design.

Soccer

Soccer uniforms are made of thin, soft fabrics. The shirt is worn tucked in to prevent it from interfering with the player's performance.

Baseball

Baseball uniforms are typically made of cotton. An undershirt is usually not worn with the summer uniform. Use accessories like a cap, belt, and socks to make the uniform look more convincing.

Kyudo (Archery)

Note that the sizes of the sleeves and collar are vastly different from those of a regular kimono. The bow should be taller than the character.

Judo

The upper half of the judo *dogi* (uniform) top is a thick fabric. The *dogi*'s top then switches to a thin fabric about waist-level. The pants are usually made of a thin fabric. The obi (sash) and collar are typically stiff.

Japanese Dress

Japanese robes should always be worn with the left side in front (so that the right side is worn on the inside). Take careful note that robes are only worn with the right side in front on the deceased as burial dress.

Yukata

The *yukata* is a cotton summer kimono. Position the obi low on the torso and draw the abdomen so that the belly appears to stick out just slightly. There is no tuck of fabric underneath the obi as there is on women's *yukata*.

Jinbe

The *jinbe* is summer clothing made of cotton and comprising a top and bottom. The seam joining the sleeve to the shoulder is distinctive. Other than the top's front closure, the remainder of the garment is reminiscent of Western clothing.

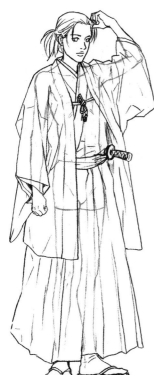

Haori-Hakama

The *haori-hakama* is formalwear, consisting of a kimono, skirt-like pants called a "hakama," and a jacket called a "haori." The formalwear *hakama* is much roomier than the *hakama* worn with the martial arts uniforms worn today. The *haori*'s hem should fall to about knee-level.

Shinobi-Shozoku

This *shinobi-shozoku* is the costume worn by ninja from the Iga region. The *zukin* (head kerchief) is a square cloth that has been draped over the head and tied at the neck. The face mask is a separate piece of cloth.

Other Specialty Costumes

Sometimes adults wear costumes as well. Many Japanese take delight in dressing in specialty costumes and have light-heartedly dubbed it, "*kosupre*" (short for "costume play.")

Waiter

The vest has a distinctive design and cuts a dashing figure. The collar and the back box pleat of the shirt distinguish the waiter's uniform from a standard button-down.

Doctor

The white lab coat favored by doctors is often double-breasted. The hemline falls below the knees.

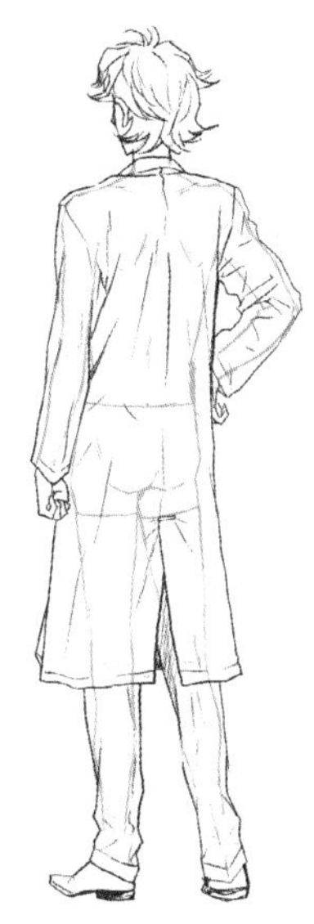

Nobleman

The fashion shown here is indeterminate in its period and country of origin. This coat was inspired by the 17th and 18th c. justaucorps.

Kannushi

The costume of the *kannushi* or Shinto priest dates back to the Heian Period (794-1193). The sleeves are long. Unlike those of a kimono, the ends of the sleeves are completely open. (A kimono's sleeve has a pouch that hangs from it called a *tamoto*. Consequently, the long, hanging portion of the kimono is closed.) The *kannushi*'s top is called a "kariginu." His footwear, which is made of lacquer, is called "*asagutsu*."

Sleepwear and Undergarments

These double as loungewear.

Pajamas

Pajamas should be baggy and have a low waist.

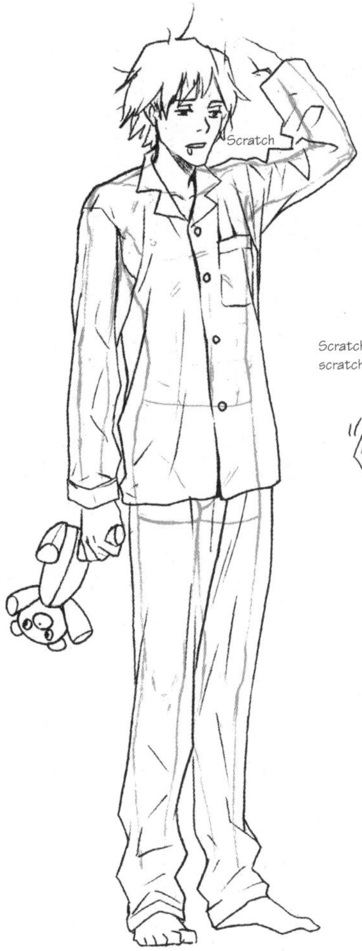

T Shirt

Undergarments

Typically constructed of thin fabrics, there is a huge variety of types of undergarments and a myriad of designs.

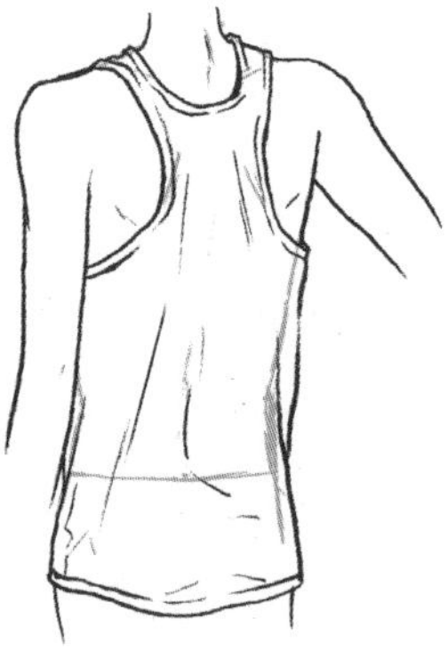

Boxers

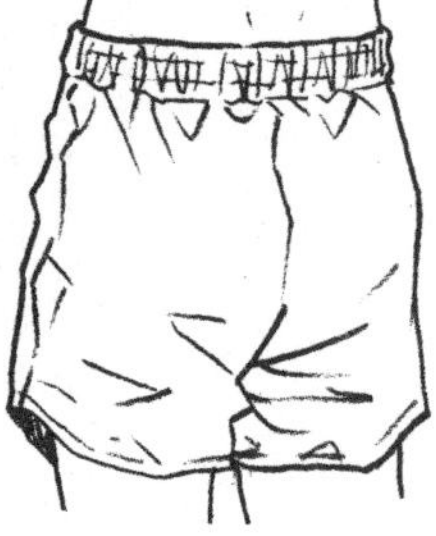

Briefs

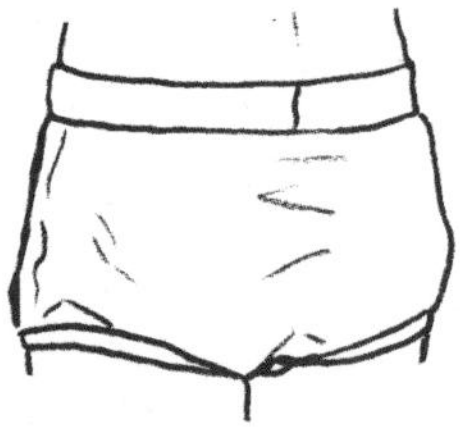

Button-Fly Boxer Briefs

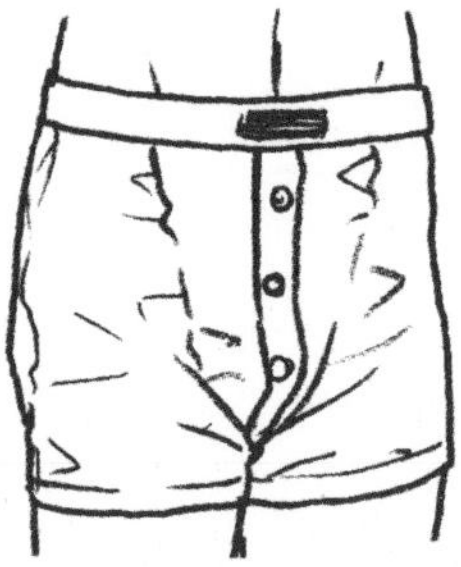

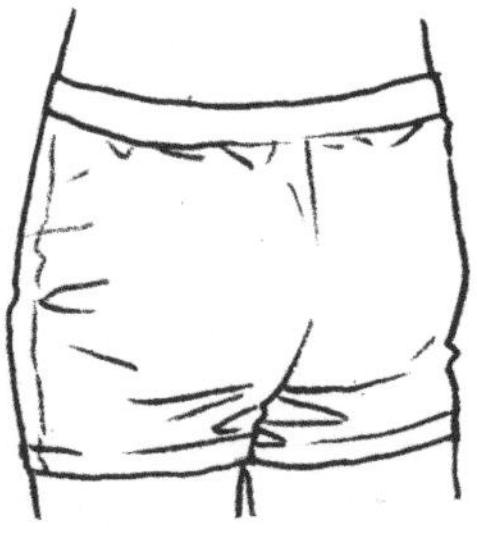

Chapter 5
Embracing Poses

Drawing Two Figures

Poses with seemingly complex compositions are actually drawn using essentially the same steps when drawing a solitary figure. Note that the two figures should be developed simultaneously. When sketching the under drawing, include those parts of the body that will not be visible in the final image, owing to one figure obscuring part of the other and the like. Look at the samples below, which show twin brothers of the same build and appearance, and study how one figure obscures part of the body of the other and vice versa, depending on the pose.

You ate my piece of cake, didn't you?

Uh huh

Compose the two figures as a single unit and develop both at the same time, m'kay?

Mommy!

Ain't brotherly love grand?

We two are as one.

Poses with Pre-established Structures

For poses with two figures wrapping their arms around each others' shoulders, one giving another a piggyback ride, and the like, the positions of elbows and torsos, and where tension and pressure play a role is predetermined. Memorizing these predetermined elements will come in handy when composing such poses on your own in the future.

One Arm Wrapped around the Other's Shoulder

Two characters wrapping their arms firmly around the shoulders of one another is a sign of close friendship. One's arm lies over the other, causing different placements of the two arms. Study how the arms are positioned in these images of two characters of the same height and build.

Figure with the Upper Arm

- The upper arm's shoulder is higher.
- The upper arm's elbow lies at a slightly oblique, downward angle from the other figure's neck.
- The upper arm is held virtually parallel to the ground plane.

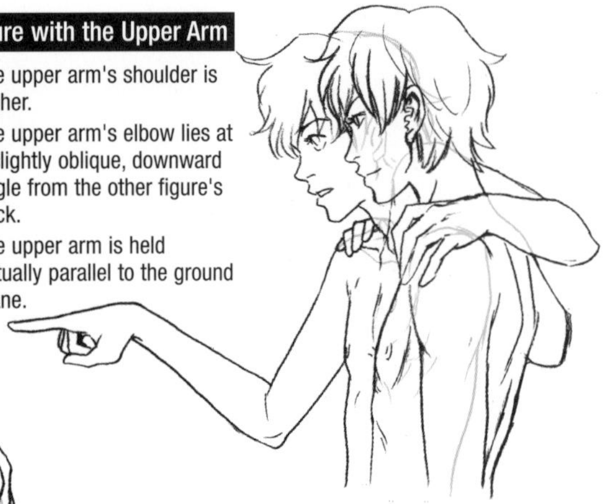

One guy's arm is on top, while the other is on the bottom, m'kay?

My arm's on top.

My arm's on the bottom.

POINT

Figure with the Lower Arm

The lower arm's shoulder is slightly dropped.
The lower arm's elbow rests just below the scapula of the other figure.
The lower arm is held almost perpendicular to the ground plane.

Supporting the Injured

In this case, one is relying on the other for support. The neck of the uninjured figure supports the upper arm of the injured figure, while holding the injured figure's wrist at chest-level. The uninjured figure's arm wraps around the waist of the injured figure. This pose could better be regarded as one character lending his shoulder to the other more than two characters with their arms wrapped around one another.

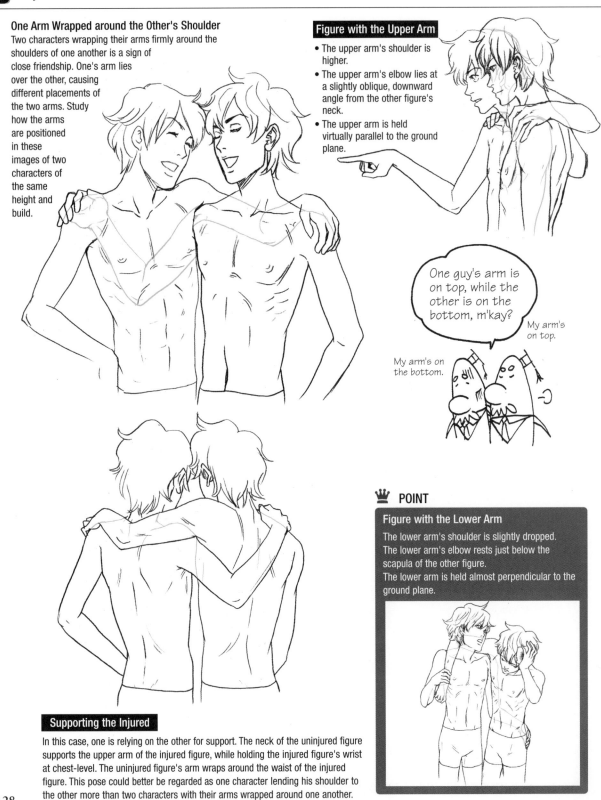

Riding Piggyback

Two characters might assume this pose if one is sick. It then becomes a vehicle for expressing the kindheartedness of the character offering to carry the other. Noting where one figure applies pressure to the other makes this pose easier to draw.

Figure Riding Piggyback

- The figure riding piggyback's pelvis rests higher than that of the figure giving the ride.
- From a front view, the torso of the figure riding piggyback tilts slightly at an oblique angle.
- The shins of the figure riding piggyback are angled forward.
- The feet of the figure riding piggyback form an inverted "V".
- One arm is hooked around the neck of the figure giving the ride.

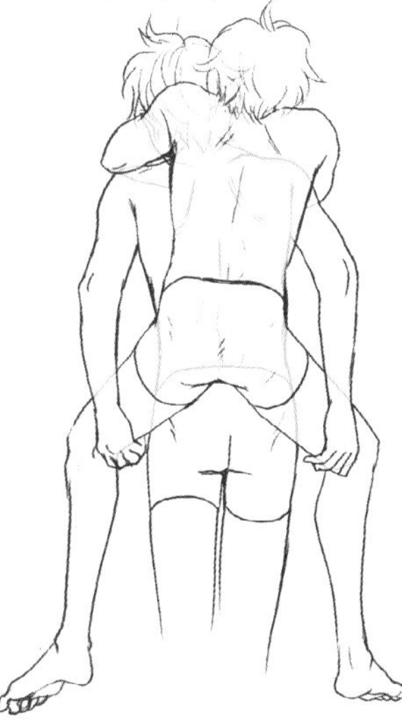

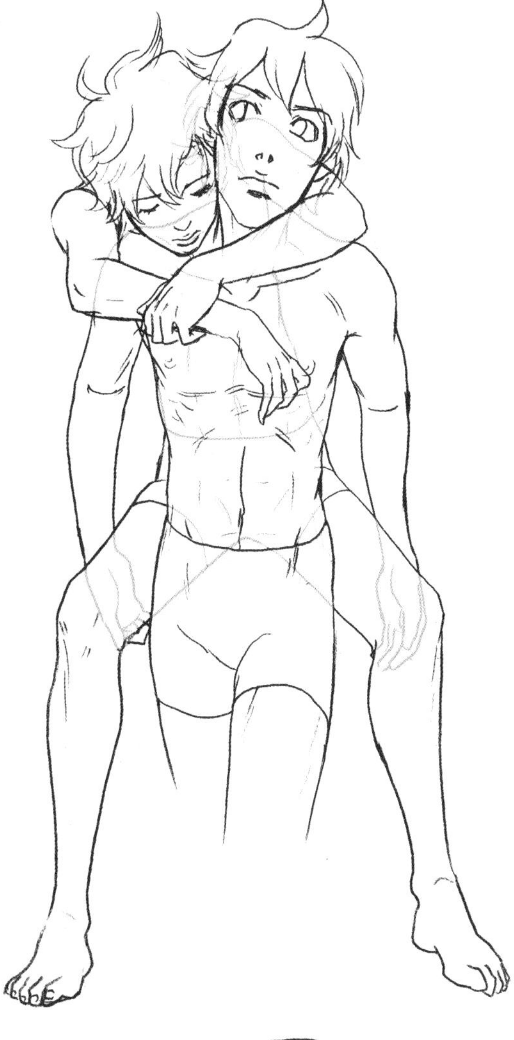

Carrying Another Piggyback

- Supporting the entire weight of the figure riding piggyback causes the upper body of the figure giving the ride to lean dramatically.
- The figure giving the ride supports the thighs of the figure riding piggyback with his hips to prevent the figure riding piggyback from falling. He also holds onto the back of the knees of the figure riding piggyback.
- The elbows of the figure giving the ride are pointed rearward.

POINT

Correct Positioning

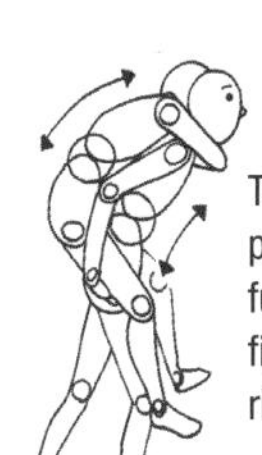

The figure riding piggyback leans his full weight into the figure giving the ride.

Incorrect Positioning

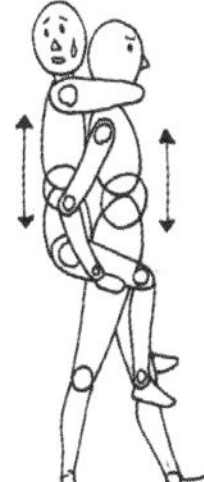

This might be an acceptable composition if the figure riding piggyback is a toddler. However, with two characters of similar height, it is implausible. The figure riding would fall.

Be certain that you draw the hips of the figure riding piggyback above those of the figure giving the ride, m'kay?

Kissing Scenes

This final lesson module covers how to compose heart-thumping kissing scenes. The trick is to show the heads tilting and to determine the placement of the noses and mouths before establishing the silhouettes. Showing the heads tilted brings the arcs traced by the eyes and noses in opposite directions. As a result, the viewer sees only one set of nostrils and only one chin. In addition, establishing the placements of the mouth and nose first allows you to avoid slip-ups and odd positionings, like one figure kissing the chin of another.

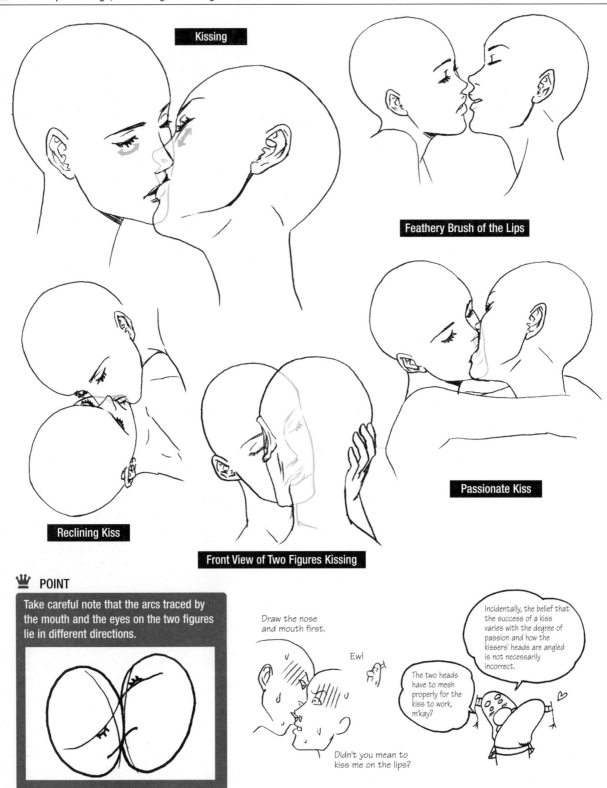

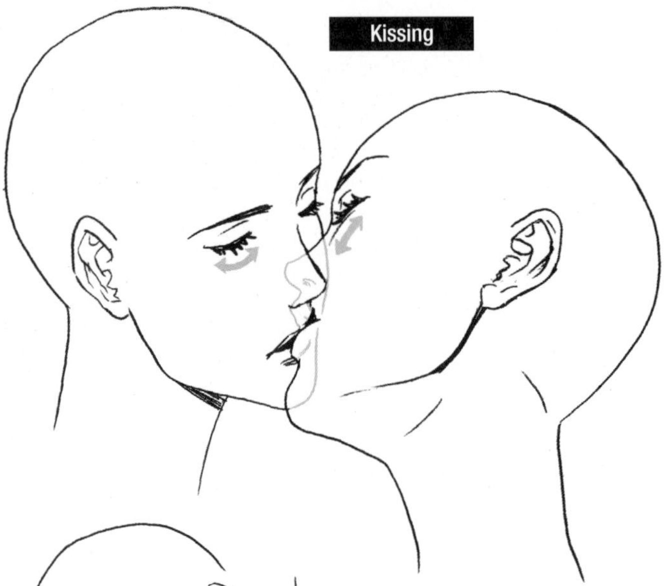

Kissing

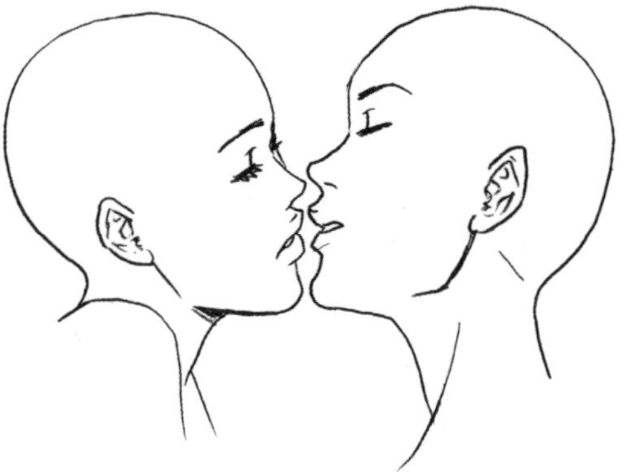

Feathery Brush of the Lips

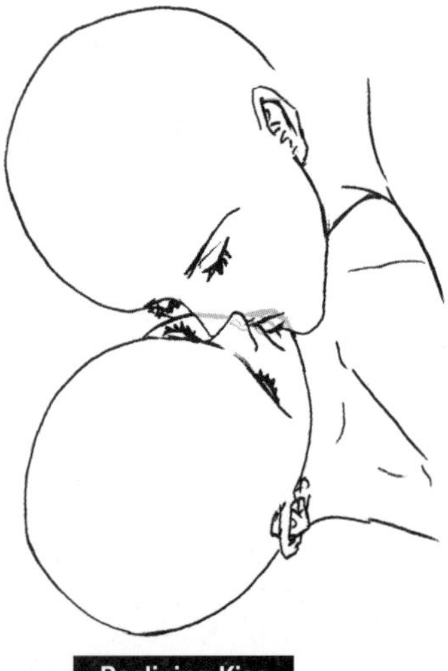

Passionate Kiss

Reclining Kiss

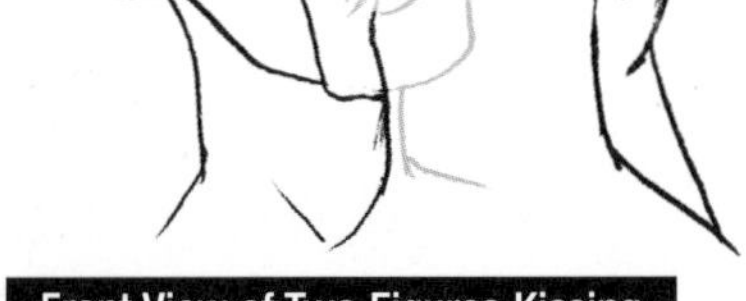

Front View of Two Figures Kissing

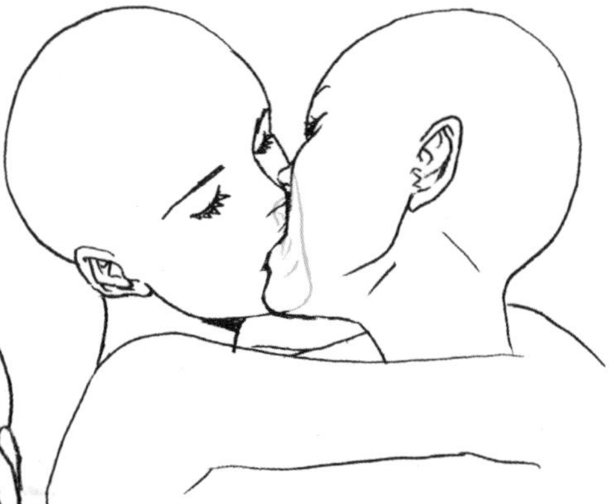

POINT

Take careful note that the arcs traced by the mouth and the eyes on the two figures lie in different directions.

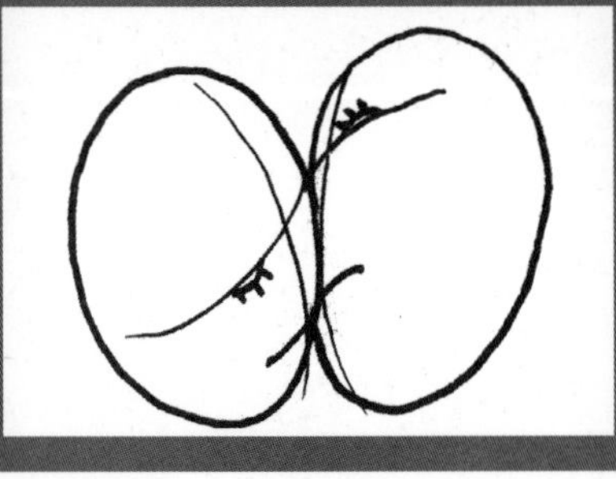

Draw the nose and mouth first.

Ew!

Didn't you mean to kiss me on the lips?

The two heads have to mesh properly for the kiss to work, m'kay?

Incidentally, the belief that the success of a kiss varies with the degree of passion and how the kissers' heads are angled is not necessarily incorrect.

STOP!

This page marks the end of the story. Go to page 144 and read the pages in reverse order from that point.

[Assistance]
Usamaru Furuya
Tamami Myo

Fin

Afterword

While I wrote this book in the manner of an instructional text, it also constitutes record of my own studies. In the beginning, I did not have much experience in drawing *bishonen*. So, I relied on the assistance of a few individuals who were not only good artists but who also had strongly developed ideas regarding *bishonen*. In other words, I sought the help of real-life Dr. *Bishonen*-types, which enabled me to design successfully my own *bishonen*.

I would like to express my sincerest gratitude to each and every one of the real life Dr. *Bishonen*'s who gave me advice, the staff at Graphic-sha Publishing, and the designers, who received my odd drawings and flights of fancy with a smile and managed to put together this book.

I hope this book proves useful to the readers out there.

Ai Kozaki

Well...
If...If I work hard, will I become an exemplary bishonen?

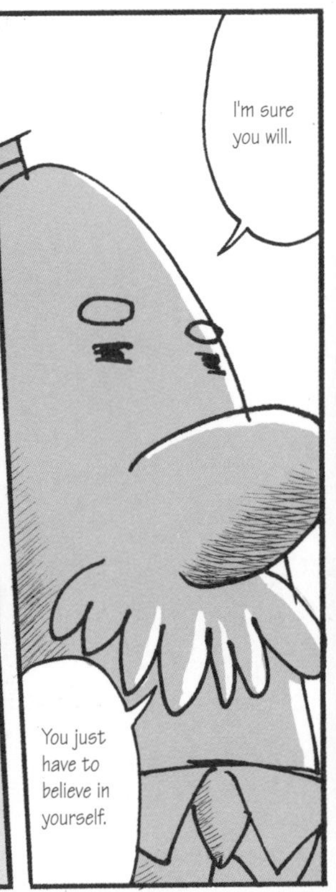

I'm sure you will.
You just have to believe in yourself.

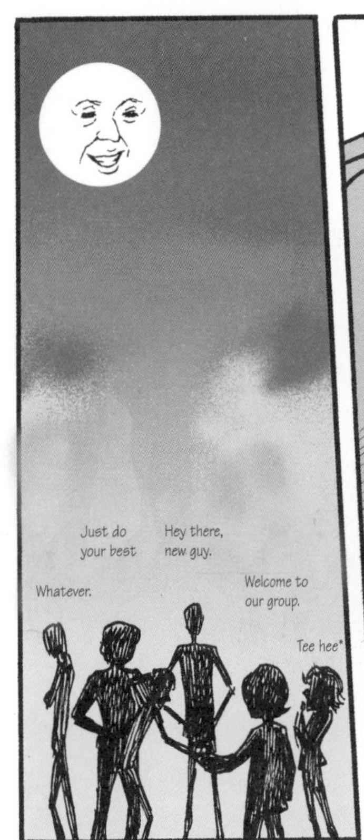

Tee hee*
Welcome to our group.
Hey there, new guy.
Just do your best
Whatever.

Bontaro Hei had now tasted the depth of what it means to be a *bishonen* and the first feeling of frustration in his young life.

Dr. Bishonen's days as a bishonen are supposed to be legendary.

Sir, were you a *bishonen* in your youth?

Just think of what I'd be now if only I hadn't gotten married.

Wait up!

Today, he had finally taken his first step toward that barren, fruitless field called, "*Bishonen*."

おしまい

The real world is better without such a troublesome creature as a *bishonen*.
Then why do they exist?

Because *bishonen* don't exist in real life, people idolize them, m'kay?
オラッ
顔はやめて!!
NON!!
ポコッ
せいっ

Nowhere?
They don't exist?

A *bishonen* researcher once made an insightful observation.
He said that *Bishonen* were like a unicorn that appeared at a lake on a moonlit night.

Because no one has actually seen one, they are immortal beings that seduce people.
They represent eternal beauty.
Unicorns?

Flap, flap, flap

If you look at it from that perspective, then there is no way I am a *bishonen*.
I'm just your run-of-the-mill good-looking guy.
ガク
Slump
If you are going to be taken in that much by a little joke in a *manga* like this, you are half the boy I thought you were.
There's no reason to be so glum, Bondaro.
ホッホッホ
Sir.

Quit ignoring me!

Dr. Bishonen, look!
What?!

These guys, look at their weird head-to-body ratios and the strange things they say and do.
Take that!
How can you call them "*bishonen*"?
Eek! I'm frightened!

Ah, I see. They are without doubt *bishonen*, m'kay?
At least, they are more legitimate *bishonen* than you are.

Huh?

You're dead meat!

Each era has something that it yearns for blindly, and *bishonen* reflect that.

Please stop fighting. Do it for me!

Bishonen suddenly become emotional for no apparent reason.

Ahrrr!

Grrr!

They are given to violent outbreaks.

Ha ha ha! Keep on fighting,

Bishonen can also be unexpectedly cruel, m'kay?

Dr. *Bishonen*'s *Bishonen* Lesson (Part IV)
The Next Generation
Bishonen in the 1990s to the Present

During the 1990s, Comiket (a.k.a. "Comic Market," the world's largest comics convention) and Yaoi* culture (*an acronym for "no climax," "no end" or "no punch line," and "no meaning" and has come to refer to homoerotic content in novels and *manga*) took strong hold, and the *bishonen* market exploded in size. The numbers of *bishonen* consumers steadily increased, ranging from elementary school-aged girls to young women in their late teens and twenties. The content ranged dramatically, and the tastes of the young female readership become increasingly compartmentalized. New *bishonen* characters appeared on the scene, one after another. Even minor, peripheral characters spellbound readers, and each *bishonen* character attracted his own following.

Today, we often see a myriad of *bishonen* character types grace a single work of *shonen manga* or *shojo manga*. There is the composed guy who wears glasses, the Prince-Charming guy, the junior student, the honor student, and many other personality types. There are also encouraging cases where a character not even remotely designed to be a *bishonen* is somehow elevated through the rosy glasses of the *manga*'s young, female readers to a dashing *bishonen*. The present market is glutted with *bishonen*.

Recent trends frequently see highly original character types with unbelievably eccentric personal philosophies and attitudes. Such personalities would surely get slapped by an adult if they actually existed.

And in the time it took to convey all this information, an artist somewhere just gave birth to a new *bishonen*.

Model:
Bishonen Academy Freshmen
Sugita Hinekure

Sugita is such an egoist that he's lost all sense of morals, m'kay?

So, who's group are you going to join?
Yikes!

I don't want to join up with any of you.
Hey! He's running away!

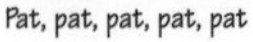
Pat, pat, pat, pat, pat

What is their problem?
They just aren't human.

Ah, there's someone with a normal head-to-body ratio.
Help! I'm being chased by people of strange body proportions.

....

Flip
プイっ
Huh? He's ignoring me.

Hey! Wait up!
Are you a manga character too?

Stop! M'kay?
The two of you were born on the same day from the same womb.
Why do you have to be so different?
やめろ～!!!

Don't judge people on appearanc es, Jotaro.
You dress like a dork.

Dr. *Bishonen*'s *Bishonen* Lesson (Part III)

The *Bishonen* Warring States Period

Bishonen in the 1980s

It was time for a change in the *bishonen* of the 1970s, who lived in dormitories and read the Bible. From *bishonen manga*, which had been completely left to its own devices, steadily emerged a new type of *bishonen*. A new generation of *bishonen*, who were light-hearted and athletic, appeared. Like the traditional *bishonen* before them, these new *bishonen* also had long eyelashes and gentle faces. However, they also had the strong, willful gaze particular to the characters of *shonen manga* (*manga* targeted at boys).

This new generation had the sensitive delicacy of *bishonen* combined with a vivacity and positive-outlook not seen for quite some time. Girls swooned.

Meanwhile, boys who were just a tad bad had become the rage in *shojo manga*. These boys were in bands and were always getting bawled out by their teachers. They wore the latest trendy fashions and had head-to-body ratios of 1:10. These *bishonen* were evolving into chic fashionistas.

While that might have been the case, both types of these new *bishonen* still maintained the beauty and evanescence of *bishonen*, and the power of this permeated throughout them.

The concept of "*bishonen*" was split by two strong forces—boys versus girls. While they were all still *bishonen*, their superficial differences were fascinating. However, both types frequently displayed a positive mindset.

The subfield of "shonenai" or "boys' love" expanded in the 1970s and 1980s, and "secondary *shonen manga* works (i.e. fanfiction *manga*) written by girls cranked up in volume.

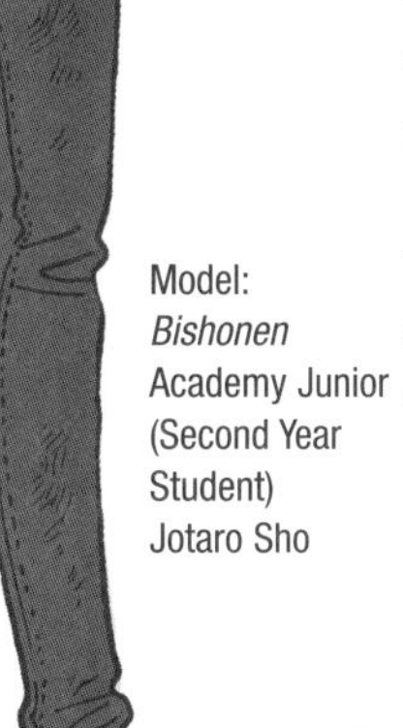

Model: *Bishonen* Academy Junior (Second Year Student) Jotaro Sho

But on the inside, they are surprisingly alike, m'kay?

Model: *Bishonen* Academy Senior (Third Year Student) Nentaro Sho

Right. Hey, if you're going to be a high school student, we've got what it takes.

You're horrid!

How cruel!
Traitor!
Grim Reaper!
I could just die!
I can't. I hardly ever read books.

No! You shut up, Nentaro!

Shut your trap, Jotaro! I'm talking to him.

Think you can take me?

No, join a band.

How about the Soccer Team?

But, doesn't their proportioning seem a little off?

Despite all the fighting, those two are talented athletes and twins, m'kay?

Bring it on!

You know NOTHING about Jim Morrison!

POKA JUKA

BOW WOW

You'll make Mom cry in Heaven.

TENYA WANYA

Yank

Dr. *Bishonen*'s *Bishonen* Lesson (Part II)
The Blossoming of *Bishonen*
Bishonen in the 1970s

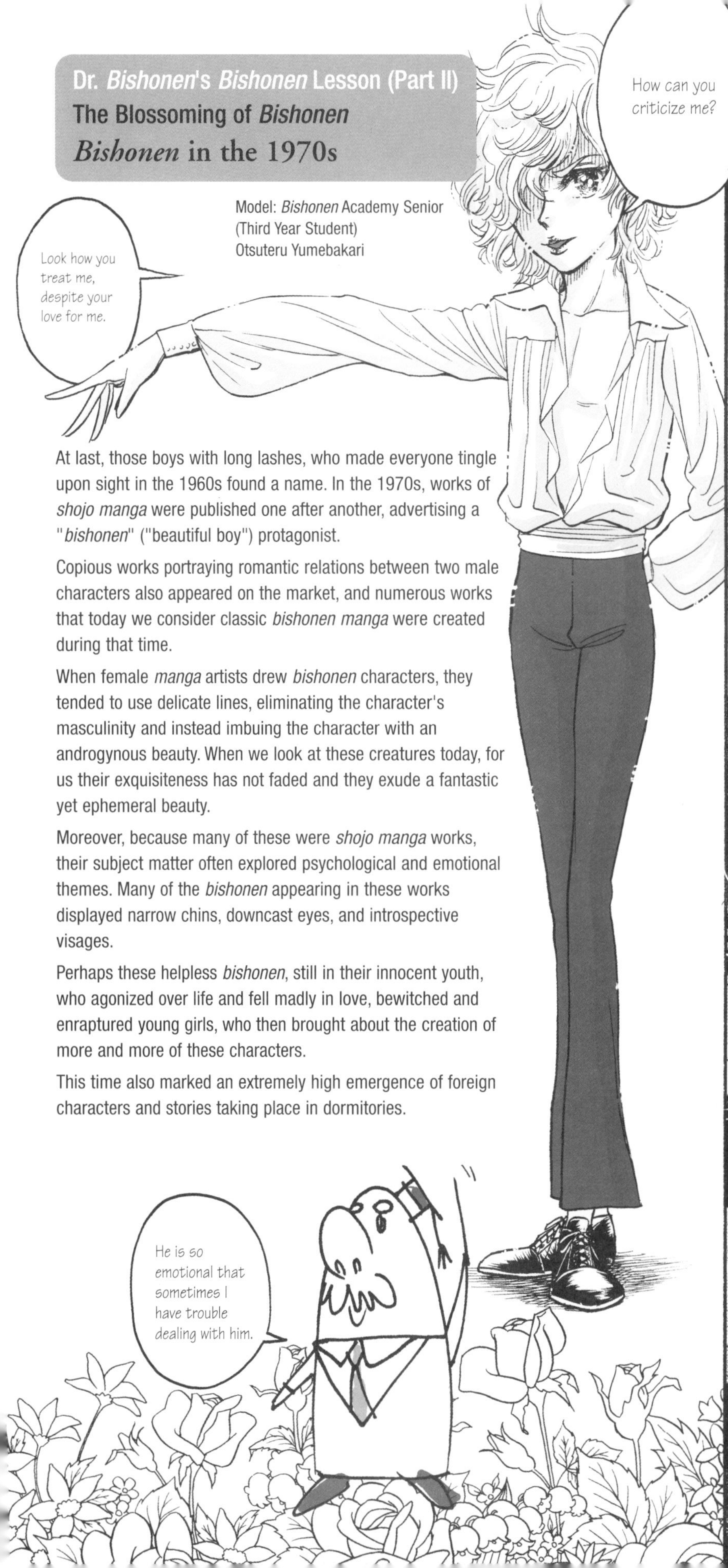

Model: *Bishonen* Academy Senior
(Third Year Student)
Otsuteru Yumebakari
How can you criticize me?
Look how you treat me, despite your love for me.
He is so emotional that sometimes I have trouble dealing with him.

At last, those boys with long lashes, who made everyone tingle upon sight in the 1960s found a name. In the 1970s, works of *shojo manga* were published one after another, advertising a "*bishonen*" ("beautiful boy") protagonist.

Copious works portraying romantic relations between two male characters also appeared on the market, and numerous works that today we consider classic *bishonen manga* were created during that time.

When female *manga* artists drew *bishonen* characters, they tended to use delicate lines, eliminating the character's masculinity and instead imbuing the character with an androgynous beauty. When we look at these creatures today, for us their exquisiteness has not faded and they exude a fantastic yet ephemeral beauty.

Moreover, because many of these were *shojo manga* works, their subject matter often explored psychological and emotional themes. Many of the *bishonen* appearing in these works displayed narrow chins, downcast eyes, and introspective visages.

Perhaps these helpless *bishonen*, still in their innocent youth, who agonized over life and fell madly in love, bewitched and enraptured young girls, who then brought about the creation of more and more of these characters.

This time also marked an extremely high emergence of foreign characters and stories taking place in dormitories.

We are born with the original sin.
If we are unable to regain our lost wings, we should at least carve a beautiful poem on our breasts and think of heaven.
生まれながらの罪人…
失った翼を取り戻すことが出来ないのなら
せめて美しい詩をこの胸に刻みつけ
天国に想いを馳せよう…
ポッカ〜ン…
I think what he's trying to say is, "Please join the Book Club."

Me? I don't think I'm the sci-fi type.
What do you mean?
Do you think you can walk away after learning this much about the Organization?
Prepare to die!
Aaaaah!
Stop right there!
やめろ!!!
Thunk
Ow!
Using force to make someone join your club? How horrid!
You should be ashamed of yourself, Mr. Inochigake.
Stand up, honey.
Oh no! Not another freak.
Uh, thanks.
"The thought of suicide is a powerful solace."
Wha'?
Nietzsche.
Have you ever contemplated death, self-righteous and gentle death?
Well...um
...
How can I get out of this?
This is my love, proof of a fallen angel.
イチョウ
Gingko

Now, now, Bondaro.
Tsk
め
That's not how you talk to a top student, m'kay?

Let go of me!
What do you think you're doing, running into me like that?

Dr. *Bishonen*'s *Bishonen* Lesson (Part I)
The Dawn of *Bishonen*
Bishonen in the 1960s

Action and adventure stories, targeted at boys constituted mainstream *manga* during the 1960s. The term "*bishonen*" had not yet infiltrated *manga*, but they certainly existed. Whether the character had a stylized head-to-body ratio of 1:4 or 1:5, his eyes would seem somehow troubled and brimming with a beleaguered air. Many put their lives in the hands of an organization and fate. Despite that some were slightly naughty bad boys or utter rogues, or even the minions of an evil organization, they were boys with a subtly mature manner, who somehow made us care. Just because they had slightly darker personalities than the other characters and had long eyelashes, why would we feel so strongly for them?

Glancing at these *bishonen*, who projected an atmosphere that was somehow different from the stereotypical good guy with a strong sense of justice, we see that they made the hearts of young girls thump with an unidentifiable pang, and the young boys idolized them.

Why don't you joint the Sci-fi Club and work for the Organization?

Model: *Bishonen* Academy Senior (Third Year Student) Kosaku Inochigake

He's the type who's easily sucked in, m'kay?

For now, I'll just show you around the quad, m'kay?
Pat, pat, pat, pat, pat
All of the students really are bishonen, aren't they?
Outta my way!
Wha'?
Bam!
Fwoomp
What a huge head!
Shhh!
They'll find us.
He's over there!
Mmph, mmph
Swat, swat, swat
All right! I got away.

Excuse me, sir.
You're Bontaro Hei, the new student, aren't you?
Welcome to Bishonen Academy!
I'm the academy's headmaster.
Now that you've enrolled in our academy, I expect you to work your hardest to become an exemplary *bishonen*, m'kay?
Dr. Bishonen
Phffth.
It feels strange to say it, but I'm a *bishonen* now.
I intend to, sir.
The real question is whether this school is up to my standards.
Yap, yap, yap, yap, yap
What a jerk.
The academy has a wide variety of students.
For now, why don't you join a club and see what the senior students have to teach you, m'kay?
Kay?

駆け出し美少年 平凡太郎

こざき亜衣

Bontaro Hei, Fledgling *Bishonen*
Artwork and Story by Ai Kozaki

Meet the Characters

Nentaro Sho
Nentaro Sho is a junior at *Bishonen* Academy and is Jotaro's twin brother (Nentaro is the older twin). Nentaro is a passionate young man and can become a little too fiery at times, but he is a kind soul and looks after the other boys. He is drawn at a 1:6 head-to-body ratio and reflects the style of a *shonen manga* character from the 1980s.

Sugita Hinekure
Sugita Hinekure is a freshman at *Bishonen* Academy. Like Bontaro Hei, who is also a freshman, Sugita is drawn using a 1990s-to-present-day style. He is a shady character and does not have a single friend. Sugita is drawn at a 1:8 head-to-body ratio.

Kosaku Inochigake
Kosaku Inochigake is a senior (third year student) at *Bishonen* Academy. He belongs to a mysterious organization and is always found engaged in some kind of mission. He reflects a style ca. 1960s and is drawn at a 1:4 head-to-body ratio.

Bontaro Hei
Bontaro Hei is a new student who transferred mid-school year. He has a cocky attitude and has just earned the title of "*bishonen.*" He is studying what it means to be a *bishonen* under Dr. *Bishonen*'s tutelage. He is still a freshman and is drawn at a 1:7 head-to-body ratio.

Dr. *Bishonen*
Dr. *Bishonen* is the headmaster of *Bishonen* Academy. While Dr. *Bishonen* is small in stature, he is a highly capable individual and is able to teach a wide range of *bishonen* subjects, ranging from how to draw *bishonen* to the history of *bishonen.* Rumor has it that Dr. *Bishonen* was quite an attractive young man, himself, when he was a lad. Now, he sets his personal needs aside in order to dedicate his energies to educating his successors. He is drawn at a 1:2 head-to-body ratio.

Jotaro Sho
Jotaro Sho is a junior at *Bishonen* Academy and is Nentaro's twin brother (Jotaro is the younger twin). He can be a little of a reprobate, but he is an affable guy. He is drawn at an implausible 1:9 head-to-body ratio in the style of a *shojo manga* (*manga* targeted at girls) character from the 1980s. Jotaro is popular amongst the ladies.

Otsuteru Yumebakari
Otsuteru Yumebakari is a senior at *Bishonen* Academy. Giving to wildly fanciful declarations, he is effeminate and is drawn in a style ca. the 1970s. Otsuteru is drawn at a 1:5 head-to-body ratio.

Our story on the history of bishonen through the decades begins here. Enjoy!